Law, Politics, and the Constitution

Central and Eastern European Forum for Legal, Political, and Social Theory Yearbook

Edited by Jürgen Busch / Péter Cserne / Michael Hein / Miklós Könczöl / Miodrag Jovanović / Marta Soniewicka

Volume 4

PL ACADEMIC RESEARCH

Antonia Geisler / Michael Hein / Siri Hummel (eds.)

Law, Politics, and the Constitution

New Perspectives from Legal and Political Theory

PL ACADEMIC RESEARCH

Bibliographic Information published by the Deutsche Nationalbibliothek
The Deutsche Nationalbibliothek lists this publication in the Deutsche Nationalbibliografie; detailed bibliographic data is available in the internet at http://dnb.d-nb.de.

Library of Congress Cataloging-in-Publication Data
Central and Eastern European Forum for Legal, Political and Social Theory (5th : 2013 : Greifswald, Germany)
Law, politics, and the constitution : new perspectives from legal and political theory / Antonia Geisler, Michael Hein, Siri Hummel (eds.).
pages cm. – (Central and Eastern European Forum for Legal, Political, and Social Theory Yearbook ; v. 4)
ISBN 978-3-631-65464-4
1. Constitutional law–Europe, Central–Congresses. 2. Constitutional law–Europe, Eastern–Congresses. 3. Constitutional law–European Union Countries–Congresses. 4. Separation of powers–Europe, Central–Congresses. 5. Separation of powers–Europe, Eastern–Congresses. 6. Separation of powers–European Union Countries–Congresses. 7. Civil rights–Europe, Central–Congresses. 8. Civil rights–Europe, Eastern–Congresses. 9. Civil rights–European Union Countries–Congresses. 10. Law–Political aspects–Europe–Congresses. I. Geisler, Antonia, editor. II. Hein, Michael, 1980- editor. III. Hummel, Siri, 1983- editor. IV. Title.
KJC4444.8.C46 2013
342.4–dc23
2014024612

ISSN 2191-8317
ISBN 978-3-631-65464-4 (Print)
E-ISBN 978-3-653-04686-1 (E-Book)
DOI 10.3726/978-3-653-04686-1

PL Academic Research is an Imprint of Peter Lang GmbH.

Peter Lang – Frankfurt am Main · Bern · Bruxelles · New York · Oxford · Warszawa · Wien

This publication has been peer reviewed.

www.peterlang.com

Table of Contents

Introduction

This volume is the 4th 'Central and Eastern European Forum for Legal, Political, and Social Theory Yearbook.' The 'Central and Eastern European Forum of Young Legal, Political, and Social Theorists' is an initiative for the cooperation and exchange of ideas among young scholars who come from, currently study or work in Central and Eastern Europe or have a research interest in the region. It evolved from a conference held in 2009 in Katowice, Poland, where some of the participants had come to realise that the meeting filled a real gap in academic exchange. Establishing the Forum was a response to the dominance of Western European and American scholarship in the field: not so much an attempt to build up a counterpower, but to reflect on our issues and to articulate our views in a distinct voice. At the same time, it was also an endeavour to connect those younger cohorts of academics whose career started at or after the turn of the millennium. The idea to form a group with a regional and generational character was further stimulated by the need to build a network of researchers who often live in close proximity of one another without knowing of each other's work. Being part of a diverse and respectful scholarly community where intellectual freedom and honesty reign over hierarchy and cynicism is an experience that is regrettably uncommon in today's academia – yet this is exactly what the Forum strives to facilitate.

The main activity of the Forum is organising annual conferences that provide an opportunity for junior scholars to present their work to an international audience of peers. After Katowice, the conferences have taken place in Budapest (Hungary, 2010), Belgrade (Serbia, 2011), Celje (Slovenia, 2012) and Greifswald (Germany, 2013), each followed by the publication of selected papers in this book series.[1] The chapters of this volume were presented and discussed on 3 and 4 May 2013 at the 5th Forum in the beautiful historical town of Greifswald in Germany near the Baltic Sea. The conference was hosted at the Alfried Krupp Wissenschaftskolleg in cooperation with the University of Greifswald. We would like to thank

1 In May 2014, the 6th Forum was held in Zagreb (Croatia); selected contributions to this conference will be published in the 5th Yearbook in 2015. The 7th Forum will be held in spring 2015 in Sofia (Bulgaria). For further information, please visit our website at [http://www.cee-forum.org].

the Alfried Krupp von Bohlen und Halbach Foundation, which generously sponsored the realisation of the conference, and the Wissenschaftskolleg's staff for their enthusiasm and hard work on-site. Additionally, we would like to express our gratitude to *Prof. Dr. André Brodocz* (University of Erfurt, Germany) who held the conference's keynote speech and consented to its publication in this volume.

About 50 participants from 14 European countries took part in the Greifswald Forum and delivered more than 40 presentations. The conference thus provided a platform for a lively and academically rigorous debate. In particular, the debates centred upon two key topics from legal and political theory that are of critical importance in the Central and Eastern European contexts of relatively young constitutional democracies and were each given attention by way of their own section. In the first section, the participants discussed two core elements of democracy and the rule of law – 'Separation of Powers & Constitutional Review.' The questions raised in particular were what the exact meaning of the term 'separation' and its manifold synonyms and alternatives could be and whether the idea of the separation of powers is still applicable to the complexity of modern polities or merely of historical importance. Furthermore, it was discussed how constitutional review could be adequately understood: as adjudication, politics in the cloak of the law, something in between – or even something completely different? Importantly, the relationship between the separation of powers and constitutional review was examined (see part I of this volume). In dialogue with these primarily theoretical questions, a number of contributions to the conference discussed the role of constitutional review in the East Central European Countries after 1989 (see part II of this volume). Finally, several panels from the first section addressed the role of constitutionalism and the separation of powers in the governmental system of the European Union (see part III of this volume).

The second section of the Forum was dedicated to 'Constitutional Rights & Obligations.' Most modern constitutions provide basic rights and freedoms for individuals and groups in order to protect them against encroachments by the state. Additionally, there is some general consent in constitutional theory as to which fundamental rights a constitution should at least guarantee. In contrast, obligations are much rarer in the constitutional landscape. Hence, it is controversially debated in legal and political theory whether constitutions should impose certain obligations on their citizens at all. Against this background, the participants discussed how constitutional obligations are related to constitutional rights and whether obligations should be incorporated in constitutions or whether they systematically violate the basic principles of liberal and democratic polities. Furthermore, the relation between rights and obligations and both the common good and the idea of a neutral state were examined. Finally, the normative foundations and challenges of ethnic parliamentary representation were discussed in this context (see part IV of this volume).

In the aftermath of the conference, 21 participants answered the Call for Papers for the Yearbook, 13 of which were selected for publication by the editors. The first part of this volume comprises three contributions on 'Constitutional Review and Separation of Powers.' In his chapter entitled 'Constitutional Courts and Their Power of Interpretation', *André Brodocz* analyses the complex phenomenon of judicial power. As this power only becomes apparent in decisions by supreme courts regarding the meaning of the constitution, judicial power is defined as the power of interpretation. In order to explain why the power of interpretation is not necessarily absolute and how its levels are characterised by special preconditions and limitations, the author distinguishes between three interdependent levels: the level of the interpreted constitution, the level of the interpreting court and the level of the interpretation. Subsequently, *Michael Hein* and *Stefan Ewert* pose the question: 'What is "Politicisation" of Constitutional Courts? Towards a Decision-oriented Concept.' They start with the observation that, although politicisation is one of the most frequently used keywords in scientific research on constitutional courts, a distinct definition of the term is lacking in many studies. In light of this, they examine the theoretical conceptions of the relationship between politics, law and constitutional adjudication that underlie the different understandings of politicisation. Based on their findings, they develop a decision-oriented concept of politicisation, which is not only suitable for many theoretical approaches, but which can also be detected in numerous empirical studies. In the final contribution to the first part, *Martin Belov* discusses the idea of the separation of powers. Under the heading 'Separation of Powers reconsidered: a Proposal for a New Theoretical Model at the Beginning of the 21st Century' he argues that the key conceptions of the separation of powers that were elaborated at the beginning of modern constitutionalism are no longer appropriate for the reality of modern states. Therefore, he introduces some alternative views with regard to the classification and delimitation of state powers. Based on these, he proposes a seven-powers model, that comprises not only the classic *trias politica* of the legislative, executive and judicial branches, but also four new powers: external, financial, patronage and symbolic.

The two chapters in the second part contribute to the empirical dimension of 'Constitutional Review in East Central European Countries.' In her contribution 'Access to Constitutional Justice in the New Hungarian Constitutional Framework: Life after the Actio Popularis?' *Katalin Kelemen* evaluates the conditions of access to the Constitutional Court after the enactment of the new Fundamental Law in Hungary in 2012. In particular, she analyses the consequences of the abolition of actio popularis and the concomitant introduction of full constitutional complaint, and she asks whether these changes to the procedural law have led to a shift in emphasis from abstract to concrete review. The second chapter, contributed by *Rafał Mańko,* is on the '"War of Courts" as a Clash of Legal Cultures: Rethinking the Conflict Between the Polish Constitutional and Supreme Court Over "Interpretive Judgements."' *Mańko* examines the tense relationship between the Constitutional Court and the Supreme Court in post-socialist Poland, mainly characterised by the fact that the Supreme Court has refused to follow the Constitutional Court's decisions on numerous occasions, claiming that they are unconstitutional, ultra vires and non-binding. An analysis of the arguments put forward by the Supreme Court and Constitutional Court in this 'war of courts' reveals that the Supreme Court prefers ultra-formalist arguments typical of the hyper-positivist legal culture of the former state-socialist period, whereas the Constitutional Court seems to prefer pragmatic arguments more typical of the contemporary Western legal culture.

The third part of this volume aims at 'Theorising the European Union: Constitution, Division of Powers, and Sovereignty.' *Marcin Pieniążek* opens this section with a chapter on 'Paul Ricœur's Thought as the Basis for the Political Theory of the European Union.' He presents a conception of social structures, interpersonal relationships and democracy related to Ricoeur's concept of the subject (*ipse*) as a basis for a political theory of the European Union. Introducing Ricoeur's definition of ethical aspiration, the argumentation starts at the microscale of the entity which characteristically represents the intention of a good life; then goes on to the meso-level, i.e. to an interpersonal relationship in broad terms; and finally aims to describe the macroscale of just political institutions. Subsequently, *Balázs Fekete* examines the 'Vertical Division of Powers from the Perspective of the Member States – Police Power in the Context of European Union Constitutionalism?' By investigating the value of this classical term of US federalism for today's EU developments, the chapter critically analyses whether Article 4 paras (1) and (2) TEU as enacted following the Lisbon reforms may be interpreted as the emergence of the concept of police power in this context.

In his contribution '"Solange, Chapter 5"? The Law of the European Union and the Sovereignty in Rulings of the Constitutional Courts in Central Europe', *Mariusz Jerzy Golecki* discusses the scope of application and the meaning of the principle of primacy of EU law. By focussing on several judgements by the constitutional courts of some of the member states on the Lisbon Treaty, the chapter concentrates on the difference between the meaning of the concept of sovereignty and its application by the different courts, and on the theoretical foundations of the potential solution to the problem of comprehensive application of the primacy principle throughout the member states. *Karolina Ristova-Asterud* devotes

her contribution to 'The Balancing Role of National Parliaments in Transforming the European Union. Towards a Parliamentary Polity.' She introduces the Lisbon Treaty as a serious step moving the EU away from de-parliamentarisation towards a path of re-parliamentarisation. The chapter shows how the recent treaty novelties regarding national parliaments affect the balance of power in the intergovernmental system of EU governance. On a more theoretical level, it explores how the shared European intellectual traditions on sovereignty have influenced these developments, and how they may further transform the EU from a dominantly intergovernmental into a parliamentary polity.

The fourth and final part, 'The Common Good, Constitutional Rights and Individual Obligations,' opens with the chapter 'The Common Good and Individual Rights' by *Szilárd Tattay*. The author seeks to elucidate the ontological presuppositions and conceptual premises underlying the classical theory of the common good and the approaches to overcoming both the reduction and the opposition of the common good and individual goods and rights. In the second contribution 'Towards a "Soft" Concept of the State Neutrality Principle', Wojciech Ciszewski aims to elaborate a formula of state neutrality resistant to the objection that it is impossible to fulfil the requirements of the neutrality principle with state institutions and public authorities. The chapter starts with the author's claim that critics often employ a very narrow definition of the state neutrality principle which makes it quite easy to demonstrate that state policies often cannot comply with such a demanding standard. After examining the most questionable assumptions of this narrow definition, an alternative definition is introduced: a formula for 'soft' state neutrality.

Subsequently, *Axelle Reiter* analyses the interaction between constitutional rights and constitutional obligations from a libertarian standpoint. Her chapter 'Another Brick in the Wall? A Libertarian Outlook on Constitutional Rights, Individual Obligations, and the Boundaries of Legal Consistency' outlines a libertarian conception, which conceives rights as personal choices derived from a general entitlement to personal autonomy. The fact that these rights are defined as absolute side-constraints on actions and obligations constitutes the author's challenge for the recognition of individual obligations in libertarian theories. Finally, in the contribution on 'Ethnic Representation in National Legislatures – Normative Foundations and Challenges', *Konstantin Sachariew* considers the normative and empirical arguments in favour of and against group representation as well as descriptive representation. The normative claim that a democratic parliament should reflect the social diversity of the population often goes together with the demand for group representation through specialised measures and institutions that expand the traditional understanding of representative government and alter the electoral competition. The chapter reviews the current literature on group and descriptive representation with a special focus on the normative debate that has formed around it.

In sum, the contributions to this Yearbook shed new light on important topics, not only in contemporary legal and political theory, but also in the legal and political developments in both Central and Eastern Europe and the European Union. We hope that the readers find the chapters inspiring and thought-provoking.

*

The publication of this Yearbook was made possible through the generous financial assistance of the Alfried Krupp von Bohlen und Halbach Foundation, Essen (Germany).

Greifswald, May 2014

Antonia Geisler
Michael Hein
Siri Hummel

Part I
Constitutional Review and Separation of Powers

Constitutional Courts and Their Power of Interpretation

André Brodocz

Abstract

Judicial power is a complex phenomenon. It is not the same as formal competence. Instead, judicial power only becomes apparent in decisions by supreme courts regarding the meaning of the constitution. In this sense, judicial power is defined more precisely as the power of interpretation. When analysing it, we must distinguish between three interdependent levels: the level of the interpreted constitution, the level of the interpreting court and the level of the interpretation. This is the only way to explain why the power of interpretation is not necessarily absolute and how each level is characterised by special preconditions and limitations.

1. Introduction

Judicial Power constitutes a central challenge for constitutionalism (Geiger 1995, c. 1007). The judiciary practices its powers through a constitutional court as soon as its decisions bind the actions of other political institutions or actors. Still, it is known that constitutional courts themselves cannot forcefully obtain obedience. Worldwide, the decisions of constitutional courts are nonetheless adhered to in most cases. But why do governments and legislators adhere to them? And why do constitutional courts expect that political institutions will do it? The question is what motivates governments and legislators on the one hand and what motivates constitutional courts on the other hand? The answer is: power.

Political institutions follow the constitutional rulings when they have recognised the power of the judiciary. And constitutional courts demand obedience from political institutions when they can expect the recognition of their power. Power is what motivates both sides (Luhmann 1988, 21). That is to say: the constitutional court must be motivated to make use of its formally assigned power to begin with. This motivation is not inherent to constitutional courts. For example: between 1947 and 2000 the Japanese Supreme Court annihilated only five decisions of the legislator, practising it's power over this political institution (Hatajiri 2003, 714). Also, the US Supreme Court made use of its formal power against Congress only twice between 1789 and 1864 (Epstein et al. 1996, 144).

This should not come as a surprise. An institution that is not able to apply sanctions does not expect to be recognised as powerful. And constitutional courts dispose of no sanctions – in contrast to the legislative or the executive. Nonetheless constitutional courts are not left completely without any sanctions. When citizens recognise the authority of their constitutional court, they expect the same from their political representatives (Vanberg 2005).

Political institutions that disregard the authority of constitutional courts must therefore expect to be punished during next elections. In this case, constitutional courts profit from the power of the citizens and their ability to sanction the government – but only when citizens trust them (Vorländer 2001, 14; see also Gibson et al. 1998, Mishler and Sheehan 1996) and recognise their authority. The recognition of authority therefore binds not only the constitutional court and the citizenry, but also a third actor – in this case the political institutions. This is independent from the fact of whether the political institutions recognise the authority of the constitutional court themselves. Still, this weakens the power of a constitutional court. The legislative institutions might, for example, revise the sentence of the constitutional court in case it is met with wide disapproval by issuing a new law.

From these short introductory comments it should have become clear that the power of constitutional courts is not the same as formal competence. Instead, the power of a constitutional court only becomes apparent in the decisions about the meaning of the constitution. In this sense, the power of the constitutional court is defined more precisely as *the power of interpretation.* The decision of a constitutional court is then based on an interpretation of the constitution that in itself constitutes a certain interpretation. According to Ernst-Wolfgang Böckenförde, this power of interpretation results from 'the connection between three elements: the precedence of the constitution, the responsibility for the mandatory interpretation of a constitution which in large parts is indefinite in its content and the lack of a recognised canon of interpretative methods.' (Böckenförde 1999, 16 [own translation, A.B.]).

In this book chapter I will present in how far these three elements that Böckenförde refers to point to *three different levels of the constitutional power of interpretation.* This analytical differentiation of three levels of the power of interpretation demonstrates in which way the power of interpretation of a constitutional court *could* be expressed. Whether a constitutional court *actually* possesses this power is empirically open – especially due to the courts inability to directly sanction.

2. The interpreted constitution

When analysing the power of constitutional courts, we must distinguish between three levels: the level of the interpreted constitution, the level of the interpreting court and the level of the interpretation. At the *level of the interpreted constitution* we can discern a power of interpretation of the constitutional jurisdiction when the interpreted constitution precedes the ordinary law. The power of interpretation of the constitutional court thus presupposes the normative precedence of the interpreted constitution at this level (Starck 2001, 3; Pieroth 2003, 299–305).

Attention must be paid to the distinction between the claim to normative precedence and it's conversion into practice. Constitutions may not convert their claim to normative precedence by themselves – to achieve this they will need a court or another actor. But constitutional courts can administer this protection only when the normative precedence of the constitution is claimed in the first place. Therefore, the normative precedence of the constitution functions as the precondition to the power of interpretation at this level.

Due to the normative precedence of the constitution, the judicial power of interpretation at the first level is characterised by a specific asymmetry: the asymmetry between the interpreted constitution and the rest of the law. This asymmetry is established by the institution that creates the constitution: the constituent power. The asymmetry between the constitution and the rest of the law provides the constitutional court with the possibility to annihilate laws (Wahl 2003, 123). The constitutional court and the constituent power thus compete at this level of the power of interpretation. The asymmetry between the constitution and the rest of the law indeed establishes the power of interpretation of the constitutional court in this competition.

This power of interpretation is not necessarily absolute. Rather, it may be subject to factual, social and temporal limitations. *Factual limitations* means: the constitution may be amended by the constituent. The extent of this limitation depends upon the requirements for a constitutional amendment (Ismayr 2003, 12; Lutz 1994, 367). High requirements for an amendment imply only a small limitation of the power of interpretation of the constitutional court, while low requirements for a constitutional amendment limit the power of interpretation of the constitutional jurisdiction to a large extent. In the US, the power of interpretation of the constitutional jurisdiction is only barely limited in this respect. To amend the constitution, it is necessary that three-quarters of the states' legislatures agree with the proposed changes (article V of the US constitution). Given this high requirement, the US constitution has only been amended 27 times over a time period of more than 200 years. Compared to this, the power of interpretation of the German constitutional court is limited to a large extent by the fact that the German Basic Law (Grundgesetz) may be amended so easily. The amendment of the German Basic Law requires only the compliance of two-thirds of each of the members of the Bundestag und the Bundesrat (article 72, II of the German Basic Law). This simple formal manner in which the German Basic Law may be amended is also mirrored in the comparable high amount of amendments that have been executed (Busch 1999). Between the years 1949 and 1998, 189 text amendments were executed by the implementation of 45 amendment laws. By comparison, the German Basic Law thus belongs among the constitutions with the highest amendment rate (Lutz 1994, 369). Nevertheless, the simple formal manner in which a constitution may be amended does not necessarily mean that a constitution will actually be amended that often. The Japanese constitution, for example, can be amended more easily than the US constitution. Still, it has not been amended more often. To the contrary, in the first 47 years it was not altered at all (ibid.). An amendment of the constitution did not seem necessary since the Japanese Supreme Court – as has been pointed out before – hardly put the normative precedency of the constitution to practice. Hence, the frequency of amendments does not depend upon the difficulty to formally amend the constitution alone (ibid., 361).

Social limitations relate to the access to the constitutional court. This limitation depends upon the fact that constitutional courts cannot activate their power of interpretation by themselves. In general, they can only initiate legal proceedings based on the request of another institution or actor. The more restrictive the access to the constitutional court is regulated, the smaller the chances for a constitutional court to practice it's power of interpretation. The manner access is granted to individual persons is central here since citizens represent the greatest quantity of potential petitioners. Constitutional courts, such as the courts in Bulgaria, France or Turkey (Brunner 2002, 236–246), which cannot be called upon by an individual, therefore face higher restraints against their power. It seems that those constitutional jurisdictions are at an advantage here which are not concentrated in one court, but are practiced more diffusely, such as in Canada, Australia, India, or Japan (Cappalletti and Ritterspach 1971, 82–84). It is in these cases that citizens may assert violations against their constitutionally guaranteed fundamental rights in every court proceeding (Brunner 2002, 197).

In contrast to this, when the monitoring of the constitution is concentrated exclusively with the constitutional court (see for the various forms of concentrated constitutional courts in Europe Comella 2004), direct access may be granted to citizens with the help of an appeal to their fundamental rights. This is the case with the German constitutional court, as well as with constitutional courts in Croatia, Lichtenstein, in Slovenia, Slovakia and Spain. In the case of the German constitutional court, individual complaints about the infringement of the constitution are therefore by far the procedures most often executed. Between the years 1952 and 2000, more than 130.000 applications for legal proceedings were filled with the court, almost 127.000 of those complaints about the infringement of the constitution (Badura and Dreier 2001, 935). On the one hand, this results in an overload of the constitutional court (Hain 2002, 102–104; Blankenburg 1998, 37–60). On the other hand, the formal necessity for activation looses its constraining impact on the constitutional court. The complaint about the infringement of the constitution thus serves as a mobilisation of citizens to enforce the constitutional law (Gusy 2001, 654).

Nevertheless, access to the constitutional court cannot only be constrained by limiting the number of potential applicants. A temporal limitation is also possible, limiting the time-span for the application process. The power of interpretation of the constitutional jurisdiction is *temporally* limited at this level through a strict limitation on the time-span spent on the constitutional supervision. The schedule is especially tight when legislation can only be examined on whether it is in accordance with the constitution *before* coming into effect, as is the case with the so-called preventive supervision (Tomuschat 2001, 257). Other constitutional courts may only become active *after* a law comes into effect. Their power of interpretation may then only be employed at a later point in time, but will not be temporally limited. This bears two eminent consequences: On the one hand, the declaration of constitutional conformity does not confer a permanent seal of approval upon a piece of legislation since these constitutional courts have the possibility to revise positive decisions in the future, a possibility which the French *Conseil constitutionnel* does not have since it is restricted to preventive action. On the other hand it is possible for these constitutional courts to examine and annihilate a piece of legislation even decades after its adoption.

3. The interpreting court

At the second level, *the level of the interpreting court*, the constitutional court competes with the rest of the courts. This competition becomes especially apparent under the condition of a diffuse constitutional jurisdiction (Brunner 2002, 195). In this case, the constitutional review of laws is not an exclusive function of one single (constitutional) court. Due to this, all US courts may suspend the application of laws that in their opinion are not in accordance with the constitution. Nevertheless, the binding effect of the precedents has installed an institutional practice in which the US Supreme Court has gained the exclusive power of interpretation over the constitution. Under this condition of competition, the power of interpretation of the constitutional court is thus based on its *interpretative precedency* over the constitution. In contrast to the interpretation of other courts, its interpretations are not subject to revisions by higher courts.

At this level, the power of interpretation is executed by the asymmetry between the *ultimate* jurisdiction and other jurisdictions. Nevertheless, this asymmetry is not always established by the constituent alone. In certain aspects, it may also be established through a law on the functioning of the constitutional court – written by the legislator. In such a way the diffuse character of the constitutional court was removed in Switzerland, Portugal, Greece and Estonia (Brunner 2002, 197).

Besides the interpretative precedence, an exclusive interpretative supremacy exists when the functions of constitutional jurisdiction rest with a court, the constitutional court, alone (as is the case with the German *Bundesverfassungsgericht*, but also the cases of the constitutional courts in Albania, Bulgaria, Italy, Croatia, Austria, Poland, Spain and Hungary). All these constitutional courts are authorised alone to interpret the constitution in a collectively binding manner. At this level, the precondition of the power of interpretation of the constitutional court rests on the fact that it occupies the exclusive function to interpret. Such a concentration of constitutional jurisdiction alone is no guarantee that the exclusive function to interpret of the constitutional court leads to a factual power to interpret over other courts. For – as can be seen in the Czech Republic – the competition between the constitutional courts and the other courts over who holds the power to interpret becomes a conflict.

In some cases like Austria, France, the Netherlands (Brunner 2002, 216; Cappelletti and Ritterspach 1971, 88) the exclusive interpretative supremacy of the constitutional court reaches to the extent at which all other jurisdiction must *always* consider the existing laws as valid. In Germany and Italy, this is different. The lower courts there must appeal to the constitutional court as soon as they consider a law to stand in opposition with the constitution or at least doubt its accordance with the constitution (see BVerfGE 1, 184). It is here that the interpretative competition between the constitutional jurisdiction and the rest of the jurisdiction becomes most apparent. At the same time this competition gets formalised which can lead to the mitigation of the competition over interpretation. In this case the relation between simple courts to the constitutional court can be understood as one of 'cooperation': The lower courts ask the constitutional court to check their doubts of the constitutional lawfulness of a norm (Korioth 2001, 59).

But when the lower courts take a norm, applicable by them, to be in accordance with the constitution, they cannot only, but *must* refrain from a constitutional examination of this norm. This structural autonomy grants them a power of interpretation that competes with the constitutional court. Different from a jurisdiction which must always act on the assumption that laws are in accordance with the constitution, these courts decide for themselves whether something is in accordance with the constitution or not. In Germany the ones who were involved in a process may after the sentence of a court object to the applications of a supposedly unconstitutional norm and bring it to the constitutional court. If a citizen feels violated in his fundamental rights because of such a norm, he can object immediately the judgement and indirectly the applied norm. At the latest in this case the competition about who has the power to interpret between the constitutional court and the other courts becomes inevitably tenuous (Korioth 2001, 60, see also Düwel 2000 and Kenntner 2005).

Still, in contrast to the constitutional court, they do not decide what is *not* in accordance with the constitution. Lower courts may thus only affirm autonomously that a piece of legislation is in accordance with the constitution, but cannot negate this status single-handedly. This has consequences for the first level of the power of interpretation since in this case the power of the legislator or the government can only be strengthened by the power of interpretation of the lower courts over the constitution.

At the same time the legislator and the government are protected from a restraint of the same power of interpretation of these lower courts. Under the conditions of a diffuse constitutional jurisdiction, this structural protection is nevertheless always a question of the institutional practice of the constitutional court. In Japan, lower courts apply their power of interpretation quite often against the political institutions. However, these decisions are then very often repealed by higher courts, the highest being the Supreme Court itself (Noll 1992, 120).

Aside from this, analysing the power of a constitutional court has to take into account, that this power can manifest itself at this level in two forms. The question of the power of interpretation will either be preliminarily answered by the institutional structure (in cases of a concentrated constitutional jurisdiction), or it will be answered over and over again in practice (in cases of a diffuse constitutional jurisdiction). Nonetheless, the power of interpretation of a constitutional court is also not limitless at this level. Especially the factual, social and temporal *range* of the constitutional law offer possibilities to set limitations for the power of interpretation of the constitutional court.

Factual limitations can be set by functionally circumventing the arena of the public law from questions of the civil and criminal law. Sometimes, this limitation still remains legally undecided. Paradoxically, the question over the range of its power of interpretation may thus even lie with the constitutional court itself. In such a way the German constitutional court maximised its own range of power in his Lüth-decision. There it states that the constitutional law does not only expresses a certain part of the law but also an objective value system which claims validity over all parts of the law (BVerfGE 7, 198 [205]). Contrary, at the Italian *Corte constituzionale* the diffuse requirements for admission allow for a regulation of a constitutional range of power. Decisive for the admission is the 'relevance.' Since the relevance is broadly understood and thus used flexible the Italian constitutional court extends its own range of power to interpret.

Socially the range of the power of interpretation of the constitutional court may be limited at this level when decisions made by the lower courts are not affected by the decisions of constitutional court. This decoupling of the jurisdiction is the case in for example Poland and Hungary (Brunner 2002, 219–220). In these cases citizens may have the constitutionality of laws examined on whose basis they were convicted. Still, the decision of the lower court cannot be annihilated, even when the constitutional court decides that the law is not in accordance with the constitution. Only the respective law loses its validity, but not the decisions based on it. The citizen filing the suit thus does not experience any direct advantage from this ruling at first. The power to interpret of the constitutional court encompasses therefore not the decisions of the ordinary courts. This limits its power of interpretation. At the same time however this leads to a decrease of the strains between the constitutional court and the other courts (Brunner 2002, 219).

In additions, the range of the power of interpretation of the constitutional court may be limited *temporally* at this level by setting the date a legal decision becomes effective. This limitation thus depends upon the fact whether the decisions of the constitutional court are binding in a temporal manner. In some cases, an annihilated law will only lose its validity when the decision of the constitutional court has been published, so that this decision is only effective in the present and future. For example, a decision of the Italian *Corte costituzionale* or the Bulgarian constitutional court then abolishes an existing law, but not the past jurisdiction and bureaucratic application based on it (Stalev 1999, 18). In contrast to this, the German constitutional court even allows for a general, retrospective annihilation that affects the present, future and past, meaning the point in time when the respective law became effective (Blasberg 2003, 17–20). Under these circumstances, the constitutional court has the possibility to annihilate a law and thus negate its existence for all time – not only in the future, but also in the past.

4. The interpretation

The first and second level of the power of interpretation have a special relation. On the one hand, the second level of the power of interpretation (the exclusive supremacy over mandatory interpretations) relies on the first level of the power of interpretation (the normative precedency of the interpreted constitution) as a necessary condition. This can be seen in England where these conditions are lacking (Creutzburg 2006, 358). Since the exclusive, mandatory interpretation of the constitution is only linked to power when the constitution to be interpreted can also make decisions about the validity of the basic law. On the other hand, the first level of the power of interpretation depends on the enforcement of its claim to normative precedence on the second level. In this case, the second level functions as a sufficient condition for the power of interpretation at the first level.

Nevertheless, both levels are not only mutually dependent upon each other as necessary and sufficient conditions. Both levels also rest on the third level of the power of interpretation: *the interpretation*. The critical condition for this is that the constitution's text cannot control its own meaning (as shown for the German constitution by Depenheuer 1988). It cannot interpret itself. And it cannot determine its interpretation (Grimm 2001, 27). Due to this, the constitutional court not only effectively secures the precedency of the constitution (Starck 1992, 196). It also practices the power of interpretation through interpretation because the method to apply norms is a mechanism to select for content and not a neutral tool to interpret content (Grimm 1987, 371). Thus, *at the third level* of a power of interpretation of the constitutional court, the *interpretation* itself comes into effect. The asymmetrical structure between different interpretations is situated at this level of the power of interpretation: on the one hand, the interpretation that the constitutional court updates, and on the other hand, the remaining potential alternatives. Here, the court competes with the judicial scientific community for the right interpretation (Schlink 1989).

Nevertheless limitations can be set on this level, but they can only be set on the arbitrariness of the interpretation. In *a factual manner*, the interpretation is limited through the interpreted: the constitutional text. Even when the text is not in command over its own wording, it can still limit the number of possible interpretations (Riecken 2003). However, it is a different question of interpretation in how far this limit reaches. Constitutional courts may also overcome these limitations of the text by allocating different sources of law or principles to the constitutional level. In that sense decided the German constitutional court in its first case that it accepts the existence of overpositive law which binds the constitutional court itself as well as the positive law (BVerfGE 1, 14 [18]). Through this, constitutional courts can free themselves from the limits of the constitutional text (Simon 1990, 156) and the will of its authors.

In a *social manner*, the power of interpretation of the constitutional court is limited by its 'societal [...] accountability' (Cappalletti 1983, 25–27). The accountability towards the general public (Hocks 2002) is made possible through the publication of the majority's and minority's opinions of the court. This publication makes the relation between the interpretation and the interpreted visible for third party members. The interpretation must then also be comprehensible to the third party members. The publication of the minority's dissenting opinions has a different function. It shows that those alternative interpretations that were not updated are still considered valid by a minority of the judges. This publication of the minority's dissenting opinions is not necessarily linked to the establishment of a constitutional court. The US Supreme Court, for example, published its first explicit dissenting opinion only in 1805, 15 years after its institutionalization (Epstein et al. 1996, 12). It took the German constitutional court 20 years to do the same (Roellecke 2001, Lamprecht 1992).

In *a temporal manner*, the power of interpretation can be limited by expectations for continuity. Their self-declared dependency on the constitutional text confronts the constitutional courts with the intentions of the authors of the constitution. Due to this, the constitutional court must always expect its interpretation of the constitution to be compared to the original will of the constituents. These expectations may not determine a single decision, but they may limit the range of possible interpretations (Leedes 1986, 15; Sunstein 1993, 94). But even this limitation can be overcome by the constitutional court since the crucial question remains which documents express the will of the constituents (for an example from the United States see Herrmann 2002, 132 ff.).

Time sets a similar limit on the court's own jurisdiction, because it also produces expectations for continuity that limit the constitutional court at this level. The US Supreme Court lives up to this expectation through its *stare decisis doctrine* determining that made decisions apply not only to the present, but also function as precedents for the future (ibid. 136). The appeal to past decisions thus turns into a central justification for new decisions. Also in the case of the German constitutional court (Schäller 2006), the jurisdiction is more and more linked to its own past decisions (Brodocz 2003). But the constitutional court can modify this limit again. On the one hand it might happen that only with a new case it becomes apparent that two decisions contradict each other in the now relevant aspect. On the other hand the constitutional court itself often decides to what extent it binds itself to previous decisions (see for a discussion about the German constitutional court Sachs 1977).

5. Conclusion

Judicial power is a complex phenomenon. When analysing it, we have to consider three interdependent levels (see table 1). But even then we fail to meet the full complexity of judicial power since judicial power only exists in practice. Thus, at the third level the constitutional court has the opportunity to limit the power of interpretation itself through methodic self-restraint (Simon 1994, 1671). Suppose a constitutional court always concentrates on the same method of interpretation. In this case, the manner in which the constitution would be interpreted could always be determined before the final decision. Thus, the judges would not have to settle for one of the different methods of interpretation anymore. Instead, they would execute the single legitimate interpretation with the help of the prevailing method. But through such a self-restraining the power of interpretation does not dissolve completely at this level for two reasons: first of all, the basic decision over the prevailing method of interpretation remains, and second of all, the power of interpretation in these cases is only shifted from court to method. We can also turn this thought around meaning a constitutional court can protect the power of interpretation at this level if it bases its interpretation on different methods (see as an example the analysis of the Lüth-case in Brodocz 2005).

This bears two important consequences. Only under this condition does the bare executor of the power of interpretation of the constitution turn into *its sovereign interpreter* at the third level of the power of interpretation; and only due to this do the first and second level of the power of interpretation become problematic: the first two levels of the power of interpretation strengthen this sovereignty by concentrating the power of interpretation on the third level with the constitutional court (second level of the power of interpretation) and hierarchizing it against the legitimate power of the legislator (first level of the power of interpretation). Nevertheless, this also means that the third level of the power of interpretation, which draws from the interpretation, may be limited preventively at the first two levels of the power of interpretation.

Finally, something else also becomes apparent. The power of interpretation that draws from the interpretation itself can unfold most effectively when it is endowed especially well on the first two levels of the power of interpretation. This interdependency also shows that the differentiation between the three levels is not a phenomenal, but rather an analytical one. This analytical differentiation becomes necessary in order to be able to describe and explain the complexity of the phenomenon 'the power of interpretation.'

Table 1: Three levels of the power of interpretation

	First level: The interpreted constitution	**Second level: The interpreting court**	**Third level: The interpretation**
Precondition	Normative precedency of the constitution	Exclusive interpretative supremacy or interpretative precedency	No control of the interpreted text over the interpretation
Asymmetry	Between the constitution and the rest of the law	Between constitutional jurisdiction and the rest of the jurisdiction	Between the updated interpretation and the remaining potential alternatives

	First level: The interpreted constitution	Second level: The interpreting court	Third level: The interpretation
Constitution of the asymmetry	By the constituent	By the constituent, the legislator and the constitutional court	Through the constitutional court itself
Competing actors	Constitutional court vs. the constituent	The constitutional court vs. lower courts	The constitutional court vs. the judicial scientific community
Factual constraint	Ability to amend the constitution	The range of the constitutional jurisdiction	The wording of the constitutional text
Social constraint	Access to the constitutional court	Circumvention of the court's jurisdiction	Publication of the dissenting opinions
Temporal constraint	Time-span for the application	Setting the date when a constitutional court's decision becomes effective	Obligation to the will of the constituent and the court's own decisions

Acknowledgements

I would like to thank Stefanie Hammer and Linda Monsees for translating and editing this chapter that is a shortened and revised version of Chapter IV.1 in Brodocz (2009).

References

Blankenburg, Erhard. 1998. Unsinn und Sinn des Annahmeverfahrens bei Verfassungsbeschwerden. *Zeitschrift für Rechtssoziologie* 19: 37–60.

Blasberg, Georg. 2003. *Verfassungsgerichte als Ersatzgeber. Entscheidungsaussprüche bei Normenkontrollen von Bundesverfassungsgericht und Corte costituzionale*. Frankfurt am Main: Peter Lang.

Böckenförde, Ernst-Wolfgang. 1999. *Staat, Nation, Europa. Studien zur Staatslehre, Verfassungstheorie und Rechtsphilosophie*. Frankfurt am Main: Suhrkamp.

Brodocz, André. 2003. Die Eigenzeit des Bundesverfassungsgerichts. Eine qualitative Analyse seiner Rechtsprechung. *Zeitschrift für Soziologie* 24: 183–217.

Brodocz, André. 2005. Lüth und die Deutungsmacht des Bundesverfassungsgerichts. In *Das Lüth-Urteil aus (rechts-)historischer Sicht. Die Konflikte um Veit Harlan und die Grundrechtsjudikatur des Bundesverfassungsgerichts*, edited by Thomas Henne and Arne Riedlinger, 271–289. Berlin: Berliner Wissenschaftsverlag.

Brodocz, André. 2009. *Die Macht der Judikative*. Wiesbaden: VS Verlag für Sozialwissenschaften.

Brunner, Georg. 2002. Der Zugang des Einzelnen zur Verfassungsgerichtsbarkeit im europäischen Raum. *Jahrbuch des öffentlichen Rechts der Gegenwart* 50: 191–256.

Busch, Andreas: Das oft geänderte Grundgesetz. In *Demokratie in Ost und West. Für Klaus von Beyme*, edited by Wolfgang Merkel and Andreas Busch, 549–574. Frankfurt am Main: Suhrkamp.

Cappelletti, Mauro. 1983. 'Who Watches the Watchman?' A Comparative Study on Judicial Responsibility. *The American Journal of Comparative Law* 31: 1–62.

Cappelletti, Mauro, Ritterspach, Theodor. 1971. Die gerichtliche Kontrolle der Verfassungsmäßigkeit der Gesetze in rechtsvergleichender Betrachtung. *Jahrbuch des öffentlichen Rechts der Gegenwart* 20: 65–86.

Comella, Victor Ferreres. 2004. The Consequences of Centralizing Constitutional Review in a Special Court. Some Thoughts on Judicial Activism. *Texas Law Review* 82: 1705–1736.

Creutzburg, Claudia. 2006. Deutungsmacht und ungeschriebene Verfassung: England. In *Die Deutungsmacht der Verfassungsgerichtsbarkeit*, edited by Hans Vorländer, 339–362 Wiesbaden: VS Verlag für Sozialwissenschaften.

Depenheuer, Otto. 1988. *Der Wortlaut als Grenze. Thesen zu einem Topos der Verfassungsinterpretation*. Heidelberg: R.v. Decker & C.F. Müller.

Düwel, Martin. 2000. *Kontrollbefugnisse des Bundesverfassungsgerichts bei Verfassungsbeschwerden gegen gerichtliche Entscheidungen.* Baden-Baden: Nomos.

Epstein, Lee, Segal, Jeffrey, Spaeth Harold J., Walker, Thomas. 1996. *The Supreme Court Compendium. Data, Decisions, and Developments.* Washington, D.C.: Congressional Quarterly.

Geiger, Willi. 1995. Bundesverfassungsgericht. In *Staatslexikon, First Issue*, edited by Görresgesellschaft c. 1006–1012. Freiburg et al.: Herder.

Gibson, James L., Caldeira, Gregory A., Baird, Vanessa A. 1998. On the Legitimacy of National High Courts. *American Political Science Review* 92: 343–359.

Grimm, Dieter. 1987. Methode als Machtfaktor. In *Recht und Staat in der bürgerlichen Gesellschaft*, edited by Dieter Grimm, 347–372 Frankfurt am Main: Suhrkamp.

Gusy, Christoph. 2001. Die Verfassungsbeschwerde. In *Festschrift 50 Jahre Bundesverfassungsgericht, Bd. 1. Verfassungsgerichtsbarkeit – Verfassungsprozeß,* edited by Peter Badura and Horst Dreier, 641–671. Tübingen: Mohr Siebeck.

Hain, Sabine. 2002. *Die Individualverfassungsbeschwerde nach Bundesrecht. Von den Vorarbeiten zu einer deutschen Verfassung bis zur Aufnahme ins Grundgesetz.* Baden-Baden: Nomos.

Hatajiri Tsuyoshi. 2003. Ein Versuch zum richterlichen Prüfungssystem unter rechtsvergleichenden Gesichtspunkten. Reformvorschläge in Japan. *Jahrbuch des öffentlichen Rechts der Gegenwart* 51: 711–723.

Herrmann, Dietrich. 2002. Der amerikanische Supreme Court und die Prinzipien von *Original Intent* und *Stare Decisis.* In *Dauer durch Wandel. Institutionelle Ordnungen zwischen Verstetigung und Transformation*, edited by Stephan Müller, Gary S. Schaal and Claudia Tiersch, 131–144. Köln et al.: Böhlau.

Hocks, Stephan. 2002. *Gerichtsgeheimnis und Begründungszwang. Zur Publizität der Entscheidungsgründe im Ancien Régime und im frühen 19. Jahrhundert.* Frankfurt am Main: Vittorio Klostermann.

Ismayr, Wolfgang. 2003. Die politischen Systeme Westeuropas im Vergleich. In *Die politischen Systeme Westeuropas,* edited by Wolfgang Ismayr, 9–54. Opladen: Leske und Budrich.

Kenntner, Markus. 2005. Vom „Hüter der Verfassung' zum „Pannenhelfer der Nation'? Zur Kontrolldichte im Verfahren der Urteilsverfassungsbeschwerde. *Die öffentliche Verwaltung* 58: 269–280.

Korioth, Stefan. 2001. Bundesverfassungsgericht und Rechtsprechung („Fachgerichte"). In *Festschrift 50 Jahre Bundesverfassungsgericht, Bd. 1. Verfassungsgerichtsbarkeit – Verfassungsprozeß,* edited by Peter Badura and Horst Dreier, 55–81. Tübingen: Mohr Siebeck.

Kriele, Martin. 1976. *Theorie der Rechtsgewinnung entwickelt am Problem der Verfassungsinterpretation.* Berlin: Duncker & Humblot.

Lamprecht, Rolf. 1992. *Richter contra Richter. Abweichende Meinungen und ihre Bedeutung für die Rechtskultur*. Baden-Baden: Nomos.

Leedes, Gary C. 1986. *The Meaning of the Constitution. An Interdisciplinary Study of Legal Theory.* Millwood (NY): Associated Faculty Press.

Luhmann, Niklas. 1988. *Macht*. Stuttgart: Enke.

Lutz, Donald S. 1994. Toward a Theory of Constitutional Amendment. *American Political Science Review* 88: 355–370.

Mishler, William and Sheehan, Reginald S. 1996. Public Opinion, the Attitudinal Model, and Supreme Court Decision Making. A Micro Analytic Perspective. *Journal of Politics* 58: 169–201.

Noll, Alfred J. 1992. *Internationale Verfassungsgerichtsbarkeit. Fragen der Verfassungsgerichtsbarkeit in Großbritannien, der USA, Frankreich, Italien und Japan*. Wien: Verlag der Österreichischen Staatsdruckerei.

Pieroth, Bodo. 2003. Das Verfassungsgericht als kommunikatives Element moderner Verfassungsstaatlichkeit. *Rechtstheorie* 34: 299–305.

Riecken, Jörg. 2003. *Verfassungsgerichtsbarkeit in der Demokratie. Grenzen verfassungsgerichtlicher Kontrolle unter besonderer Berücksichtigung von John Hart Elys prozeduraler Theorie der Repräsentationsverstärkung*. Berlin: Duncker & Humblot.

Roellecke, Gerd. 2001. Sondervoten. In *Festschrift 50 Jahre Bundesverfassungsgericht, Bd. 1. Verfassungsgerichtsbarkeit – Verfassungsprozeß,* edited by Peter Badura and Horst Dreier, 363–384. Tübingen: Mohr Siebeck.

Sachs, Michael. 1977. *Die Bindung des Bundesverfassungsgerichts an seine Entscheidungen.* München: Vahlen.

Schäller, Steven: Präjudizien als selbstreferentielle Geltungsressource des Bundesverfassungsgerichts. In *Die Deutungsmacht der Verfassungsgerichtsbarkeit*, edited by Hans Vorländer, 205–234. Wiesbaden: VS Verlag für Sozialwissenschaften.

Schlink, Bernhard. 1989. Die Entthronung der Staatsrechtswissenschaft durch die Verfassungsgerichtsbarkeit. *Der Staat* 28: 161–172.

Simon, Dieter. 1990. Zäsuren im Rechtsdenken. In *Zäsuren nach 1945. Essays zur Periodisierung der deutschen Nachkriegsgeschichte*, edited by Martin Broszat, 153–167 München: R. Oldenbourg.

Simon, Helmut: Verfassungsgerichtsbarkeit. In *Handbuch des Verfassungsrechts der Bundesrepublik Deutschland,* edited by Ernst Benda, Werner Maihofer and Hans-Jochen Vogel, 1637–1677 Berlin et al.: de Gruyter.

Stoyan Stalev. 1999. *Verfassungssysteme im Umbruch. Eine rechtsvergleichende Untersuchung zu Bulgarien, Rumänien und Slowenien.* Baden-Baden: Nomos.

Starck, Christian. 2001. Das Bundesverfassungsgericht in der Verfassungsordnung und im politischen Prozeß. In *Festschrift 50 Jahre Bundesverfassungsgericht, Bd. 1. Verfassungsgerichtsbarkeit – Verfassungsprozeß,* edited by Peter Badura and Horst Dreier, 1–32. Tübingen: Mohr Siebeck.

Sunstein, Cass R. 1993. *The Partial Constitution*. Cambridge (MA) et al.: Harvard University Press.

Tomuschat, Christian. 2001. Das Bundesverfassungsgericht im Kreise anderer nationaler Verfassungsgerichte. In *Festschrift 50 Jahre Bundesverfassungsgericht, Bd. 1. Verfassungsgerichtsbarkeit – Verfassungsprozeß,* edited by Peter Badura and Horst Dreier, 246–288. Tübingen: Mohr Siebeck.

Vanberg, Georg. 2005. *The Politics of Constitutional Review in Germany*. Cambridge: Cambridge University Press.

Vorländer, Hans. 2001. Der Interpret als Souverän. Die Macht des Bundesverfassungsgerichts beruht auf einem Vertrauensvorschuß, der anderen Institutionen fehlt. *Frankfurter Allgemeine Zeitung* (17. April).

Wahl, Rainer. 2003. *Verfassungsstaat, Europäisierung, Internationalisierung*. Frankfurt am Main: Suhrkamp.

Court Rulings
German Federal Constitutional Court

Decision of 23 October 1951, BVerfGE 1, 14
Decision of 20 March 1952, BVerfGE 1, 184
Decision of 15 January 1958, BVerfGE 7, 198

What is 'Politicisation' of Constitutional Courts? Towards a Decision-oriented Concept

Michael Hein and Stefan Ewert

Abstract

'Politicisation' is one of the most frequently used keywords in public discourse and scientific research on constitutional courts. However, whereas the concept of judicialisation, which is equally important in this field of research, has been the subject of considerable discussion in political and legal theory, a distinct definition of the term politicisation is lacking in many studies. In light of this, we address the question of how politicisation of constitutional courts can adequately be understood. To this end, we examine the theoretical conceptions of the relationship between politics, law and constitutional adjudication that underlie the different understandings of politicisation. Based on our findings, we develop a decision-oriented concept of politicisation, which is not only suitable for many theoretical approaches, but can also be detected in numerous empirical studies.

1. Introduction

'Politicisation' is one of the most frequently used keywords in public discourse and scientific research on constitutional courts. On many occasions, these courts are publicly blamed for taking political rather than legal decisions, for illegitimately overstepping the bounds of constitutional law, for intervening in the politics of the day and for exceeding their competencies to the disadvantage of parliament and government. However, in political and legal research on constitutional courts, politicisation also features as one of the central analytical terms used. It can be found in numerous studies that deal with political influences on or political consequences of constitutional adjudication (instead of others, see Alivizatos 1995; Stone Sweet 2000; Grimm 2001; Lietzmann 2006; Lembcke 2007; Bornemann 2007; Hönnige 2009; Garoupa 2009; Engel 2011; Bartels and Johnston 2012; Hein 2012; Hein and Ewert 2013).

A brief overview of these diverse uses does not only demonstrate that the term politicisation emerges with manifold meanings, but also that a distinct definition of the concept is often lacking. According to Basil Bornemann (2007, 77) a large part of the debate is characterised 'by merely a vague understanding of the relevant basic terms and causal mechanisms.'[1] Whereas the somewhat antonymous

1 All German-language quotations are translated by the authors.

concept of judicialisation, which is equally important in the research on constitutional courts, has been the subject of considerable discussion in political and legal theory (see Rehder 2010), much less attention has been paid to the concept of politicisation. A significant hint in this regard is the fact that this term has been completely left out in anglophone political science encyclopedias and handbooks so far (see Magill 1996; Bealey 1999; Whittington, Kelemen and Caldeira 2008; Goodin 2009; McLean and McMillian 2009; Badie 2011). As a matter of course, this can be traced to the US-American political science tradition of conceptualising judges as 'politicians in robes' (Sheldon 1970, xi), i.e. as politically interested actors that do not systematically differ from other political actors. However, even in US-American research the concept of politicisation has gained in importance in recent years (see Stone Sweet 2000; Garoupa 2009; Engel 2011; Popova 2012).

Nevertheless, the state of the art regarding the terminology and conception of 'politicisation' falls far short of the central role that it plays in constitutional court research. In light of this, we address the question of how it can adequately be defined. To this end, we will firstly give a brief overview of the various uses of the term in social sciences in general (2). Subsequently, we will show which theoretical conceptions of the relationship between politics, law and constitutional adjudication underlie the different concepts of politicisation in the relevant studies on constitutional courts (3). Based on our findings, we will finally develop a decision-oriented concept of politicisation, which is not only suitable for many theoretical conceptions, but which can (at least implicitly) also be found in many empirical studies (4).

2. Politicisation – a brief literature overview

In general, 'politicisation' describes 'making previously non-political persons or issues political' or, in other words, the 'process and/or result of the expansion of politics, especially of the power to take socially binding decisions and to penetrate previously non-political fields such as private life or private economic activity' (Schmidt 2000, 630). Virtually all social spheres and objects can be targets of politicisation. As a consequence, there are manifold applications of this term in social research. For instance, it appears in connection to the *economy*, often under the more specific heading of 'democratisation', denoting the introduction of democratic decision-making mechanisms at the level of individual companies, economic branches or the economic system in general (see Fricke and Wagner 2012). A similar application can be found when it is used in the context of *universities* (see Nullmeier 2001). *Ethnicity* and *religion* are also often analysed as being politicised in the sense that they have become politically relevant factors or fulfil political purposes (see Wierzcholska 2012; Schröter 2006). With regard to the *law*, politicisation is commonly used as a synonym for positivisation, i.e. the historical process of introducing political legislation as the most important legal source (see Grimm 2001, 16–17).

Politicisation can also refer to the *constitution*, here in the specific sense of 'inserting short-term political issues into the constitution, thereby removing them from the disposition of the "simple" parliamentary majority, as well as stripping them of the subsequent political discourse' (Scholz and Meyer-Teschendorf 1998, 10). Concerning *public administration*, politicisation describes 'the substitution of political criteria for merit-based criteria in the selection, retention, promotion, rewards, and disciplining of members of the public service' (Peters and Pierre 2004, 2). Politicised public authorities, therefore, do not exclusively function in compliance with legal provisions, but can be subject to semi-legal or even illegal political directives. In the political science's sub-discipline of international relations, the concept of politicisation has recently been used to describe the 'de-technocratisation' of *supra- or international decision-making processes*, in particular with regard to the European Union. In this context, policy decisions are seen as 'politicized when they are drawn into the public light' (Zürn, Binder and Ecker-Ehrhardt 2012, 73). Furthermore, several studies discuss the politicisation of the *society* as a whole. Here, the term denotes the penetration of the society by its political system. As is the case with the economy and the universities, we often encounter the concept of 'democratisation' here (see Czerwick 2011, 222–223). Finally, in some older studies, politicisation was used to refer to the political socialisation of people (see Easton 1957, 397–400).

If we take a closer look at research on judicial institutions, especially constitutional courts, two fundamental meanings of politicisation can be distinguished. In most cases, the term refers to a political *influence on* courts, i.e. the trials, the judges and the decision-making process. Hence, it focuses on the *input side* of courts (instead of others, see Schmitt 1929, 1931; Loewenstein 1952/53; Hesse 1995; Stone Sweet 2000; Grimm 2001; Hönnige 2009; Höpner 2010; Engel 2011; Bartels and Johnston 2012). Less frequently, the term is used to describe political *consequences of* judicial decisions, i.e. it refers to the *output side* of courts (see Alivizatos 1995; Lietzmann 2006). Finally, very rarely, both the input and the output dimensions are combined (see Bora 2003).[2]

2 For a detailed description and typologisation of the definitions of politicisation of constitutional courts in the history of political and legal sciences, see Hein and Ewert (2014, with further references).

3. Constitutional adjudication between politics and law

The following subsections indicate which theoretical interpretations of the relationship between politics, law and constitutional adjudication underlie these different concepts of the politicisation of constitutional courts. They can be divided into three groups: approaches that understand constitutional adjudication as a purely legal process (subsection 3.1), approaches that conceptualise it as an entirely political process (3.2), and approaches that define it as *both* a legal *and* a political process (3.3).

3.1 The naive approach

'The naive approach'– as we would like to call it, using a neat expression put forward by Ingwer Ebsen (1985, 108) – conceptualises constitutional adjudication as a purely legal process, solely oriented towards the norms of the constitutional law. This view can be traced back to Alexander Hamilton's (1788) considerations on judicial review in the Federalist Papers. Furthermore, it corresponds to the 'self-image of constitutional adjudication as a non-political, purely legal institution' (Brodocz 2009, 51). This self-image seems to be typical for many constitutional courts and can be identified e.g. in the works of many former and current German constitutional judges. According to Ernst Friesenhahn (1954, 150), the Federal Constitutional Court (FCC) has 'only to control that the *norms* of the constitution are complied with by the legislature.' The Court makes an exclusively '*norm-based decision*' and hence does not take part 'in the creative formation of the people's political life.' The Constitutional Court can 'only *unfold* [...] what is contained in the constitution, equally recognisable for the other state bodies' (ibid., 158). Therefore, the FCC is 'merely a servant of the law and must always remain fully aware of its non-political function' (ibid., 159, all emphases in original).

Similarly, Erich Kaufmann identifies a clear distinction from constitutional adjudication: 'all *political* issues are excluded from it. [...] I would say, quite plainly: matters are political, if there are no legal norms for their solution' (Kaufmann 1952, 4, emphasis in original). Even today, clearly the majority of FCC judges share the view that the court only conducts constitutional *interpretation* and thus performs a purely legal activity which does not contain any political element (see Kranenpohl 2010, 341–343, 409–419 and 458–463).

Rested upon such a basic understanding, the concept of politicisation denotes a normatively problematic political influence, which jeopardises the role of adjudication in constitutional adjudication. According to Konrad Hesse – another former FCC judge –, the specifics of constitutional law (in particular the relative indeterminateness of its norms) neither withdraw from the cases

> the character of legal matters, nor from the decision the character of legal decisions. [...] Despite the peculiarities of its task, therefore, constitutional adjudication is adjudication. Its decisions are, therefore, not political decisions in disguise that are in contradiction with the nature of real adjudication, inevitably leading to the politicisation of the judiciary (Hesse 1995, 241).

As the term 'naive approach' already suggests, this understanding of politics, law and constitutional adjudication is neither theoretically nor empirically convincing. It negates the fact that constitutional courts are often required to decide on matters for which they cannot find clear answers in the constitutional text. As Robert A. Dahl (1957, 280) put it, 'it is an essential characteristic of the institution that from time to time its members decide cases where legal criteria are not in any realistic sense adequate to the task [...]; that is, the setting of the case is "political."' The majority of constitutional courts cannot – contrary to what the aforecited quotation of Erich Kaufmann suggested – simply flinch from deciding these kinds of cases. Therefore, constitutional adjudication frequently contains political elements. Although this occurs within the framework of court proceedings and the judges might try to orient themselves solely by means of constitutional norms to the best of their knowledge and beliefs, they are often required to act beyond a constitutionally determined scope. Even if 'provisions are formulated as clearly and as coherently as possible, they can raise questions when it comes to solving a concrete case' (Grimm 2009, 27).[3]

3.2 The fatalistic approach

The exact opposite of the 'naive' view can be referred to as the *'fatalistic approach'*, which understands constitutional adjudication to be a purely political process. Paradigmatic of this is Carl Schmitt, who distinguishes legislation and adjudication, but not politics and law. Instead, Schmitt considers every social place political once there are conflicts to be waged and decisions to be made. Accordingly, a constitutional court is only an option for 'an *obvious violation of the constitution* that can be ascertained beyond doubt', against which 'the court

3 For a recent example of such an only seemingly clear case, please refer to a dispute before the Polish Constitutional Tribunal (PCT) in 2011 concerning the meaning of Article 98, paragraph 2 of the Polish Constitution, according to which parliamentary elections have to take place on 'a non-working day.' To improve their chances in the upcoming elections, the governing coalition had tried to extend the ballot to two days. This seemingly unequivocal breach of the constitution caused one of the most controversial decisions of the PCT, in which no less than eleven (!) of the 15 judges issued dissenting opinions (Polish Constitutional Tribunal 2011).

exercises a repressive and vindicatory kind of justice' (Schmitt 1931, 31, emphasis in original). What Schmitt is referring to are explicit violations of constitutional rules with direct legal effects, such as election procedures.[4] Apart from these narrowly defined cases, however, especially in the case of decisions on the constitutionality of laws,

> there is no "purely legal matter" and the court decision is a far cry from a judicial decision, i.e. a far cry from justice. [Instead,] the judge is in a position to take or avert political measures and to become politically active in a way that makes him a powerful factor in domestic or even foreign policies (ibid., 31–32).

Leading to the same consequence, Alec Stone Sweet interprets the behaviour of constitutional judges within his rational-choice-based approach as purely utility-maximising, self-interested and strategic – i.e. similar to that of politicians. Hence, political conflicts before the constitutional court are only formally transformed into legal ones. 'Legislators easily and naturally express their ideological differences as conflicts about the nature and content of rights' (Stone Sweet 2000, 197). Similarly, the judges primarily strategically look for suitable legal justifications for their (in fact politically-motivated) decisions. Admittedly, Stone Sweet defines rational behaviour as being embedded in social and cultural norms and rules. Notably, the law is 'at least partly autonomous from personal preferences' (ibid., 26), but these norms and rules seem to be nothing more than framework conditions for actions that are actually political. Finally, Hans J. Lietzmann defines constitutional adjudication as a political process taking place in a society which 'subjects all matters of distribution to a controversial political distinction that requires legitimisation.' Therefore, the German FCC's attempts to find 'ways of a pre-political and legal dispute settlement' are doomed to failure (Lietzmann 2006, 282).

The concepts of politicisation suggested by the three authors discussed here do not, contrary to the 'naive approach', refer to the content and the function of deciding constitutional issues, because these decisions are by definition understood to be political. Politicisation rather denotes the process of transferring this political task to judicial procedures and institutions. The term is thus placed at the institutional level: Not the function of (constitutional) adjudication, but the institution of the court is politicised. Similar to the 'naive approach', the 'fatalistic' one is hardly convincing either. Whereas the former takes no account of the fact that constitutional adjudication solely on the basis of legal criteria is often impossible, the

---

4 As the Polish example has shown (see note 3), drawing the line in this way is empirically untenable.

latter negates the considerably narrower scope of action for constitutional courts in comparison to parliaments and governments. These courts are required to consider relatively restrictive procedures; are usually only able to act at the request of other actors or when certain legally defined situations occur; and are strongly governed by constitutional norms regarding the consequences of their decisions. Particularly in the legislative arena, a constitutional court is usually only able to prevent and appeal, i.e. it can act only as 'negative legislator' (Kelsen 1929, 26). In contrast, the court can act constructively, i.e. as 'positive legislator' (ibid.), only – if at all – in certain cases (e.g. when a regulation cannot be postponed) or indirectly (through the indication of conceivable provisions that are in line with the constitution). Above all, however, just like any other court, the constitutional court must use legal norms as the basis for its decisions. To put it in a nutshell: The fact that constitutional adjudication is subjected to political influences and has political consequences does not justify the argument that it is not essentially adjudication. If this is disregarded, the specific characteristics of constitutional courts cannot be identified.

3.3 The realistic approach

Whereas the 'naive approach' labours under 'a political blind spot', the 'fatalistic' one is not able to acknowledge 'the legal viewpoint.' In contrast, a position in the middle, which we would like to call the *'realistic approach'* to politics, law and constitutional adjudication, keeps both eyes open. This view can be deduced from the works of many authors in different variations and theoretical frameworks (see e.g. Kelsen 1929, 1930/31; Loewenstein 1952/53; Dahl 1957; Häberle 1980; Grimm 2001; Bora 2003; Garoupa 2009; Höpner 2010; Bartels and Johnston 2012). All these authors share a basic understanding of constitutional adjudication as a legal process that is both subject to political influences and has political consequences. In this sense, Hans Kelsen (1930/31, 67) already claimed:

> By authorising the judge within certain limits to weigh conflicting interests and to decide conflicts in favour of one party or another, the legislator delegates to him a capacity of lawmaking and thus a power that gives the judicial function the same "political" character that the legislature has, albeit to a lesser extent.

Among the current generation of German constitutional judges there are also some jurists who subscribe to this position. In Uwe Kranenpohl's (2010, 409) seminal interview study on the FCC, an anonymously cited judge states:

> By making legal decisions you always shape policies, too. If you, like me, are convinced that concretisation also means transforming something vague into something specific, which is

> not possible through understanding but through decision, when you say: "decision-making power is a characteristic of politics", then this means that, in this sense, political opportunities can also reside in a judge.

However, this emphasis on the political attributes of constitutional adjudication does not lead to the 'fatalistic' position of denying its judicial character, because even in cases where a constitutional court 'issues far-reaching directives [...], it still functions "judicially." The choice between "law or politics" proves to be false choice!' (Häberle 1980, 72–73). Besides, the binding force of the law on constitutional adjudication is one of the court's central sources of legitimacy. It represents a vital condition for its success, because this is the basis from which the court can exercise authority and build trust (see Vorländer and Brodocz 2006).

Thus, in the 'realist' view the term politicisation denotes two interacting phenomena: the variable extent of the political influences on the constitutional court and the court's scope for political decision-making facilitated by the relevant constitutional provisions. *Ex negativo*, the former FCC judge Dieter Grimm has summarised the most important aspects of such an understanding of politicisation:

> The separation of law and politics at the level of the application of the law does not mean that the process of judicial application of the law is inherently non-political, i.e. leaving no room for creative decisions [...]. Such an *inherent de-politicisation* of the application of the law would presuppose that the legal norms adopted by the legislature could fully determine how all individual cases are decided. However, there is no legal rule of which the application does not sometimes raise questions, which the judge has to answer by concretisation and interpretation. Influences from the judge's prior understanding, personal background and socialisation, as well as political and ideological preferences, are then inevitable. [...] Nevertheless, there is still a difference, because a priori application of the law takes place in a *normatively narrowed framework* (Grimm 2001, 26–27, emphases added).

4. A decision-oriented concept of politicisation

In what follows, we will propose a *decision-oriented concept of politicisation.* Bringing the central aspects of the previous discussion together and aiming for a theoretically and empirically convincing understanding of politicisation that conveys the aforementioned general definition of 'making [something] political' (Schmidt 2000, 630), four basic decisions arise: First of all, we restrict the term 'politicisation' to exclusively denote – direct and indirect – *influences on* constitutional court *decisions* (i.e. the court in general, the trials, the judges, and the decision-making process). Second, our concept is a *functional* and not an institutional one, i.e. politicisation refers to constitutional adjudication as a process, but not to constitutional courts as organisations. Third, our concept of politicisation fits into the *'realistic'* framework, as this is the most convincing of the three theoretical approaches. Finally, fourth, the concept is *solely analytical*. However, this final basic decision does not exclude the use of our concept in normative studies, which e.g. criticise certain types of politicisation as negative (for whichever normative reasons).

In the framework of the 'realistic approach', politics and law can generally be understood as functional sub-areas of modern society, each operating autonomously and performing one specific function. Whereas the function of politics is to provide the capacity to make collectively binding decisions, the function of law is to establish and stabilise normative expectations (see Luhmann 1990, 73–74; 2004, 94 and 148). In this arrangement, the constitutional court is an organisation in which politics and law regularly meet (see Bornemann 2007, 83–88). First and foremost, this refers to the *output side* of the court. Its decisions often yield not only legal, but also political consequences, because the court,

> especially within its constitutional review power, makes collectively binding decisions and therefore fulfils a genuinely *political function*. [...] The constitutional court acts [...] as the *final political authority*, because it has the competence to revise or confirm collectively binding decisions [of the political branches, M.H./S.E.] by its own collectively binding decisions (Bornemann 2007, 86, emphases in original).

Therefore, the constitutional court belongs to the '*constitutively* multi-referential organisations', that 'are not *definitively* ascribed to any functional system but operate with multiple references – and which thus act as intermediaries between different sub-systems' (Bode and Brose 2001, 118, emphases in original). However, as mentioned previously, our concept of politicisation refers exclusively to the *input side* of the decision-making process. Constitutional judges do not necessarily need to base their decisions solely on legal (especially constitutional) criteria. Instead, the judges may also be subject to numerous political influences, most notably individual political party affiliations and policy preferences. The latter can also reflect ethical and religious ties or the socio-cultural backgrounds of the judges. Due to the aforementioned fact that the openness for such political influences is often an inevitable consequence of the relatively wide scope for decision-making, which is only framed but not determined by the constitution, the question is not *whether* constitutional courts are politicised, but rather *to what extent*.

Despite its specific dual position in politics and law, the constitutional court still acts with a *legal primary orientation*. Externally, the court 'refers to the medium of the legal system and not to the political medium of power. It takes collectively binding decisions, but in doing so it refers to the distinction legal – illegal' (Bornemann 2007, 87). Internally, the court similarly orientates itself primarily by means of legal norms, at least in principle; political considerations are only of secondary importance (see Kranenpohl 2010, 461–463).

In this light, a decision-oriented concept of politicisation can basically be built upon the systems-theoretical understanding of politicisation as developed by the sociologist Alfons Bora. Bora starts with a general definition of processes such as 'politicisation', 'judicialisation', 'economisation', 'scientification', etc. Based on the aforementioned ideas of multi-referentiality and primary orientation, he interprets these phenomena as processes in which the primary orientation of one organisation 'is superimposed by another one' (Bora 2003, 206). Politicisation of organisations with a legal primary orientation (especially courts and prosecution offices) is therefore defined as

> the replacement of legal system references by specific political ones, observable in the communications and interactions of organisational systems […]. Replacement of the system reference in single communicative episodes means that a legally coded act of communication is expectable, but a different code appears (ibid., 207).

In addition to this political influence on the court or the judicial institution concerned, politicisation also denotes the resulting consequences for the *modus operandi* of the organisation and the possible external communicative connections:

> Focussing on the communications specific to functional systems, there is no communicative connection after the change of reference; a communication using the political medium of power does not perpetuate the communications of the legal system. […] Politicisation is […] to be understood as change of the primary programming at the level of organisations (ibid.).

Therefore, politicised court decisions cannot be further processed in the legal system.

Bora's concept is only partly convincing, because it *simultaneously exceeds and limits* the phenomenal domain of politicisation. On the one hand, it includes the output side of constitutional courts in an implausible manner. It hardly seems conceivable that politicised court judgements cannot find a communicative connection in the legal system, because court decisions are by definition legal acts. They might be 'covert political decisions' (Hesse 1995, 241), but even then it is extremely unlikely that a constitutional court *explicitly* uses the political rather than the legal code in its external communication. Instead, the legal system will never have a way around acknowledging constitutional adjudication *as adjudication*.[5]

---

5 As a matter of course, this does not imply that other courts always follow the constitutional court rulings.

On the other hand, politicisation in the sense of political influences on the judges and their decisions does not only take place when 'a legally coded act of communication is expectable, but a different code appears' (Bora 2003, 207). Rather, political influences also – if not in the majority of cases –have an effect behind the 'façade' of purely legal arguments. In the FCC, for instance, the judges only explicitly express their political opinions extremely rarely, although 'time and again [...] unspoken mutual accusations of being a party activist <appear>' (FCC judge, anonymously cited in Kranenpohl 2010, 475). In addition, the judges themselves often do not realise how their individual orientations, preferences and socialisations influence their work.

Thus, from the perspective of the 'realistic approach' and based on an understanding that focusses on all possible political influences on constitutional adjudication, our decision-oriented understanding of politicisation reads as follows: *Politicisation of constitutional adjudication means that a court decision is not or not exclusively taken based on legal criteria, but is (co-)determined by political influences, especially the judges' political party affiliations and policy preferences.* Politicisation thus refers to the case that judges either are (consciously or unconsciously) influenced in their search for the most convincing legal solution to the present constitutional matter by their political preferences or considerations regarding political appropriateness, or even decide a case on the basis of political criteria and then prepare a legal reasoning to support this. Politicisation defined in this manner can generally be used in the frameworks of all theories that fall under the 'realistic approach.' This is confirmed by the fact that this understanding can implicitly be found in many empirical studies (see e.g. Lembcke 2007; Hönnige 2009; Höpner 2010).

5. Conclusion

'All work in political science starts with *terminological work*' (Kreisky 2012, 29, emphasis in original), because the theoretical coherence and empirical precision of terms and concepts have a determining influence on the quality of theories and empirical studies. The task is therefore 'to clearly and consistently describe empirical conditions with apt concepts' (ibid., 31). The latest state of the art in referring to the politicisation of constitutional courts did not meet this criterion. In this chapter we have put forward a proposal to remedy these terminological and conceptual shortcomings by proposing a concept that encompasses central aspects of the existing concepts of politicisation and is additionally compatible with many empirical studies.

Future research should pre-eminently set out to study the *variety* of possible political influences on constitutional courts. So far, politicisation through the appointment of judges (see e.g. Hanretty 2012; Garoupa 2009; Hönnige 2009) and politicisation via direct manipulation of judges (see e.g. Popova 2012) have been examined almost exclusively. In contrast, studies of other potential politicising factors largely remain to be conducted. Above all, the studies should focus on the political, legal and organisational cultures (see Kranenpohl 2010, 439–494), the content of the controversial legal norms (see Sieberer 2006) and the procedural rules of the courts, especially regarding the types of proceedings (see Hein and Ewert 2013; Hein 2012).

Acknowledgements

We would like to thank the participants of the colloquium at the Chair in Political Theory and History of Political Ideas, especially Hubertus Buchstein and Thomas Lenz, as well as Tomasz Pietrzykowski, for their helpful comments.

References

Alivizatos, Nicos C. 1995. Judges as Veto Players. In *Parliaments and Majority Rule in Western Europe*, edited by Herbert Döring, 566–589. Frankfurt/Main, New York: Campus.

Badie, Bertrand (ed.) 2011. *International Encyclopedia of Political Science*. Los Angeles: Sage.

Bartels, Brandon L., and Johnston, Christopher D. 2012. Political Justice. Perceptions of Politicization and Public Preferences Toward the Supreme Court Appointment Process. *Public Opinion Quarterly* 76: 105–116.

Bealey, Frank. 1999. *The Blackwell Dictionary of Political Science. A User's Guide to Its Terms*. Oxford: Blackwell.

Bode, Ingo, and Brose, Hanns-Georg. 2001. Zwischen den Grenzen. Intersystemische Organisationen im Spannungsfeld funktionaler Differenzierung. In *Organisation und gesellschaftliche Differenzierung*, edited by Veronika Tacke, 112–140. Wiesbaden: Westdeutscher Verlag.

Bora, Alfons. 2003. Recht und Politik. Krisen der Politik und die Leistungsfähigkeit des Rechts. In *Der Begriff des Politischen*, edited by Armin Nassehi and Markus Schroer, 189–216. Baden-Baden: Nomos.

Bornemann, Basil. 2007. Politisierung des Rechts und Verrechtlichung der Politik durch das Bundesverfassungsgericht? Systemtheoretische Betrachtungen zum Wandel des Verhältnisses von Recht und Politik und zur Rolle der Verfassungsgerichtsbarkeit. *Zeitschrift für Rechtssoziologie* 28: 75–95.

Brodocz, André. 2009. *Die Macht der Judikative*. Wiesbaden: VS Verlag für Sozialwissenschaften.

Czerwick, Edwin. 2011. *Politik als System. Eine Einführung in die Systemtheorie der Politik*. München: Oldenbourg.

Dahl, Robert A. 1957. Decision-Making in a Democracy: The Supreme Court as a National Policy-Maker. *Journal of Public Law* 6: 279–295.

Easton, David. 1957. An Approach to the Analysis of Political Systems. *World Politics* 9: 383–400.

Ebsen, Ingwer. 1985. *Das Bundesverfassungsgericht als Element gesellschaftlicher Selbstregulierung. Eine pluralistische Theorie der Verfassungsgerichtsbarkeit im demokratischen Verfassungsstaat.* Berlin: Duncker & Humblot.

Engel, Stephen M. 2011. *American Politicians Confront the Court. Opposition Politics and Changing Responses to Judicial Power.* New York: Cambridge University Press.

Fricke, Werner, and Wagner, Hilde (eds.) 2012. *Demokratisierung der Arbeit. Neuansätze für Humanisierung und Wirtschaftsdemokratie*. Hamburg: VSA.

Friesenhahn, Ernst. 1954. Wesen und Grenzen der Verfassungsgerichtsbarkeit. *Zeitschrift für schweizerisches Recht* 73: 129–162.

Garoupa, Nuno. 2009. The Politicization of the Kelsenian Constitutional Courts: Empirical Evidence. In: *Empirical Studies of Judicial Systems*, edited by Huang, Kuo-Chang, 149–195. Taipei: Academia Sinica.

Goodin, Robert E. (ed.) 2009. *The Oxford Handbook of Political Science.* Oxford: Oxford University Press.

Grimm, Dieter. 2001. *Die Verfassung und die Politik. Einsprüche in Störfällen.* München: Beck.

Grimm, Dieter. 2009. Constitutions, Constitutional Courts and Constitutional Interpretation at the Interface of Law and Politics. In *The Law/Politics Distinction in Contemporary Public Law Adjudication*, edited by Bogdan Iancu, 21–34. Utrecht: Eleven International Publishing.

Häberle, Peter. 1980. *Verfassungsgerichtsbarkeit zwischen Politik und Rechtswissenschaft. Zwei Studien*. Königstein/Ts.: Athenäum.

Hamilton, Alexander. 1788. Federalist No. 78. The Judiciary Department. In *The Federalist Papers*, edited by id., James Madison and John Jay, 589–598. La Vergne: Ingram 2007.

Hanretty, Chris. 2012. Dissent in Iberia: The ideal points of justices on the Spanish and Portuguese Constitutional Tribunals. *European Journal of Political Research* 51: 671–692.

Hein, Michael. 2012. Macht oder Recht? Der Einfluss der Verfahrensarten auf die Politisierung südosteuropäischer Verfassungsgerichte. In: *Herrschaft in Südosteuropa. Kultur- und sozialwissenschaftliche Perspektiven*, edited by Mihai-D. Grigore, Radu Harald Dinu and Marc Živojinović, 55–78. Göttingen: V&R unipress.

Hein, Michael, and Ewert, Stefan. 2013. Do the Kinds of Action Influence the Politicization of Constitutional Courts? A Measurement Proposal and First Empirical Evidence from a Paired Comparison. *Paper presented at the 7th ECPR General Conference*, Bordeaux, 4–7 September.

Hein, Michael, and Ewert, Stefan. 2014. *Verfassungsgerichte zwischen Macht und Recht. Terminologische und konzeptionelle Überlegungen zum Begriff der Politisierung.* Manuscript, currently under review.

Hesse, Konrad. 1995. *Grundzüge des Verfassungsrechts der Bundesrepublik Deutschland.* Heidelberg: Müller, 20th ed.

Hönnige, Christoph. 2009. The Electoral Connection: How the Selection of the Pivotal Judge affects Oppositional Success at European Constitutional Courts. *West European Politics* 35: 963–984.

Höpner, Martin. 2010. Warum betreibt der Europäische Gerichtshof Rechtsfortbildung? Die Politisierungshypothese. *Sozialer Fortschritt* 59.5: 141–151.

Kaufmann, Erich. 1952. Die Grenzen der Verfassungsgerichtsbarkeit. *Veröffentlichungen der Vereinigung der Deutschen Staatsrechtslehrer* 9: 1–16.

Kelsen, Hans. 1929. Wesen und Entwicklung der Staatsgerichtsbarkeit. In *Wer soll der Hüter der Verfassung sein?*, edited by Robert Chr. van Ooyen, 1–57. Tübingen: Mohr Siebeck 2008.

Kelsen, Hans. 1930/31. Wer soll der Hüter der Verfassung sein? In *Wer soll der Hüter der Verfassung sein?*, edited by Robert Chr. van Ooyen, 58–105. Tübingen: Mohr Siebeck 2008.
Kranenpohl, Uwe. 2010. *Hinter dem Schleier des Beratungsgeheimnisses. Der Willensbildungs- und Entscheidungsprozess des Bundesverfassungsgerichts*. Wiesbaden: VS Verlag für Sozialwissenschaften.
Kreisky, Eva. 2012. 'Durch die Eiswüste der Abstraktion'? Begriffs- und Theoriearbeit in der Politikforschung. In *Theoriearbeit in der Politikwissenschaft*, edited by ead., Marion Löffler and Georg Spitaler, 21–32. Wien: Facultas.wuv.
Lembcke, Oliver. 2007. *Hüter der Verfassung. Eine institutionentheoretische Studie zur Autorität des Bundesverfassungsgerichts*. Tübingen: Mohr Siebeck.
Lieckweg, Tania. 2001. Strukturelle Kopplung von Funktionssystemen 'über' Organisation. *Soziale Systeme* 7: 267–289.
Lietzmann, Hans J. 2006. Kontingenz und Geheimnis. Die Veröffentlichung von Sondervoten beim Bundesverfassungsgericht. In *Das Bundesverfassungsgericht im politischen System*, edited by Robert Christian van Ooyen and Martin H. W. Möllers, 269–282. Wiesbaden: VS Verlag für Sozialwissenschaften.
Loewenstein, Karl. 1952/53. Konflikte zwischen Regierung und Justiz. *Archiv des öffentlichen Rechts* 78: 260–284.
Luhmann, Niklas. 1990. *Political Theory in the Welfare State*. Berlin, New York: de Gruyter.
Luhmann, Niklas. 2004. *Law as a Social System*. Oxford: Oxford University Press.
Magill, Frank N. (ed.) 1996. *International Encyclopedia of Government and Politics*. London: Fitzroy Dearborn.
McLean, Iain, and McMillian, Alistair (eds.) 2009. *The Concise Oxford Dictionary of Politics*. Oxford: Oxford University Press, 3rd ed.
Nullmeier, Frank. 2001. Von der Demokratisierung der Universitäten zum Hochschulmanagement. Über die Widerständigkeit des Akademischen. In *Stationen des Wandels. Rückblicke und Fragestellungen zu dreißig Jahren Bildungs- und Geschlechterforschung. Festschrift für Ingrid N. Sommerkorn-Abrahams*, edited by Bettina Hoeltje, 75–85. Münster, Hamburg, London: Lit.
Peters, B. Guy, and Pierre, Jon. 2004. Politicization of the Civil Service. Concepts, Causes, Consequences. In *Politicization of the Civil Service in Comparative Perspective. The Quest for Control*, edited by id., 1–13. London: Routledge.
Polish Constitutional Tribunal. 2011. *Judgment of 20 July 2011, Ref. No. K 9/11, official English translation*. [http://trybunal.gov.pl/fileadmin/content/omowienia/K_09_11_EN.pdf, accessed on 25.03.2014].
Popova, Maria. 2012. *Politicized Justice in Emerging Democracies. A Study of Courts in Russia and Ukraine*. New York: Cambridge University Press.
Rehder, Britta. 2010. What is Political about Jurisprudence? Courts, Politics, and Political Science in Europe and the United States. *Contemporary Readings on Law and Social Justice* 2.1: 100–129.
Schmidt, Manfred G. 2010. Politisierung. In *Wörterbuch zur Politik*, 630–631. Stuttgart: Kröner, 3rd ed.
Schmitt, Carl. 1929. Das Reichsgericht als Hüter der Verfassung. In *Verfassungsrechtliche Aufsätze aus den Jahren 1924–1954. Materialien zu einer Verfassungslehre*, 63–109. Berlin: Duncker & Humblot, 3rd ed. 1985.
Schmitt, Carl. 1931. *Der Hüter der Verfassung*. Tübingen: Mohr.

Scholz, Rupert, and Meyer-Teschendorf, Klaus G. 1998. 'Politisiertes' Verfassungsrecht und 'Depolitisierung' durch Verfassungsrecht. *Die Öffentliche Verwaltung* 51: 10–18.

Schröter, Susanne. 2006. Politisierung von Religion und Sakralisierung von Politik. Lokale und nationale Konflikte zwischen Moslems und Christen in Indonesien. In *Religiosität in der säkularisierten Welt. Theoretische und empirische Beiträge zur Säkularisierungsdebatte in der Religionssoziologie*, edited by Manuel Franzmann, Christel Gärtner and Nicole Köck, 357–374. Wiesbaden: VS Verlag für Sozialwissenschaften.

Sheldon, Charles H. 1970. *The Supreme Court. Politicians in Robes.* Beverly Hills: Glencoe Press.

Sieberer, Ulrich. 2006. Strategische Zurückhaltung von Verfassungsgerichten. Gewaltenteilungsvorstellungen und die Grenzen der Justizialisierung. *Zeitschrift für Politikwissenschaft* 16: 1299–1323.

Stone Sweet, Alec. 2000. *Governing With Judges. Constitutional Politics in Europe.* Oxford: Oxford University Press.

Vorländer, Hans, and Brodocz, André. 2006. Das Vertrauen in das Bundesverfassungsgericht. Ergebnisse einer repräsentativen Bevölkcrungsumfrage. In *Die Deutungsmacht der Verfassungsgerichtsbarkeit*, edited by Hans Vorländer, 259–295. Wiesbaden: VS Verlag für Sozialwissenschaften.

Whittington, Keith E., Kelemen, R. Daniel, and Caldeira, Gregory A. (eds.) 2008. *The Oxford Handbook of Law and Politics.* Oxford: Oxford University Press.

Wierzcholska, Agnieszka. 2012. Polen, Juden, Tarnowianer? Die Politisierung von Ethnizität im Polen der 1930er Jahre. *Osteuropa* 62.10: 41–52.

Zürn, Michael, Binder, Martin, and Ecker-Ehrhardt, Matthias. 2012. International Authority and its Politicization. *International Theory* 4.1: 69–106.

Separation of Powers reconsidered: a Proposal for a New Theoretical Model at the Beginning of the 21st Century

Martin Belov

Abstract

'Separation of powers' is a classic concept in political and legal theory. However, the key approaches that were elaborated at the beginning of modern constitutionalism are no longer appropriate for the reality of modern states. This chapter aims at introducing some alternative views with regard to the classification and delimitation of state powers. By means of a reassessment of the criteria for state powers differentiation, a seven-powers model is proposed, that comprises not only the classic *trias politica* of the legislative, executive and judicial branches, but also four new powers: external, financial, patronage and symbolic. Moreover, the difference between substantial, personal and symbolic policy-making is taken into account.

1. Introduction

'Separation of powers' is a classic interdisciplinary topic of modern philosophy, constitutional theory and political science. Almost all social sciences work with or at least tackle some issues that belong to the concepts of powers' separation and powers' distribution, because these two intertwined – partially overlapping and partially dichotomic – concepts concern key problems of the social order, the constitutional order included. In particular, these problems are the prevention of power abuse, an optimum between distribution and concentration of power, the manageability of social and power diversity, and the establishment of a functional governmental structure. Furthermore, 'Separation of powers' is a brand name for complex institutional systems, a core element of democratic ideology and common heritage of the Western legal tradition and constitutional civilisation.

The idea of separation of powers is both rigid and open to transformation: It is rigid if we stick to the 'constitutional orthodoxy' (see Tanchev 2009) of the classic theories developed by Montesquieu, Locke, the Federalists, Constant etc. If we want to preserve thc pantheon of thought that has been erected in the founding centuries of modern constitutionalism, the theory of separation of powers becomes a 'sacred cow.' Thus, howcvcr, dcaling with this topic is mere 'constitutional archaeology' that digs in the temples of already lost civilisations of our ancestors – or even 'constitutional occultism' (ibid., 22) in the form of calling the spirits from the past to preserve us from the uncertainty of the future with its new demons. As a matter of course, modern social sciences should be familiar with the traditional concepts of their disciplines. However, reading the 'holy books of constitutionalism' and pretending that they contain an unavoidable truth is simply unrewarding.

Therefore, we should search for paradigms that explain current issues and provide solutions for current problems. Of course, it is not wise to destroy the bridges that brought us to modernity or to neglect our intellectual heritage. It is necessary to step on the shoulders of the giants from the past and to continue the search for light in the tunnel of time. But we have to understand the traditional concepts in the light of the current issues pending upon our destiny and to adapt the classic matrices to the modern contexts. Thus, the separation of powers must be tackled as a concept that is open for transformation. This transformation has normative, theoretical as well as empirical aspects. However, the core ideas remain, namely that the constitution should guarantee a certain level of power polycentrism and that checks and balances are needed in order to ensure limited and responsible government and to prevent abuse of power (see Friedrich 1974).

The classic separation of powers theories of Charles de Montesquieu (1748), John Locke (1764), the Federalists (Madison, Hamilton and Jay 1788) and Benjamin Constant (1872) contain several common key features. They insist on the provision of a rational distribution of roles among the key political actors and a scheme for power polycentrism. Moreover, they ascribe competences to the state institutions that are supposed to guarantee both limited and effective government. In addition, there is a perpetual focus of most (but not all) classic theories on the legislative, executive and judicial powers, whereas they diverge with regard to other fields of governmental activity. Modern constitutional theory is challenged to preserve these cornerstone ideas, but also to further develop them in order to assure contextual adequacy with regard to current constitutional systems and discourses. The aim of this chapter is to extract the permanent core of the separation of powers theory, to expose the common basis of all sustainable approaches and to make some proposals for its adjustment to the current situation.

2. Theorising about separation of powers theory

2.1 What is a separation of powers theory?

I would like to start the critical assessment of the classic separation of powers theories with a question that might seem oversimplified at a first glance: What is a separation of powers theory? Posing such a question is legitimate, because we sometimes discuss the details of certain concepts while losing the underlying theoretical idea. The very idea of separation of powers consists of three dimensions: first, it is a cornerstone of the 'ideal constitution' of democracy and the rule of law (theoretical dimension; see Tanchev 2003, 112); second, it describes concrete polycentric constitutional systems or prescribes an 'ideal' one (empirical dimension); and third, it is a comprehensive constitutional model for power polycentrism (normative dimension). Separation of powers *theories* constitute only the first dimension, but take into consideration the second and the third ones. These theories contain a normative ideology which prescribes a constitutional and political model based on a certain idea for the institutional design of a well-arranged society. Furthermore, they are analytical matrices which allow scientists, politicians and active citizens to presuppose and superimpose a set of criteria in order to reform, model and critically analyse their political and constitutional systems. Consequently, separation of powers theories accomplish both cognitive and normative functions.

Separation of powers theories were developed in the early modern age (late 17th until late 19th century) as a cornerstone for the establishment of a new political project: the constitutional nation state. It was by and large an elitist construct. The impetus behind it was the will of the enlightened bourgeoisie to become a leading force in the society and to have at least equal share in the state power with the monarch and the aristocracy (or, as in the case of Montesquieu, the motivation was exactly contrary: to protect the powers of the aristocracy against the arising demands of the bourgeoisie). In this context, separation of powers promised a power sharing scheme which could be satisfactory to both the old and the new elites. Notwithstanding its origin, the theory for separation of powers was a very appealing intellectual product which had all substantial and symbolic qualities in order to be sold with great profit on the market of ides of Western modernity: It was comprehensible, logical, rational, systematic and adequate to its social context.

Furthermore it was politically appealing in several aspects. First, it was plausible to parts of the old aristocratic elite while at the same time being written with golden letters on the banner of the new wealthy and ambitious bourgeois elite. The separation of powers aimed at the establishment of a rational and negotiable power distribution scheme, allowed for partial continuation of the aristocratic powers, reinforced control mechanisms over the monarch that had been lost to some extent during the era of absolute monarchies and it granted feasible advantages for the 'new rich', i.e. the bourgeoisie, in order to integrate it in the ruling elite. Moreover, it was not a form of co-optation in the 'old estates' granted 'from above', but an approach of legal guarantees. Hence, the separation of powers was less revolutionary idea than it might seem. It was to some extent a continuation of the theories for mixed government that had existed since the ancient times (see Riklin 2006). In its earlier versions, separation of powers theories established institutional polycentrism based on the idea that some of the institutions (most notably the monarch and/or the second parliamentary chamber) serve as repositories of the old privileged classes whereas other institutions (namely the lower chamber) function as channel for the interests of the 'lower' classes. Thus, the initial and conservative variants of the separation of powers' theories enabled the constitutional fusion of monarchy, aristocracy and limited democracy into a modern version of the mixed government.

Second, separation of powers theories promised prosperity to a wide range of social circles, because it assured representation and responsiveness through the parliament and equal treatment, formal justice and legality through the courts. At the same time it guaranteed the authority and the efficiency of the state as a tool for social reforms. Normative ideas and ideologies often emancipate themselves from the intents of their originators and the original contexts in which they had been created. This is also the case with the separation of powers principle: Initially launched as an intellectual weapon of the bourgeoisie, it became a concept with universal value and recognition.

Third, separation of powers theory fulfilled the rationality claim of the Enlightenment era. Although many modern constitutional paradigms, theories and concepts are a product of rationalism and constructivism, the separation of powers theory was rational *per se:* It evolved as a result of two types of mental exercises – the *induction* of empirical facts and evidences of social and political life through observation and analysis as well as the *deduction* of a system of normative statements from previously constructed principles that pretend to be universally valid. If the human mind is able to gain systematic knowledge of nature and universe, as it was proven by the scientific revolution in the natural and life sciences during the last centuries, it should be also capable of creating a well-established society and a state that is built on a plan which was drawn up in advance. That way, so the hope of 'enlightened politics', human kind can be freed from the necessity of historical co-incidences and can rationally create its own political existence by a fundamental plan named 'Constitution.' This document will contain a reasonable scheme for power division, power distribution and power sharing formalised as 'separation of powers.'

It should be taken into account that the separation of powers principle is in its theoretical dimension both prescriptive and descriptive. It is prescriptive because it tries to impose a theoretical scheme on the existing factual relations of a distinct society. At the same time it is descriptive for the reason that a working model for separation of powers can only be implemented if the social conditions for its adequate functioning do exist.

As already mentioned, *the second dimension* of the separation of powers is the *empirical* one. Most of the theories are partially based on a description of a certain constitutional system or the presumption of the pre-existence of an 'ideal', 'best' or 'target' state model. For instance, both Montesquieu and Locke used the English constitution as model for their theories; Madison, Hamilton and Jay defended the virtues of the proposed US constitution and Benjamin Constant attributed his *pouvoir neutre* to the king in the institutional design of the French Constitutional Charter of 1814. Obviously, these selections of concrete political systems are deliberate and not accidental. Instead, the choices are predetermined by political, theoretical or mere personal preferences.

In its *normative dimension*, separation of powers might be defined also as a comprehensive political and constitutional model for creation and preservation of power polycentrism. Most of the classic theories pretend to contain a holistic model for the institutional infrastructure of the state. The intellectual pathos behind the classic theories is to bring rationality and order to the political sphere.

Instead of intermediate historical conclusion, I would like to answer one additional question: Why do we need a separation of powers theory today? The answer is that modern political philosophy and constitutional theory need a comprehensive paradigm against which existing constitutional orders and political systems can be compared and evaluated. Another function of this theory is to generate legitimacy for these social structures. Moreover, the transfer and transplantation of normative concepts and ideas as well as of institutional design is simply impossible or at least difficult without a theoretical background. Finally, the separation of powers theory gives a coherent abstract response to authoritarianism and totalitarianism. It provides the constitutional and political discourse with the already mentioned compromise power sharing scheme.

2.2 What are the features that a separation of powers theory should possess?

Before discussing the necessary features of a separation of powers theory, the question should be answered how a separation of powers theory is made. Such a theory can be built in a more philosophical, positivist or sociological perspective – either separately or in a certain combination. The philosophical approach consists in the speculative creation of an abstract model; the positivist approach in analysing empirical constitutional models and focusing on a chosen model or by creating comparative typologies; and the sociological approach is based on the assessment of 'law in action.' The classic theories typically had concrete 'enemies' to fight with, institutions to promote and goals to achieve. Some of them aimed at limiting the role of the monarch and enhancing the powers of the parliament, while, in contrast, others were a defence of the monarchic principle and the prerogatives of the aristocracy. At the beginning of the 21st century, however, the scheme of interests, alliances and controversies is neither as clear as in the early modern age, nor it is the same as in the 17th–19th centuries. In particular, the discussion does not centre anymore around conflicts between certain social classes.

Hence, contemporary scientists are to some extend released from the necessity to fight for specific political and institutional interests. They and can thus 'choose not to choose sides' and create more 'neutral' separation of powers theories. They can try to map out the institutional demarcation lines that are typical for a distinct society or for a group of countries or to elaborate models and classifications of the separation of powers schemes that exist in a comparative perspective without demonising some of them while paying emotional tribute to others. A modern separation of powers theory can be achieved through deconstruction of old theories and constitutional models as well as the induction of elements from different empirical models by virtue of comparative and historical analysis. As a result, such a theory might be more adequate to the contemporary plurality of political systems. Furthermore, it might be useful to combine all three aforementioned approaches, i.e. the philosophical, the positivist and the sociological one. This can provide the necessary degree of abstract arguments permitting logical generalisations. At the same time, the general statements can be proven on the basis of the norms and the facts given by comparative legal and political research.

Keeping this preliminary considerations in mind, I suggest a modern separation of powers theory to possess the following four key features: First of all, this theory must not be focused on institutions. The scheme 'one power – one institution – one function', which can be found in some of the classic theories, is practically impossible. Institutions are not constitutional fortresses functioning in isolation from one another. This has never been the reality in any historical or contemporary constitutional order. The approach to limit the powers of each institution to only one state function is doomed to failure. Even in constitutional systems with rigid separation of powers like e.g. the USA, there are tools for institutional co-operation.

Second, a modern separation of powers theory should use the functional approach though it must not be obsessed with the creation of a non-controversial system of state functions. Governance is a process that can be institutionalised in advance only partially. Furthermore, state functions are inevitably overlapping. Just to give some examples: The adoption of the state budget is both part of the legislative and financial management function. The conclusion of an international treaty on crediting mechanisms does not only concern the two functions just mentioned but also the functions of external policy determination and external policy execution. Not least, the appointment of diplomats combines both the executive function and personal policy.

Third, a modern separation of powers theory has to expose the way the *state* institutions are functioning while taking into account the influence of *all* veto players (see Tsebelis 2002), i.e. those belonging to the state and those belonging to the public sphere. In particular, the influence of political parties and other intermediary institutions causes again a deviation from the scheme 'one power – one institution – one function.' It perforates the formal borders between the state institutions and simultaneously imposes new power division lines.

Fourth, a modern separation of powers theory has to take into account the spheres of social reality towards which the state powers are typically directed. The main domains of systematically intertwined social relations that are liable to common governance by the state institutions have to be regarded as a factor that influences the separation of powers matrix and the institutional design provided by constitutional and public law.

These four features have to be applied simultaneously in order to create a more comprehensible though not necessarily non-contradictory picture of the constitutionally enshrined institutional polycentrism. This approach allows for the creation of a theory that takes into account both constitutional statics and dynamics, both the state and the public sphere, and it combines the advantages of institutionalism and functionalism. As a result the separation of powers theory that I am proposing is based on a re-reading of the classic concepts. Furthermore, it rests on the tripartite classification of personal, substantial and symbolic policy: *Personal policy* means the hiring and firing of state office holders resulting from the system of patronage power rights granted by the constitutional law. *Substantial policy* encompasses all decisions concerning the determination of all political priorities of the state, their implementation and control.[1] *Symbolic policy*, finally, is the communication and explanation of the state policies to the general public (vertical), but also between the state institutions (vertical).

To sum up, an adequate separation of powers theory must apply a system of tree combined criteria for the delimitation of state powers and their classification: The first criterion is the spheres of social reality towards which the powers of the state institutions are typically directed. The second criterion is the function(s) a state body or a veto player performs. This function must not be presumed but should be based upon a set of competences that serve as tools for its accomplishment. The third criterion is the institution(s) performing that function(s) directed towards the respective durable group of social relations. Hence, there might be a partial overlapping of state powers due to divergence of the three criteria. Such overlapping may consist in the (partial) performance of the same function by different institu-

1 For policy determination, policy execution and policy control as key functions of the state, see Loewenstein 1962.

tions and/or the performance of different functions by the same institution. Therefore, the proposed theory insists on the *relative* and not on the absolute *nature* of the *separation of powers model*. It does not maintain an 'inevitable truth' or create a non-changeable everlasting conceptual scheme. On the contrary, it aims at achieving an inductive, normatively and sociologically verifiable theory that is not limited to description but also contains abstract conceptualisation.

Finally, the proposed theory goes beyond the classic *trias politica* by delimiting additional state powers. The existence of the classic legislative, executive and judicial powers will not be denied. However, they neither have remained static and exclusive during the history of the separation of powers idea, nor exhaustively describe the scope of state powers. The latter already holds true for the earlier stages of the development of constitutionalism but becomes even more evident in the current age of multilevel governance (see Pernice 2006) and neo-constitutionalism (see Tanchev 2003, 212). Therefore, the new roles and tasks ascribed to the state in the 20th and 21st century as well as the consequences of multilevel constitutionalism in the European Union enhance the process for state power differentiation.

3. Conceptualising new state powers

There are four powers which have to be added to the classic *trias politica:* the external, the financial, the patronage and the symbolic power. What I suggest not to add is a separate military power. Although it was frequently regulated even in distinct chapters of several constitutions until the 19th century, the majority of current constitutions do not contain such specific provisions. Moreover, the separation of a military power might have the potential to threaten the democratic order. The *external and the financial powers* are constructed predominantly by virtue of extraction of elements that are traditionally ascribed to the legislative and executive powers. This is deliberately done through a combined application of the abovementioned three criteria. The differentiation of these two 'new' powers is legitimated by the importance and autonomy of the spheres of social relations that are object of regulation. The functioning of the state in the context of international relations as well as public finance management are social sectors that are quite distinct from the rest of the socio-political relations. Furthermore, they are object of both norm setting and governmental activities that can be separated from one another only artificially. In contrast, the emancipation of *patronage power and symbolic power* has another justification. It is based on the abovementioned delimitation of substantial, personal and symbolic policy. Whereas the legislative, executive, judicial, external and financial powers concern substantial policy making, the patronage power is a tool for accomplishment of the personal and the symbolic power of the symbolic and discursive policy making.

3.1 The external power

The external power is based on John Locke's (1764, 324–328) concept of federative power. As a matter of course, the idea of a separate external state power or function is much older than Locke's concept (see e.g. Giannotti 1534, 62). However, Locke gave real prominence to the idea of that specific branch in the modern political and constitutional discourse. In the second treatise of government he defends the idea that there should be a separate state power which manages the functioning of the state in the context of its international relations. In contrast to Locke, the term 'external power' is preferable in comparison to 'federative power', because it is more neutral and focuses on the targeted function. Furthermore, Locke uses the term 'federative' in its pre-modern notion, which is quite misleading today because the external power is an attribute of all states and not reserved for federal states.

The function realised by the external power consists in the participation of the state in the international relations and thus concerns the field of substantial policy. There are several typical tasks for the external power, above all the representation of the state in the international relations vis-à-vis other states or international organisations, in international conferences, by the negotiation and conclusion of international treaties as well as their implementation in the national legal order. These tasks are fulfilled by multiple institutions. These are predominantly the government, the ministers, the head of state, the diplomats and the parliament. The distribution of the external power among them depends on the form of governance. The presidents of the presidential, semi-presidential and super-presidential republics as well as the monarchs in absolute and constitutional monarchies are the key players in the external power. In parliamentary monarchies and parliamentary systems, however, this domain broadly belongs to the prime minister, whereas the head of state is a rather nominal and symbolic figure, largely dependent on the will of the government and the parliamentary majority.

The constitutional offices which represent the state in the international relations are, above all, the head of state, the head of government, the foreign minister (as well as to a lesser extend the ministers), the diplomats and consuls. Additionally, such powers are attributed to state organs that are allowed to represent collective national institutions, e.g. the presidents of the parliament and the constitutional court. Usually the negotiation and conclusion of international treaties is a right that falls into the sphere of competence of the government and the head of state. The implementation of such treaties in the national legal order typically varies according to their subject matter. The most important treaties need parliamentary ratification, whereas for other agreements governmental sanction is often sufficient.

Until the late 19th and the early 20th century the status of parliaments in the external power was rather weak. Although the ratification of the most important treaties and sometimes decisions on war and peace were subject to parliamentary decisions, many constitutions allowed the monarch a secret external policy and did not provide for mechanisms for parliamentary control over the activity of the government in international relations. Since then, there has been a gradual gain in parliamentary competences in the external power, although it still remains a field of dominance of the leading executive institutions. Within the context of the European Union, the integration process further enhances the role of national governments in external policy making despite some efforts for the improvement of the information and controlling rights of the national parliaments.

3.2 The financial power

The financial power is related to the planning, predetermination, management and control of public finances. Some of its components are usually attributed to the legislative power whereas other are assumed to be part of the executive power. However, it should be a distinct state branch of substantial policy making. The financial power belongs to multiple institutions, most notably the government, the minister of finance, the parliament and – in some governmental systems – the head of state. All other institutions that collect or spend public money also participate in the financial power. This holds especially true for (local) self-government institutions.

The core of the financial power is the state budget, the budgetary process and the collection of taxes and dues. Here, the key players are the government, the minister of finance, the budgetary parliamentary committee and the parliament. The drafting of the state budget and its implementation are typically monopolised by the government. In contrast, the Parliament holds the exclusive right to adopt the budget as well as control its implementation. Having in mind budgetary blockades in the history of early modern constitutionalism, the majority of today's constitutions contain provisions concerning budgetary blockades and provide for different means for resolving such conflicts between parliament and government. The head of state usually has a rather moderate or even nominal participation in the financial power. This was not the case in the monarchical constitutionalism until the 19th century where the monarch was the leader of government thus also predetermining its financial policy. Contemporary heads of state might have the nominal right to introduce the governmental draft budget, to conclude financial treaties or to release persons from their public financial duties. The granting of financial amnesties is usually excluded from the competence of the heads of state and is attributed to the powers of the Parliament.

The negotiation, conclusion and adoption of finance treaties are competences that fall into the scope of both the external and the financial power. The distribution of these competences typically follows the logic that has been already discussed with regard to the external power. Finally, the public financial control is also an important part of the financial power of every modern state. It is accomplished by the parliament, distinct auditing institutions and in some countries even by specialised courts. In sum, the analysis clearly demonstrates the reasonableness of delimiting a separate financial power. This is due to the fact that the function for public financial management involves the coordinated action of many institutions that traditionally belong to different 'classic' state powers. Consequently, the financial power is neither a legislative nor an executive nor a controlling power but a hybrid that encompasses elements of all of them.

3.3 The patronage power

The patronage power models and determines the personal policy of the state. It concerns the recruitment and management of personnel for the state institutions. It is an important determinant for the way the state really functions since the legal institutional design is only the frame which gives opportunities for veto players to act (see Tsebelis 2002). The patronage power was neglected in many classic separation of powers theories.[2] There are two main reasons for this lack. First, the power to appoint and dismiss persons to different state positions are mostly conceived as part of the general competence of the state organs. Hence, patronage competences are understood as subordinate to the 'main' competences of the state institutions. This way, however, the importance of the personal policy in comparison with the substantial policy is simply disregarded. Second, the term patronage power has gained a negative connotation. This is due to the fact that it has been traditionally used for the denomination of Mafia type of recruitment of personnel based on the principle 'appointment in return for past or future favours.' Hence, patronage is often understood as a synonym for corruption and nepotism. However, alternative terms like 'constitutive power', 'constituent power', 'empowering power' or 'appointment power' are misleading and incorrect. They

2 A notable but rare exception is Donato Giannotti's version of a mixed government theory, which distinguishes four state powers or functions: legislation, external policy, jurisprudence and the election to public positions (see Giannotti 1534, 62).

either reflect other dimensions of the state activity that have nothing to do with the personal policy, do not encompass the competences for dismissal of public office holders or are truly artificial.

Personal policy is a very important component of modern constitutional and political systems. Therefore, a distinct concept encompassing all the competences to appoint and dismiss the holders of different state offices should be developed. The patronage power has a legitimate existence which is based on the cumulative application of the three abovementioned criteria for delimitation of the state power branches. It belongs to multiple institutions as well as to the people (the electorate) and indirectly to institutions of the public sphere. Furthermore, the recruitment of the political elite and the selection of office holders for the state institutions certainly is a distinct function. Moreover, the patronage power is focused on the specific sphere of social relations concerning the personal policy of the state.

There are different aspects of patronage power that can be distinguished on the basis of several criteria: According to its *predetermination and effect*, positive patronage power concerns the appointment and negative patronage power the dismissal of office holders. With regard to the *institution* to which the patronage competence belongs, we can differentiate between patronage power of the people, of public institutions and of state institutions. Hence, the concept of patronage power exceeds the sphere of the state. It demonstrates the functional conjunction between civic society, public sphere and the state.

The patronage power can be concentrated in one and the same institution or it can be internally divided among several institutions. In the latter case, one can distinguish between simultaneous and consecutive division of the patronage power. In case of a simultaneous division, different state organs can appoint and eventually dismiss certain office holders. It results in the existence of quotas. Typical examples of simultaneous division are the appointment schemes for constitutional court judges, supreme judicial councils, media councils, governing bodies of central banks and managing boards of other state agencies. In these cases, the powers to elect or appoint the office holders are usually divided between parliament, government, head of state, supreme courts etc. In contrast, the division of patronage power is consecutive if the office holder is appointed by one institution on proposal of another institution. For example, the high administrators, the diplomats and consuls and the high ranking police and military officials are in many countries appointed and dismissed by the head of state on proposal of the government, the prime minister or a minister.

Both the simultaneous and the consecutive division of patronage power have the purpose to allow for a balanced and limited government by virtue of dispersion of the personal politics among different institutions. This is achieved in different manner. The simultaneous separation of patronage power enshrines permanent checks and balances in the personal staff of the constituted institution that are not limited to the moment of the appointment or election of the office holders. It aims at constant representation of different institutional and political interests that have to mutually block biased or corrupted decision making. The consecutive separation of patronage power, in contrast, is focused on the appointment and dismissal process. Its purpose is to allow for double checking of the legal and substantial prerequisites for the just and effective hiring or firing of state officials.

3.4 The symbolic power

Finally, the symbolic power is focused on the symbolic policy of the state. It is accomplished through different constitutional competences comprising the issuing of political acts, the participation in public events, the holding of public speeches etc. Hence, the main devices of the symbolic power are the political acts that serve as tools for constitutional communication. The functional catalogue of the symbolic power includes public opinion formation, political communication, demonstration and explanation of decisions taken with the purpose of gathering public support or vice versa the imposition of public blame. The symbolic power belongs mainly to institutions that have representative and symbolic functions and possess the right to issue political acts. Consequently, the key actors are the heads of state, the prime minister and the parliament, whereas courts and administrative bodies are supposed to have only limited influence on the symbolic policy of the state.

4. Conclusion

This chapter should be rather understood as a challenge to the classic bastions of thought than as a comprehensive and fully elaborated theoretical effort. It tried to put central questions on the table, but not to give final answers. The limited volume of the chapter does not allow for a sufficient clarification of the raised issues. For instance, I have not analysed the temporal aspect of the separation of powers. Furthermore, the configuration and the current problems of the 'classic' powers, i.e. legislative, executive and judiciary, have not been tackled at all. Finally, the relation between the executive power and the 'new powers' presented above has to be clarified. However, the chapter should serve as the starting point for a reconsideration of the traditional dogmas of the separation of powers idea. Its contribution is threefold: reconstructing and reassessing traditional problems of statehood, proposing a set of criteria for state power delimitation, and (re-)introducing new aspects of constitutional power polycentrism.

References

Constant, Benjamin. 1872. *Cours de politique constitutionnelle ou collection des ouvrages publiés sur le gouvernement représentatif.* Paris: Guillaumin.

Friedrich, Carl J. 1974. *Limited Government. A Comparision.* Englewood Cliffs: Prentice-Hall.

Giannotti, Donato. 1534. *Die Republik Florenz.* München: Fink 1997.

Locke, John. 1764. *Two Treatises of Government.* London: A. Millar et al.

Loewenstein, Karl. 1962. *Political Power and the Governmental Process.* Chicago, London: University of Chicago Press, 2nd ed.

Madison, James, Hamilton, Alexander, and Jay, John. 1788. The Federalist Papers. New York: Penguin 1987.

Montesquieu, Charles Louis de Secondat de. 1748. *The Spirit of Laws.* Amherst: Prometheus Books 2002.

Pernice, Ingolf. 2006. Teorija i praktika na Evropejskija konstitucionnen săjuz [Theory and Practice of the European Constitutional Union]. In *Jubileen sbornik na Departament 'Pravo' [Anniversery Publication of the Law Department]*, edited by Rumen Vladimirov et al., 7–34. Sofia: Nov Bălgarski Universitet.

Riklin, Alois. 2006. *Machtteilung. Geschichte der Mischverfassung.* Darmstadt: Wissenschaftliche Buchgesellschaft.

Tanchev, Evgeni. 2003. *Văvedenie v konstitucionnoto pravo [Introduction to Constitutional Law].* Sofia: Sibi.

Tanchev, Evgeni. 2009. The Lisbon Treaty within and without Constitutional Orthodoxy. In *Ceci n'est pas une Constitution – Constitutionalisation without a Constitution?* Edited by Ingolf Pernice and Evgeni Tanchev, 22–44. Baden-Baden: Nomos.

Tsebelis, George. 2002. *Veto Players. How Political Institutions Work.* Princeton, New York: Princeton University Press.

Part II
Constitutional Review in East Central European Countries

Access to Constitutional Justice in the new Hungarian Constitutional Framework: Life after the *Actio Popularis*?

Katalin Kelemen

Abstract

This chapter aims at presenting and evaluating the conditions of access to the Hungarian Constitutional Court after the enactment of the new Fundamental Law and the new Constitutional Court Act on 1 January 2012. The abolition of *actio popularis* and the concomitant introduction of full constitutional complaint opened a new scenario for the Hungarian Constitutional Court in which a shift of emphasis from abstract to concrete review may be expected. Two years after the entering into force of the new scheme it is possible to make an early evaluation of the practice based on the new framework. How are these new forms being used by the complainants and interpreted by the Court? Can we already delineate the new trends of case-law?

1. Introduction

In April 2011, after a remarkably short debate that lasted two weeks only, the Hungarian Parliament adopted a new constitution, named Fundamental Law (*Alaptörvény*).[1] Hungary was the only formerly socialist country that did not approve a new constitution after the breakdown of the communist regime. In the 2010 elections the right-wing coalition (Fidesz-KDNP) won two-thirds of the seats in the unicameral Parliament. Consequently, the new government could draft and approve a new constitution without the participation of the opposition (see Kelemen 2011). As to the composition and the powers of the Constitutional Court, only parts of the rules can be found in the text of the Fundamental Law (in Articles 6, 24 and 37). In order to have a complete picture of the changes brought to the system of constitutional review, we have to take a look on the new Constitutional

1 The official English translation is available at [http://www.kormany.hu/en/news/the-new-fundamental-law-of-hungary, accessed on 28.02.2014]. The original Hungarian version in force since 1 April 2013 (after the adoption of four amendments) is available at [http://www.kozlonyok.hu/nkonline/MKPDF/hiteles/MK13055.pdf, accessed on 28.02.2014]. The English translation of the Fourth Amendment adopted on 11 March 2013 is available at [http://lapa.princeton.edu/hosteddocs/hungary/Fourth%20Amendment%20to%20the%20FL%20-Eng%20Corrected.pdf, accessed on 28.02.2014].

Court Act, too, adopted in November 2011.[2] Both the new Fundamental Law and the new Constitutional Court Act entered into force on 1 January 2012.

This chapter aims at presenting and evaluating one particular aspect of the new scheme: the access to the Constitutional Court and its impact on the Court's traditionally activist type of constitutional review. There have been significant changes. The abolition of *actio popularis* and the concomitant introduction of full constitutional complaint opened a new scenario for the Court in which a shift of emphasis from abstract to concrete review could have been expected. Indeed, the constitutional review of judicial decisions was not among the competences of the Hungarian Court before this reform. There was an instrument, by legal scholars called normative constitutional complaint, which could be used in the ambit of legal proceedings before an ordinary court against legal norms applied by that court and not against the judgment itself.[3] The Fundamental Law adds also a third version of constitutional complaint that can be filed against a legal provision which directly violates constitutional rights, i.e. without a judicial decision.[4]

Now that there is no more *actio popularis*, constitutional complaints have become much more relevant in Hungarian constitutional justice. Before 2012, complainants preferred the *actio popularis* to the normative constitutional complaint, as it did not require any proof of personal interest or exhaustion of remedies, and there was no deadline. Furthermore, the Constitutional Court tried to make up for the absence of a full constitutional complaint and to bring ordinary court judgments in its sphere of competence by applying the concept of living law (*élő jog*), borrowed from the Italian Constitutional Court, and by making general statements similar to the German Federal Constitutional Court's *Leitsätze* (see Sólyom 2001,175–178). Two years after the entering into force of the new scheme it is now possible to make an early evaluation of the practice based on the new framework: Is there life for the Hungarian Constitutional Court after the abolition of the *actio popularis*? In other words, has the abolition of this type of proceeding been really compensated by the introduction of two new forms of constitutional complaint? How are these new forms used by the complainants and interpreted by the Court? And will these changes lead to less "political" decisions?

---

2 Act no. CLI of 2011. The official English translation is available at [http://www.mkab.hu/download.php?d=64, accessed on 28.02.2014]. For a comment and summary see Kelemen 2011a.

3 See art. 48 of the old Constitutional Court Act (Act no. XXXII of 1989), available at [http://www.1000ev.hu/index.php?a=3&param=8630, accessed on 28.02.2014].

4 See art. 24 (2) d) FL.

2. The rich competences of the Hungarian Constitutional Court before and after 2012

The Hungarian Constitutional Court has been for a long time considered to assert one of the widest constitutional jurisdictions in Europe (see Sadurski 2009, 1), notwithstanding it could not deal with full constitutional complaints before 2012. Until the adoption of the new Fundamental Law the *actio popularis* ensured unlimited access to the Court for natural and legal persons against any piece of legislation, without time-limit, the payment of a fee, the obligation of being represented by a lawyer or the requirement of being a citizen of the country. This unlimited access led inevitably to an excessive caseload of the Court, which in more than one occasion suggested to the legislator to abolish the *actio popularis* and to introduce the full constitutional complaint instead (see Lábady 1991, 385–390; Sólyom 1991, 176). In contrast, decisions of ordinary courts could not be brought before the Constitutional Court but only in relation to a normative constitutional complaint, which however did not review the constitutionality of the judicial decision but that of the law applied by the decision. Even though, as mentioned above, in its first two decades of functioning the Constitutional Court tried to make up for this absence by applying the concept of living law and statements of general principle. According to this concept, the constitutionality of the challenged provision is to be reviewed by having regard to the meaning it assumed during its application in practice, and not by considering a literal interpretation of its wording.[5]

The wideness of the Court's powers had moreover contributed to its very large jurisdiction that also included *a priori* or preventive review, indirect review, constitutional interpretation, the review of referendum orders, the resolution of conflicts of competence, the dissolution of local representative bodies and the removal from office of the President of the Republic. All these competences were preserved in the new constitutional framework, and they are not rare among European constitutional courts.[6] Nevertheless, the Hungarian Court's jurisdiction is particularly open. This openness is manifested both in the standing to raise constitutional issues before the Court and in the possible bases for review. Until 2012 the accessibility of the Court was the largest a legislator could conceive: anybody could initiate constitutional review (via *actio popularis*), and additionally the Court had

5 The concept was used for the first time by the Court in 1991 in the so-called *Jánosi* case (Decision no. 57/1991 [XI. 8.] AB of 11 May 1991).

6 In contrast, there are other competences that the Hungarian Constitutional Court does not have, e.g. the power to adjudicate the constitutionality of political parties.

the possibility to exercise it *ex officio*.[7] As to the possible basis for review, besides the provisions of the Constitution it may include also international treaties, both before and after 2012. Until 2012 the Court also had the power to check the legality of local government decrees, which moved to ordinary courts in 2012, and to review the constitutionality of any sub-legislative act. The review of decisions of the National Electoral Commission moved to the Supreme Court (*Kúria*).

2.1. Changes in the a posteriori *abstract review*

The biggest change brought to Hungarian constitutional justice by the new Fundamental Law and Constitutional Court Act has been, undoubtedly, the abolition of *actio popularis*. It has been subject to a large debate in which several arguments and counter-arguments were raised. As already mentioned, before 2012 the rules concerning the access to the Court were very generous. Besides being open to anyone, regardless direct and individual interest, the Court could also use a wide range of norms as basis for review (the Constitution and international treaties) to check the constitutionality of a wide range of acts (international treaties, legislative and other normative acts,[8] and omissions of the legislator, but not judicial decisions). Thus an ordinary citizen or even a foreigner could challenge an act of the Parliament or the Government (including their passivity), without being required to prove his or her personal interest in the case. The intention was to ensure a quick and efficient transition from the socialist to a democratic regime. Since Hungary, similarly to the vast majority of the post-Socialist countries, chose the road of legal continuity and did not abolish all the old laws at once in order to build up a new legal system from scratch, it was for the newly elected Parliament and the newly established Constitutional Court to free the legal system from those old Socialist norms which had lost their legitimacy (see Sólyom 2003, 151). At the same time, however, popular actions opened the door to bring political questions before the court, such as the position of the Head of the State.

The introduction of *actio popularis* in 1989 was an achievement of the Round Table negotiations between the Communist Party and the opposition groups.

---

7 In Central and Eastern Europe, this competence exists also in Macedonia, Montenegro and Serbia. In Russia it was abolished in 1994 and in Poland in 1997.

8 Art. 32/A (1) of the old Constitution referred to 'legal norms' (*jogszabályok*) as the possible object of constitutional review. Therefore, the Constitutional Court always refused to review individual decisions, even if they take the form of normative acts (see Decisions no. 6/1994 [II.8.] AB and 45/1997 [IX. 19.] AB). The only exception was if the individual decision contained in the legal norm violated a fundamental right; this was considered by the Court as an abuse of power by the legislator (see Decision no. 5/2007 [II.27.] AB).

Art. 32/A inserted in the Constitution established a constitutional court for Hungary. This article, even though very short and concise, being the result of a compromise, provided explicitly only for an abstract constitutional review of legislation. However, it also contained two other rules of fundamental importance: the Court had the power to annul unconstitutional laws and everyone had the right to initiate proceedings.[9] Therefore, the abolition of the *actio popularis* required a constitutional amendment. The new Fundamental Law does so by omitting to provide that everyone has the right to initiate proceedings. At the same time it provides that the Court examines 'any piece of legislation for conformity with the Fundamental Law at the request of the Government, one-fourth of the Members of Parliament or the Commissioner for Fundamental Rights.'[10] In March 2013, the Fourth Amendment to the Fundamental Law extended the right to initiate proceedings of *a posteriori* review to the President of the Supreme Court and the Prosecutor General.[11] All these actors may challenge a law in case of violation of an international treaty.[12] Thus the basis for review has not been limited by the new legal framework.

In order to evaluate the consequences of these changes, we have to examine them within the new legal framework. Already during the drafting stage of the Fundamental Law, the Venice Commission expressed its opinion on the matter, stressing that 'the availability of an *actio popularis* in matters of constitutionality cannot be regarded as a European standard', and its abolition, if accompanied by the introduction of the full constitutional complaint, cannot be regarded as 'an infringement of the European constitutional heritage' (European Commission for Democracy Through Law 2011, 11–12). The criticism that emerged in relation to the reform feared for the counter-majoritarian function of the Constitutional Court, and according to a group of Hungarian NGOs the legislator would have transformed the *a posteriori* constitutional review from being an instrument for the protection of rights into a weapon of the opposition and the government.[13]

9 All the other competences adduced above, which made the Hungarian Constitutional Court one of the widest constitutional jurisdictions in Europe, were introduced by the Constitutional Court Act.

10 Art. 24 (2) e) of the Fundamental Law.

11 See art. 12 (2) of the Fourth Amendment; for a comment see Kelemen (2013).

12 Art. 24 (2) f) of the Fundamental Law and art. 32 of the new Constitutional Court Act.

13 See the *Analysis of the new rules on the Constitutional Court* prepared jointly by the Hungarian Helsinki Committe, EKINT and TASZ, three NGOs, at p. 8, available in Hungarian at [http://www.ekint.org/ekint_files/File/tanulmanyok/abtv_elemzes_20111028_final.pdf, accessed on 28.02.2014].

However, the Fundamental Law does not limit the access to the Court to the opposition and the Government, but gives this right also to a third actor, the Commissioner for Fundamental Rights (i.e. the Ombudsman). In its comparative study on individual access to constitutional justice the Venice Commission explicitly recommended that the mandate of the Ombudsman should include 'the possibility of applying to the constitutional court of the country for an abstract judgment on questions concerning the constitutionality of laws and regulations or general administrative acts which raise issues affecting human rights and freedoms' (European Commission for Democracy Through Law 2011b, 18).

Thus the question emerges: is the Ombudsman able to fill in the space left by the abolition of the *actio popularis*? The official statistics of the Constitutional Court do not give account of the number of proceedings initiated by the Ombudsman,[14] but we find detailed data in the Ombudsman's annual report to the Parliament: In 2012, he received 758 complaints in which the complainant asked him to raise an issue before the Constitutional Court.[15] He decided to initiate the proceedings of the Court in 20 of these cases and in four additional cases *ex officio*. By the end of January 2013 the Court had decided 12 of the cases initiated by the Ombudsman, and in seven of these it accepted his legal opinion. Especially due to the extensive media attention received by his challenge of the Transitional Provisions of the Fundamental Law, which were declared invalid by the Constitutional Court in December 2012,[16] he attracted a large number of complaints. Thus it seems that the Ombudsman is very active in initiating proceedings before the Constitutional Court, even if his resources are not unlimited. This holds especially true since the new Fundamental Law has kept only one of the four former Ombudsman positions. Moreover, the Ombudsman will not exercise his right in case of violation of other constitutional principles such as the separation of powers or judicial independence.

---

14 The official statistics are available at [http://www.mkab.hu/dokumentumok/statisztika, accessed on 28.02.2014].

15 Annual Report 2012, available at [http://www.ajbh.hu/eves-beszamolok, accessed on 28.02.2014], 93. In 2012 the Ombudsman received 7,861 complaints in total (ibid., 322). At the moment of finalising this chapter the Annual Report 2013 was not yet available.

16 The Transitional Provisions were declared invalid on the ground that they were enacted in excess of the constitutional delegation of power to enact transitional provisions, but they contained also substantive and not only temporary rules (Decision no. 45/2012 [XII. 29]). The English translation of the decision is available at [http://www.mkab.hu/letoltesek/en_0045_2012.pdf, accessed on 28.02.2014].

Finally, it is important to draw attention to a peculiar and unprecedented limitation of the Court's powers. Art. 37 (4) of the Fundamental Law provides that

> '[a]s long as state debt exceeds half of the Gross Domestic Product, the Constitutional Court may, within its competence set out in Article 24 (2) b–e), only review the Acts on the state budget and its implementation, the central tax type, duties, pension and healthcare contributions, customs and the central conditions for local taxes [...] due to violation of the right to life and human dignity, the right to protection of personal data, freedom of thought, conscience and religion, and with the rights related to Hungarian citizenship.'[17]

As several observers have pointed out, the list does not contain a number of rights that would also deserve similar protection, such as the right to property, the principle of equality or the right to fair trial (see Tilk 2011, 15; Jakab 2011, 282–283). The Fourth Amendment extended this restriction even further. A new paragraph 5 inserted in art. 37 now provides that in the case of statutory provisions which entered into force during the period when the state debt exceeded half of the GDP, the restriction shall also apply if the state debt no longer exceeds half of the GDP, even if only in respect of this period.[18] The Venice Commission clearly condemned this unprecedented and solely politically motivated restriction of a constitutional court's powers (European Commission for Democracy Through Law 2011a, 20; id. 2012, 10).

This provision, however, still leaves some space for the review of budgetary and tax laws. Due to the fact that it explicitly refers to the competences set out in art. 24 (2) b–e) of the Fundamental Law while not including point f) of the same paragraph, international treaties may also serve as a basis for review of budgetary and tax laws. Review for the violation of an international treaty may be requested, as already mentioned above, by the same actors as abstract *a posteriori* review. It seems rather odd and illogical that there is such a serious restriction of constitutional review in relation to budgetary and tax laws, while they may be challenged without any limitation for the violation of an international treaty. It also seems to contradict the government's political rhetoric on the 'sovereignty of Hungary', as in this way budgetary and tax laws may violate the Hungarian Fundamental Law but not international treaties (see Jakab 2011, 282). Moreover, including human dignity among the rights that may not, in any event, be violated by budgetary and tax laws also reduces the restriction's practical effect, as the right to human dignity has always been interpreted broadly by the Constitutional Court which treated it as

---

17 Apart from this, the Constitutional Court maintains the unrestricted right to annul the related acts for non-compliance with the procedural requirements for drafting and publication.

18 This extension had been already done by the Transitional Provisions and then been incorporated in the Fundamental Law.

a 'mother right.' In fact, shortly after the adoption of the restriction, the Constitutional Court struck down a tax provision that imposed, with retroactive effect, a 98 per cent tax on severance payments which exceed the 3.5 million HUF threshold. According to the Court this retroactivity was an affront to human dignity.[19] In conclusion, it became obvious that, notwithstanding the new restriction, the Court finds its way to review budgetary and tax laws.

2.2. Constitutional complaints before and after 2012

The instrument of constitutional complaint, which existed only in its normative version before 2012, played a very limited role in the first twenty years of Hungarian constitutional justice. As long as the *actio popularis* existed, it made little sense for a complainant to wait for the final decision of the ordinary judge to challenge a law applied against him in the proceedings, while she could do so immediately through an *actio popularis*. Now that this type of proceeding has been abolished, the *normative constitutional complaint* has acquired fundamental importance, and ordinary citizens cannot initiate the proceedings of the Constitutional Court without showing a direct and individual interest. Today a private person is compelled to wait for the decision of the ordinary judge before he may challenge the law applied against him.

The new legal framework, however, also contains two new forms of constitutional complaint. The so-called *full constitutional complaint* is established by the Fundamental Law,[20] while the *direct constitutional complaint* is introduced by the new Constitutional Court Act.[21] The former, also called 'real complaint' (see Gárdos-Orosz 2012, 307), may be submitted against a judicial decision that violates the complainant's constitutional rights after all possible legal remedies have been exhausted.[22] The latter, instead, is an extension of the normative complaint which, exceptionally, may be used against a legal provision directly. It means that it is not required that the contested provision is being applied by an ordinary court, if it becomes directly effective. We can find a similar instrument in Austrian constitutional justice, called *Individualantrag*, that may be applied to challenge a general act if it is directly applicable to the complainant or an individual act if it is addressed to her.[23]

---

19 See Decision no. 37/2011 (V.10.) AB. An English summary is available at [http://www.mkab.hu/case-law/translations, accessed on 28.02.2014].

20 See art. 24 (2) d).

21 See art. 26 (2).

22 The detailed rules are set out in art. 27 of the new Constitutional Court Act.

23 See art. 139 (1) of the Austrian Constitution.

The explanatory notes attached to the bill presented in Parliament make explicit reference to German constitutional justice as a model for the new regulation. A significant difference from the German solution is that the Hungarian Constitutional Court Act does not include administrative acts among the acts that may be challenged before the Court. It is also true, however, that the German Federal Constitutional Court interprets the requirement of exhaustion of all legal remedies very strictly, so in practice only a very small part of constitutional complaints are directed against an administrative act, since most of these may be brought before an administrative court (Lorz 2005, 176).

Like the full constitutional complaint, the direct complaint represents a novelty of equal importance in Hungarian constitutional justice. This third form of constitutional complaint, which follows the German and Austrian models, is the one intended to replace the former *actio popularis*, as it may be lodged against a law directly, without being preceded by a judicial or administrative decision. There is, however, a deadline set by the Constitutional Court Act: 180 days, i.e. six months, after the entry into force of the challenged law.[24] An equally significant restriction in comparison to the *actio popularis* is the requirement of proving direct concern, a condition open to interpretation.

Finally, an important new provision allows the Constitutional Court to filter constitutional complaints and to admit only those cases which raise constitutional law issues of fundamental importance' or, in the case of full complaints, if the judicial decision is 'significantly affected by a conflict with the Fundamental Law.'[25] According to the explanatory notes this rule also represents the reception of a German solution. Indeed, the German Federal Constitutional Court applies these criteria to reject the overwhelming majority of constitutional complaints (Luther 2000, 197).[26] Therefore, the requirement of being of fundamental constitutional significance offers a great liberty to the constitutional court in selecting the cases to hear.[27]

---

24 Art. 30 (1) of the new Constitutional Court Act. It is a stricter deadline than the one set by the German Federal Constitutional Act which limits the filing of direct complaints to one year from the coming into force of the challenged law (see BVerfGG § 93, par. 3). The time-limit set for full complaints is instead double of the German one: sixty days instead of one month (art. 30 (1) of the Hungarian Constitutional Court Act and BVerfGG § 93, par. 1).

25 Art. 29 of the new Constitutional Court Act.

26 BVerfGG § 93a, par. 2.

27 The question of filtering constitutional complaints is a rather controversial issue in German scholarship. Many scholars point out that the consequence of this rule is that the Court is not obliged to give reasons for not hearing a case. The German Court attaches a reasoning

3. The court practice based on the new rules

3.1. Statistics from 2012–2013

Statistical data on the case-load of the Hungarian Constitutional Court is available until December 2013. The following tables summarise the relevant data:

Table no. 1: Pending and started cases between January 2012 and December 2013:

Form of action / Period	Cases pending on 1 January 2012	Cases started in 2012	Cases pending on 1 January 2013	Cases started in 2013
Normative complaint	274	80	32	36
Full complaint	0	353	73	125
Direct complaint	10	295	90	38
Indirect review	90	65	50	49
Preventive review	1	1	2	0
A posteriori abstract review	16	25	22	13
Constitutional interpretation	0	2	0	2
Conflicts of competence	1	0	0	0
Review of electoral decisions	21	15	3	0
Opinion on the dissolution of a local representative body	0	0	0	1
Total	**413**	**836**	**272**	**264**

Source: Official website of the Hungarian Constitutional Court [http://www.mkab.hu/dokumentumok/statisztika, accessed on 28.02.2014], own compilation.

Table no. 2: Certain kinds of decisions delivered in 2012–2013

Form of action / Year	2012	2013
Inadmissible constitutional complaints	184	149
Other inadmissible actions	320	110
Actions rejected on the merits	100	140
Annulled judicial decisions	0	5
Annulment of legal norms	29	53
Constitutional interpretation	2	1
Quashed cases	24	4

Source: Official website of the Hungarian Constitutional Court [http://www.mkab.hu/dokumentumok/statisztika, accessed on 28.02.2014], own compilation.

to the decisions declaring the inadmissibility of a complaint in about 75 percent of the cases (see Kommers 1997, 19–20).

A lot of interesting information may be retrieved from these numbers which offer an insight in the first two years of the Constitutional Court's work after the reform. In order to interpret the numbers correctly, it is important to know that all pending popular actions submitted before 1 January 2012 by complainants who do not have the right of access before the Constitutional Court according to the new rules extinguished with the entering into force of the new legal framework. However, there was the possibility to re-file these actions as a normative or direct constitutional complaint, if the requirements specified in art. 26 of the new Constitutional Court Act were met.[28] The deadline set for the re-submission of popular actions as constitutional complaints was 31 March 2012. This circumstance explains the high number of normative (354) and direct complaints (305) handled by the Court in 2012, and the drop in this number in 2013 (only 36 new normative and 38 new direct complaints). Quite obviously, many petitioners of popular actions that concerned an older proceeding could neither raise their issue again as a normative complaint (due to the short time-limit set by the new legal framework), nor as a direct complaint (because the contested law must not entered into force longer than six months before). According to the statistical data published by the Court, 224 of the 707 normative and direct complaints pending on 1 January 2012 or started during 2012 were re-submitted old popular actions. It seems clear that after the end of this transitional period the full complaint will represent the overwhelming majority of constitutional complaints submitted to the Court.

3.2. Case-law

As it emerges from Table no. 2, in the first two years of its operation the Constitutional Court denied the admissibility of 333 constitutional complaints, while among those decided on the merits only five cases led to the annulment of a judicial decision. These numbers show that the admissibility criteria provided by the new Constitutional Court Act are strict and are being applied strictly by the Court. The requirement of 'fundamental constitutional importance' provided by art. 29 of the new Constitutional Court Act has played, as it could have been expected, a fundamental role in the selection of cases. The Constitutional Court made clear very early that it would not act as a last instance jurisdiction and would not supervise the practice of the ordinary courts and their substantive findings and interpretations of the law if it did not clearly violate the Fundamental Law.[29] Moreover,

---

28 See art. 71 (1) and (3) of the new Constitutional Court Act.

29 In Decision no. 3077/2012 (VII. 26.) AB the Court refused to hear a complaint which contested the constitutionality of inconsistent court practice in relation to the interpretation of

legal norms that regulate details will not be considered as being of fundamental constitutional importance.[30]

An extensive interpretation of the 'fundamental constitutional importance' requirement is represented by cases in which the Court rejected a complaint on the ground that they raised already decided questions.[31] It certainly is a frequently used basis for decisions of inadmissibility. It also shows that the Court is not shy to use old case-law based on the old Constitution, notwithstanding the provision introduced by the Fourth Amendment, according to which all previous decisions of the Constitutional Court delivered before the entry into force of the new Fundamental Law lose their effectiveness.[32] It also happened, on the other hand, that the Court simply declared the lack of constitutional importance of the issue, without giving further explanation. It did so in a case concerning a challenge against a provision the Act on Civil Servants providing for lower salary for higher-up officers of local governments than for officers of government agencies,[33] and in a case concerning a challenge against a provision of the Code of Civil Procedure.[34]

The second part of the admissibility criteria set by art. 29, concerning normative complaints, requires that the judicial decision shall be significantly affected by a conflict with the Fundamental Law. In a case concerning the constitutionality of a municipal decree the Constitutional Court stated that its decision, i.e. the annulment of the challenged provision, also has to affect the final outcome of the case. If it cannot produce the effect desired by the complainant, the issue cannot be considered of fundamental constitutional importance.[35]

---

a criminal offense. The Court argued that it would not review legal dogmatic questions of substantive criminal law unless it clearly contradicts widely accepted scientific findings.

30 In Decision no. 3065/2012 (VII. 26.) AB the Court considered a provision not entitling the authors of musical scores to a reprographic fee (unlike authors of other kinds of intellectual work) a detail of the law of intellectual property, which does not amount to a question of fundamental constitutional importance.

31 See Decisions no. 3074/2012 (VII. 26.) AB, no. 3080/2012 (VII. 26.) AB, and no. 3081/2012 (VII. 26.) AB.

32 Section 5 of the Closing and Miscellaneous Provisions of the Fundamental Law (see also Kelemen 2013).

33 See Decision no. 3076/2012 (VII. 26.) AB. The complainant invoked the principle of non-discrimination. The Court in its reasoning simply states that the issue does not raise any constitutional question of fundamental importance.

34 See Decision no. 3078/2012 (VII. 26.) AB. The contested art. 260 of the Code does not allow for revision of a decree issued in a winding-up procedure.

35 See, e.g., Decision no. 3089/2012 (VII. 26.) AB in which the Court found that annulling the challenged municipal decree would not lead to a reduction of the taxes to be payed by the complainant.

It seems that the Constitutional Court has adopted a strict interpretation of the admissibility criteria also with regard to the direct complaint. Tax laws, for example, have been declared not to be directly applicable norms already in more than one occasion, as taxes are assessed and collected by the tax authority.[36] In a similar manner, pension laws cannot be challenged directly by a person who is not yet retired, and in any case the complaint is to be filed against the individual decision of the public pension agency and not against the law. Thus a constitutional complaint cannot be based on a supposed future violation of the complainant's rights.[37]

The first full constitutional complaint that led to the annulment of a judicial decision was filed by a liberal political party (LMP). The case concerned a decision of the police denying authorisation for the organisation of an event on a national holiday in Heroes' Square in Budapest.[38] Even though the ordinary court decided in favour of the complainant, the event could not be held, as the judgement had been delivered too late. According to the Constitutional Court the ordinary court, by not making a timely decision, violated the right of assembly enshrined in Art. VIII of the Fundamental Law.[39]

4. Conclusion

According to Victor Ferreres Comella constitutional courts can be located along a spectrum of 'purity' as to the functions they exercise. A constitutional court would not be 'pure' when, apart from reviewing legislation, it has some other functions (see Ferreres-Comella 2009, 6–7). From this perspective the Hungarian Constitutional Court has moved from the middle to one extreme of the spectrum. Before the entering into force of the new Fundamental Law, it performed some additional tasks, although its main activity was still review of legislation. After the reform, however, with the abolition of *actio popularis* and the introduction of full constitutional complaint, it can be considered one of the 'less pure' constitutional courts in Europe, together with the German, Austrian and Spanish ones, since in terms of everyday practice, its main function is not to determine the constitutionality of

36 See Decisions no. 3079/2012 (VII. 26.) AB, no. 3082/2012 (VII. 26.) AB and no. 3085/2012 (VII. 26.) AB.

37 See Decision no. 3090/2012 (VII. 26.) AB; see also Decision no. 3020/2012 (VI. 21.) AB.

38 The authorisation was denied because the local government of Budapest had already conceded the same area for the same national holiday to the office of the mayor. However, later the mayor abandoned the idea of organising an event in Heroes' Square.

39 See Decision no. 3/2013 (II. 14.) AB.

legislation any more. Only roughly half of the cases started in 2013 (136 of 264, see table 1) concerned this function.

As mentioned in the introduction, a shift of emphasis from abstract to concrete review may be expected in Hungarian constitutional justice.[40] This prediction seems to be confirmed quite clearly by the statistics for the moment.[41] Another point that is becoming evident is that the admissibility criteria provided by the new Constitutional Court Act are interpreted strictly by the Court: in 2012 and 2013 it refused to hear 504 and 399 cases, respectively (see table 2). Even if the Court has become less open, as it cannot be reached by anyone at any time any more, that does not mean that political questions may not be raised after the reform. The ombudsman's standing and the maintained opportunity for preventive review still give rise to politically sensitive cases.

As the Venice Commission also observed, the abolition of the *actio popularis* is not at all problematic from the viewpoint of the rule of law (see European Commission for Democracy Through Law 2012, 12). However, it is an exceptional instrument in the panorama of European constitutional justice. The introduction of full constitutional complaint, in contrast, extends the reach of the Hungarian Constitutional Court's powers, as it now also examines the constitutionality of judicial decisions. These reforms are undoubtedly transforming the Hungarian model of constitutional justice, but the early evaluation of the practice provided in this chapter has shown that the Court aims at upholding continuity with its previous case-law and its previous role in the Hungarian legal system.

References

European Commission for Democracy Through Law (Venice Commission). 2011. *Opinion on Three Legal Questions Arising in the Process of Drafting the New Constitution.* Opinion no. 614/2011 [http://www.venice.coe.int/webforms/documents/default.aspx?pdffile=CDL-AD%282011%29001-e, accessed on 28.02.2014].

European Commission for Democracy Through Law (Venice Commission). 2011a. *Opinion on the New Constitution of Hungary.* Opinion no. 621/2011 [http://www.venice.coe.int/webforms/documents/default.aspx?pdffile=CDL-AD%282011%29016-e, accessed on 28.02.2014].

40 All three types of constitutional complaint lead to concrete review, since they necessarily involve a concrete legal controversy (in the case of the normative and full complaints) or a concrete real-life situation (in the case of the direct complaint).

41 Only in 13 of 264 cases started in 2013 the Court has had to exercise abstract review (see table 1).

European Commission for Democracy Through Law (Venice Commission). 2011b. *Study on Individual Access to Constitutional Justice.* Study no. 538/2009. Strasbourg: Council of Europe.

European Commission for Democracy Through Law (Venice Commission). 2012. *Opinion on Act CLI of 2011 on the Constitutional Court of Hungary.* Opinion no. 665/2012 [http://www.venice.coe.int/webforms/documents/default.aspx?pdffile=CDL-AD%282012%29009-e, accessed on 28.02.2014].

Ferreres Comella, Victor. 2009. *Constitutional Courts and Democratic Values. A European Perspective.* New Haven, London: Yale University Press.

Gárdos-Orosz, Fruzsina. 2012. The Hungarian Constitutional Court in Transition from Actio Popularis to Constitutional Complaint. *Acta Juridica Hungarica* 53: 302–315.

Jakab, András. 2011. *Az új Alaptörvény keletkezése és gyakorlati következményei* [The Adoption of the New Fundamental Law and Its Practical Consequences]. Budapest: HVG-ORAC.

Kelemen, Katalin. 2011. Constitution-making in Hungary: The final stage. In *Diritti Comparati* (9 April) [http://www.diritticomparati.it/2011/04/constitution-making-in-hungary-the-final-stage.html, accessed on 28.02.2014].

Kelemen, Katalin. 2011a. Hungary: The new Constitutional Court Act. In *Diritti Comparati* (15 December) [http://www.diritticomparati.it/2011/12/hungary-the-new-constitutional-court-act.html, accessed on 28.02.2014].

Kelemen, Katalin. 2013. A Flexible Constitution: The 4th Amendment to the Hungarian Fundamental Law. Part I and Part II. In *Diritti Comparati* (20 and 25 March) [http://www.diritticomparati.it/2013/03/, accessed on 28.02.2014].

Kommers, Donald. 1997. *The Constitutional Jurisprudence of the Federal Republic of Germany.* Durham et al.: Duke University Press, 2nd ed.

Lábady, Tamás. 1991. A populáris akció és az egyéni jogvédelem biztosítása az alkotmánybírósági eljárásban [Popular Action and the Protection of Individual Rights in the Constitutional Court's Procedure]. *Magyar Jog* 7: 385–390.

Lorz, Ralph Alexander. 2005. Standing to raise constitutional issues in Germany. In *Standing to raise constitutional issues: Comparative perspectives*, edited by Richard S. Kay, 163–194. Bruxelles: Bruylant.

Luther, Jörg. 2000. La giustizia costituzionale nella Repubblica Federale di Germania. In *Esperienze di giustizia costituzionale. Tomo I*, edited by Jörg Luther, Roberto Romboli, and Rolando Tarchi, 159–198. Torino: Giappichelli.

Sadurski, Wojciech. 2009. *Twenty Years After the Transition: Constitutional Review in Central and Eastern Europe.* Legal Studies Research Paper No. 09/69. Sydney Law School [http://ssrn.com/abstract=1437843, accessed on 28.02.2014].

Sólyom, László. 2001. *Az alkotmánybíráskodás kezdetei Magyarországon* [The Outset of Constitutional Justice in Hungary]. Budapest: Osiris.

Sólyom, László. 2003. The Role of Constitutional Courts in the Transition to Democracy. *International Sociology* 18: 133–161.

Tilk, Péter. 2011. Az Alkotmánybíróság eljárásának korlátozása és az ehhez vezető események [Restriction of the Constitutional Court's Jurisdiction and the Events Leading to It]. *De iurisprudentia et iure publico* 2011/2: 1–16 [http://www.dieip.hu/2011_2_16.pdf, accessed on 28.02.2014].

‘War of Courts’ as a Clash of Legal Cultures: Rethinking the Conflict Between the Polish Constitutional Tribunal and the Supreme Court Over ‘Interpretive Judgments’

Rafał Mańko

Abstract

Since 1986, Poland has had its Constitutional Tribunal, placed outside the structure of ordinary judiciary. Since 1993, this court has been issuing ‘interpretive judgments’ in which it decides that a certain statutory rule is constitutional only under a certain interpretation. On numerous occasions the Supreme Court has refused to follow the Constitutional Tribunal’s decisions, claiming that they are unconstitutional, *ultra vires* and non-binding. An analysis of the arguments put forward by both courts in this ‘war of the courts’ reveals that the Supreme Court prefers ultra-formalist arguments typical of the hyperpositivist legal culture of the former state-socialist period, whilst the Constitutional Tribunal seems to prefer pragmatist arguments, more typical to contemporary Western legal culture. The article concludes that behind the ‘war of the courts’ in Poland there is a clash of legal cultures and attempts at identifying the reasons for it.

1. Introduction

The establishment of a separate, specialised constitutional court, placed outside the structures of the ordinary judiciary often leads to constitutional conflicts (Comella 2011, 273). Such conflicts are defined as ‘quarrels in which either two or more actors draw upon the same constitutional competence or one actor claims a competence that draws the diapproval of another’ (Hein 2011, 3), in this case the actors in question being the constitutional court and the ordinary courts, usually the supreme court. Famous examples include Germany (Heun 2011, 182), Italy (Garlicki 2007, 54–56), South Africa (Michelman 2011, 286–287) the Czech Republic (Sadurski 2005, 22–23; Kühn 2011, 194–195, 200–207) or recently Spain (Leslie 2006, Turano 2006). One could even go as far as to say that such conflicts, especially some forms of questioning the authority of the constitutional court by the chief court of the ordinary judiciary, are a commonplace struggle for power and prestige between highest courts, which can be ascribed, *inter alia*, to the judges’ inclination to expand their power, authority and competences (Garlicki 2007, 64–65), especially that a newly created constitutional court is viewed with envy by the existing ordinary judiciary (Sadurski 2005, 21).

Following the German model Poland has had, since 1986, a separate Constitutional Tribunal (*Trybunał Konstytucyjny*, ‘TK’), distinct from the Supreme Court

(*Sąd Najwyższy*, 'SN'), established in 1917, and the Chief Administrative Court (*Naczelny Sąd Administracyjny*), established in 1980. This division of power within the apex of the Polish judiciary has led to conflicts. In the Polish case, the 'war of the courts' between the TK and SN has been focused on the binding force of those TK judgments which declare that a certain statutory rule is constitutional only under a certain interpretation ('interpretive judgments'). The SN has, on several occasions, openly refused to follow such decisions, claiming they are unconstitutional, *ultra vires* and not binding. This chapter will analyse the arguments used by the two contenders in the Polish 'war of the courts' on the basis of a case study, regarding one of the battles of that 'war.' The analysis will show that the SN displays a tendency to cling to the hyperpositivist, ultra-formalist legal culture typical of the former state-socialist period, whilst the TK seems more inclined to employ a pragmatist, instrumentalist and realist argumentative style. This will lead me to the conclusion that behind the Polish 'war of the courts' there is actually something deeper than only a struggle of power – it is a clash of legal cultures and a struggle for ideological hegemony between the post-socialist hyperpositivism (nurtured by the SN) and the new European legal pragmatism (detectible in the style of the TK). I will explain this difference between the two courts by proposing to link the style of adjudication with such factors as institutional history, career trajectories of judges, the relevant auditorium and the place of each court in the structure of the judiciary.

Despite praise of the style of the TK and criticism of the style of the SN, the contentions of this essay should be read as relating to the context of the 'war of the courts', in which the TK is more pragmatic, and the SN more hyperpositivist. However, this does not imply an unqualified endorsement of the judicial style and case-law of the TK in general, especially that, as persuasively shown by Dębska (2013a, 330–338; 2013b, 226–251), it still remains tainted by a number of formalist features itself, such as 'guru style', one-sidedness of argumentation, magisterial and deductive argumentation, inherent in Polish legal culture (Mańko 2005, 541–542). Nevertheless, it seems that it is the TK, rather than the SN, which is evolving in the desirable direction towards a more transparent culture of adjudication (Mańko 2005, 548).

In order to avoid terminological confusion, I will explicitly define the key notions of 'formalism' and 'pragmatism.' I will understand 'formalism' as an approach to law which concentrates on linguistic and logical analysis of legal texts, whilst factoring out political, social and economic considerations, treats systemic coherence of the law as a value, draws a sharp distinction between legislation and adjudication (Gray 2003, 478; Matczak 2007, 64–66). As its opposite, I will treat 'pragmatism' which I will understand as an approach to law which treats law as a means to attaining political, economic, social, cultural and other aims, which shifts focus from legal texts to purposes, interests, and policies, as well as legal actors, legal institutions and law in action (Hesselink 2001, 73; Gray 2003, 479). I will characterise hyperpositivism (defined in section 2) as permeated with an extreme form of legal formalism.

The chapter is structured as follows: I first introduce the notion of 'hyperpositivism' as a salient feature of Polish legal culture (section 2), then I present crucial socio-political data about the TK and SN (section 3), before discussing the constitutional framework of the 'war of the courts' (section 4). The main part of the chapter is devoted to the case study (section 5), before ending with conclusions which are an attempt to explain the detected phenomenon (section 6).

2. Hyperpositivism in Polish Legal Culture

Following World War II, Poland found itself in the Soviet block and its legal culture was subject to a strong influence of the USSR (Mańko 2013b). A salient feature of Soviet legal culture, starting from the Stalinist period, was so-called 'hyperpositivism' – an extreme form of textual positivism, also referred to as 'primitive positivism' (Zirk-Sadowski 2006, 308–309). Although initially born out of a reception of Western European legal ideas (classical positivism), Soviet hyperpositivism developed a number of distinct features making it a unique phenomenon (Mańko 2013a, 218). Paradoxically, the Soviet bloc experienced a rise of hyperpositivist legal thinking in the aftermath of Stalinism, owing to the belief that formalism could place checks on totalitarianism; at the same time, in the West, German lawyers associated formalism *with* totalitarianism, and moved away from it towards a more transparent, pragmatic and informal legal culture (Hesselink 2001; Kühn 2004, 535; Kühn 2011, 154–157).

Hyperpositivism as a paradigm of legal theory and practice can be defined by resorting to four fundamental features (Mańko 2013a, 218), which have a typological character and need not always be present with the same intensity. First of all, hyperpositivism is based on the notion of a 'limited law', meaning that only texts emanating from the State are considered to be 'the law' (Sadurski 1984, 203; Izdebski 1986, 18; Łętowska 1997, 56; Kühn 2004, 540–541; Mańko 2005, 534; Kühn 2011, 209; Mańko 2013a, 218–219). The law, rather than being conceived as a form of social practice or a system of principles, values and rules, is reduced to a set of written texts – codes and statutes. General principles, customary norms, case-law or doctrinal writings are denied the status of law (Mańko 2013a, 218–219). The dichotomy of binding (law) vs. non-binding (hence, 'non-law') is strongly emphasised (Kühn 2011, 273). The notion of law in hyperpositivism can, therefore, be described as hermetically closed, as opposed to softer forms of positivism.

Secondly, hyperpositivism reduces legal interpretation to the grammatical and logical exegesis of texts considered as being part of the 'law' (Łętowska 2002, 43; Kühn 2011, 207–208; Mańko 2013a, 219). There is a belief in 'only one correct' interpretation of a text, usually its 'literal' interpretation (Łętowska 2002, 43).

Thirdly, hyperpositivism nurtures a reductionist vision of a judge as someone performing an automatic act of 'subsumption' of facts under legal rules (Mańko 2005, 534–535; Zirk-Sadowski 2006, 308–39; Milej 2008, 68–69; Mańko 2013a, 219–220).

Finally, hyperpositivism entails a high degree of formalism, whereby judges prefer to decide cases on formal, rather than substantive grounds and the formal side of the law enjoys precedence over the underlying substantive issues (Kühn 2004, 555; Milej 2008, 69; Uzelac 2010, 383–385, Kühn 2011, 204–207; Mańko 2013a, 220).

Whereas this description could in a way fit to many Western European legal cultures in the 19th century, it must be emphasised that hyperpositivism is a social phenomenon directly linked to the particular historical setting of Actually Existing Socialism and as such reflects the reduced social role of lawyers in that system (Mańko 2013a, 222–224). Its persistence after the transformation from state socialism to capitalism may be viewed as a legal survival, i.e. an example of a phenomenon of legal culture which persists despite the disappearance of its original socio-economic foundation (Mańko 2013a, 215–216).

3. Socio-Political Background of the Two Courts

An underlying assumption of this chapter is the existence of a causal link between the socio-political background of a judicial body and the legal culture of its individual members and the body as a whole; hence the need of inquiring into the institutional history of the TK and SN, the social background and career paths of their members, and the place of the two courts in the structure of Polish judiciary. The two institutions differ sharply with regard to all these features.

The SN, established in 1917, has enjoyed almost 100 years of uninterrupted existence, save for the period of WW II (Malec 2011). Despite the two radical socio-economic transformations experienced by Poland in the 20th century, it even managed to maintain a relatively high continuity of its judicial personnel (Bereza 2011). Following the transition to capitalism, the SN's term was ended prematurely (Bereza 2011, 285); however, among the 57 new appointees, 38% originated from the pre-1990 SN (Kozielewicz 2011, 302), and the others mainly from career judges. In contrast, the TK's history is much shorter – it has been operational only since 1986, originally intended as a means of boosting the legitimacy of the military dictatorship of Geneneral Jaruzelski (Mażewski 2011, 333; Dębska 2013b, 103–104). Until 1990, it was a weak institution, more of an advisory body than a real constitutional court (Sadurski 2005, 1; Mażewski 2010, 127), since its decisions on the unconstitutionality of statutes were subject to the parliamentary review. After 1990 its position was strengthened, especially after the creation of a direct complaint to the TK, available against a statutory rule which served as a basis of determining the rights and duties of an individual in a definite manner.

The two courts differ as regards the social background of its members. The SN is dominated by career judges, the majority of whom (75%) do not hold a PhD (SN website, 2013). The system of judicial appointments at the SN favours the reproduction of the judicial elite: the SN itself screens candidates and forwards its selection to the National Council of the Judiciary (KRS), which makes the final selection and presents it to the President (SN Act 2002, KRS Act 2011). In practice the KRS, itself is a corporate body representing judges, who constitute 68% of its members (KRS website 2013; Sadurski 2005, 57), rejects roughly 34% of SN candidates (data for 1990–2006, see Kozielewicz 2011, 369). In practice, neither Parliament, nor the public opinion are involved actively in the selection process.

In contrast to the SN, the process of appointment of TK Justices is much more transparent, political and contested, involving civil society and the media (Sadurski 2005, 15–16; Safjan 2008, 10). Appointments are voted in the lower house of the Polish Parliament (*Sejm*) by ordinary majority, allowing the ruling coalition to impose its preferred candidates (Sadurski 2009, 5; Zdziennicki 2013). The candidates must either be fully qualified academics, or legal practitioners with 10 years' experience (TK Act 1997, SN Act 2002). Until now, of all TK Justices 80% were academics (out of which 36% pure academics), 50% had links with politics, whilst only 36% Justices originated from the judiciary in general, and 3% were career judges without other experience; 21% Justices were practitioners, usually with some kind of political background (Dębska 2013b, 184, 196–197, 205).

For most judges at the SN, an appointment to the court is the last step in their professional career. The ambitions of TK Justices seem to go further, and former Justices have been appointed to the Court of Justice of the EU, the European Court of Human Rights, the SN, as well as to the post of the Ombudsman (Dębska 2013b, 206).

4. The 'War of the Courts' in Poland

The legal axis of the war of the courts in Poland is the issue of the so-called 'interpretive judgments' of the Constitutional Court. An interpretive judgment is a decision in which a constitutional court 'declares a legal rule under scrutiny to be in conformity with the Constitution, provided that a norm deducted from the rule will have a content determined by the Court' (Sulikowski 2008, 50–51; see also Florczak-Wątor 2006, 93–103, 150–152; Sadurski 2009, 22). Interpretive judgments are issued by Western European constitutional courts, including the Italian, German and French (Florczak-Wątor 2006, 94; Garlicki 2007, 54; Kühn 2011, 240). Interpretive judgments are considered to be 'an efficient instrument of management – rationalisation of the law, furthering changes in an appropriate direction identified by constitutional courts.' (Sulikowski 2008, 52).

In this context it should also be added that between 1989 and 1997 the Constitutional Court enjoyed the power to issue abstract, binding interpretations of statutes (Constitution 1952 as from 8.4.1989; TK Act 1985 as from 19.7.1989). This right was inherited from the socialist period, when the Council of State – an equivalent of the Presidium of the Supreme Soviet – enjoyed this power between 1952 and 1989. The fact that the Constitutional Court had enjoyed this right before it was it was taken away by the 1997 Constitution is often relied upon by the SN (see e.g. SN 17.12.2009, III PZP 2/09, para II.3).

In general, within the Polish 'war of the courts', the SN has displayed a tendency towards employing hyperpositivist and ultra-formalist arguments, whereas the TK has rather preferred pragmatic, instrumentalist and realist arguments. First of all, the SN bases its arguments on the 'literal meaning' of the text of the Constitution and TK Act, pointing out that 'interpretive judgments' are not mentioned there as a separate category (e.g. III PZP 2/09, para. II.6). Secondly, the SN relies on the hyperpositivist sharp distinction between 'creating' law (allegedly only by the legislature) and 'applying' law, and uses this argument to accuse TK of law-making, which is to make interpretive judgments *ultra vires* (e.g. III PZP 2/09, II. 5) and contrary to the division of powers between the legislative and judiciary (SN 25.4.2007, IV CSK 34/07; SN 17.11.2008, I CO 23/08; III PZP 2/09, II.20). The SN is programmatically deaf to any purposeful arguments, stating that '[p]ragmatic reasons [...] do not entitle the Constitutional Court to [...] enter the sphere reserved for the law-maker' (III PZP 2/09, II.11). The obvious fact that judges create the law, and in particular that '[c]onstitutional judges *make the law* through interpreting the constitution' (Stone Sweet 2012, 827; see also Hein 2011, 17), still escapes the SN's hyperpositivist imagination. The 'analogy between the function of the judge and the function of the legislator' (Cardozo 2010, 49), noted by American scholars already in the 1920s, and accepted in Western Europe at least after World War II (Wieacker 2000, 421; Kühn 2004, 537; Kühn 2011, 87–88, 197–198; Mańko 2013a, 221), still remains outside the cognitive capacity SN judges who repeat the mantra that 'courts in the Republic of Poland *apply* the law, but do not *create* it' (IV CSK 34/07, emphasis added). Thereby, they refuse to recognize what 'has always been recognized, at least by the realists, that judicial interpretation entails some component of lawmaking' (Garlicki 2007, 66). The SN also rejects TK's comparative law arguments in favour of interpretive judgments, stating that the 'judicial practice of constitutional courts of other states should not be uncritically transferred, replicated or copied' (III PZP 2/09, II.7).

On the other hand, TK has resorted mainly to pragmatic arguments to support its practice, underlining that a legal rule has more than one interpretation (TK 11.12.2001, SK 16/00), that if a rule is capable of being interpreted in conformity with the Constitution, it would be too harsh to strike it down completely (TK 15.9.1999, K 11/99). The TK considers its interpretive decisions as binding on the entire judiciary (TK 6.7.2005, SK 27/04).

5. Case Study: Conflict over Retrospective Application of a Case Selection Mechanism by the SN Civil Chamber

In order to illustrate the difference in the style of adjudication of the TK and SN, I will resort to a case study – a conflict over the interpretation of two rules of Polish civil procedure, one introducing a case selection mechanism in proceedings before the SN in civil matters, and another regarding the reopening of civil proceedings following a TK decision favourable for an applicant.

The cassation in civil matters, introduced to Polish civil procedure in 1996, was a form of third-instance proceedings available to litigants as a matter of right. Hence, the SN could not refuse to hear a case on account of its insignificance for the development of the law. This led to a serious overload of the SN's docket and persuaded the legislature to introduce a case selection mechanism. The act introducing the case selection mechanism contained an intertemporal rule which provided that cassations filed before its entry into force should be subject to the old rules, both as regards the requirements for their 'filing', and as to 'deciding' them. This relatively plain language was initially understood at face value by the SN, which was working hard through its overloaded docket. However, at some point the SN came up with the apparently brilliant idea of reinterpreting the intertemporal provision in a way which would allow it to reject all the 'old' cassations for want of a significant legal issue. Faced with the need of overcoming the plain meaning of the intertemporal provision, the SN (17.1.2011, III CZP 49/00) resorted to a sophisticated form of linguistic and logical trickery, aimed at presenting its interpretation as compelling and justified as a *literal* interpretation of the rule. Strangely (for a legal realist, at least), it did not try to balance the public interest of the administration of justice (clearing up of the SN's docket, and hence speeding up of proceedings for all litigants) with the private interest of those litigants, who had filed their cassations under the old rules (who would retroactively be deprived of their procedural right to be heard, on a point of law, in third-instance proceedings). Instead, the SN concentrated on the linguistic level, relying on the fact that the old provisions are to apply to the 'filing' of cassations and 'deciding' upon cassations brought under the old rules. Drawing upon dictionary definitions from the 1960s, the SN argued that in between the litigant's act of 'filing' and the SN's act of 'deciding', there is still room for an additional act of 'selecting', and this selection process is to be governed by the new law. It also drew on the intertemporal rules of the socialist Code of Civil Procedure ('CCP') to propose a general principle of retrospective application of new procedural rules to pending cases. This allowed the SN to rely on the classical canon of strict interpretation of exceptions to treat 'filing' and 'deciding' as exceptions to the general rule of applying the new rules to cassations filed before the entry into force of the new rules. The SN thus treated the legal rules in an instrumental way, eager to broaden the scope of its judicial discretion, but simultaneously factoring out any concerns for the social justice of the outcome.

The style of the TK within the battle over the retrospective application of the case selection mechanism in civil proceedings was, in comparison, much more pragmatic. In its first case on the topic (18.2.2004, SK 12/03), it made the realist assumption that it would not analyse the controversial intertemporal rule in the abstract, but would rather concentrate on its interpretation adopted by the SN. On the basis of parliamentary proceedings, the TK found that SN's interpretation departs from the obvious intent of the legislature. However, instead of entering into a polemic on this basis (and adopting an intentionalist position with regard to legal interpretation), the TK accepted the SN's reading of the rule as a legal fact and went on to evaluate it in the light of constitutional values and principles. Framing its analysis as a balancing exercise, the TK identified three applicable principles: a rigorous, though not absolute prohibition of retroactive laws (application of new law to facts in the past); secondly, a limitation on retrospectiveness (application of new law to existing legal relationships), and thirdly, the principle of protection of vested rights of individuals. Entering the details, the TK identified two conflicting interests: the public interest in the immediate application of the new procedural rules, even to pending cases (for the sake of speeding up proceedings at the SN), and on the other hand, the individual interest of having the old procedural rules applied to pending cases. The TK also underlined the principle of trust, pointing out that litigants had filed their petitions for cassation on the understanding that a certain set of procedural requirements would apply.

In conclusion, the TK acknowledged that fighting the backlog on the SN's docket is an important public interest which justified the introduction of a case selection mechanism to cassation proceedings, but nevertheless it is not an overriding interest which would justify a retrospective introduction of this new requirement. The TK pointed that petitioners, at the time of filing their cassations, could not have even known the new rules, which were introduced only later. By applying those requirements retrospectively, the SN was committing a denial of justice. On the basis of a balancing of interests, the TK came to the conclusion that with regard to those litigants who had filed their petitions for cassation before the entry into force of the new rules, the protection of their trust in the justice system must prevail over pragmatic needs of combating the SN's backlog. It invited the SN to revise its case-law on the topic in order to opt for an interpretation of the intertemporal rule conforming to the Constitution.

When litigants, armed with TK's interpretive judgment in their favour, tried to reopen proceedings to have their cassations heard, the SN blatantly refused (6.3.2003, I CO 7/03), relying this time on a highly formalist interpretation of a detailed rule in the CCP governing the reopening of proceedings following a TK judgment. The relevant rule provided for reopening of civil proceedings which ended with a 'judgment.' However, the technical term for the SN's decision refusing to hear a cassation is not 'judgment' but 'order.' In a hyperpositivist spirit, drawing on this terminological flaw in the CCP rule, the SN refused to reopen cassation proceedings, despite TK's interpretive judgment in their favour. The SN also raised a series of formalist arguments questioning the binding force of TK's interpretive judgment, condemning it as a form of 'law-making.' It also added that since 1997 the TK has not enjoyed the power to issue abstractly binding interpretations of statutory rules, and therefore interpretive judgments have the form of a 'non-binding interpretation.' Finally, the SN relied on a formalist reading of the principle of judicial independence, stating that independence of the SN and ordinary judiciary means that they are free to interpret statutes by themselves, without being bound by TK's precedent.

Faced with the SN's refusal to reopen proceedings, litigants came back to the TK, this time complaining against the CCP rule on the reopening of proceedings, applied by the SN in a formalistic manner to their detriment (2.3.2004, SK 53/03). Analysing the constitutionality of that rule, the TK pointed out that the framers of the Constitution clearly wished to create a remedy which would allow having a case which had been decided on the basis of an unconstitutional rule, reopened and decided once again in conformity with the Constitution. This constitutional right of the individual must find its embodiment in the ordinary rules governing the civil, criminal and administrative procedure. Conceding that the drafting quality of the contested CCP rule may give rise to doubts, the TK nevertheless invited the SN to give it an interpretation in conformity with the Constitution or to rely on other CCP rules which would permit to achieve the result prescribed by the

Constitution. The TK even gave the SN specific suggestions as to which of the already existing rules in the Code of Civil Procedure could be used to set aside an order which has been based on an unconstitutional rule. Therefore, hoping that the SN would take a flexible and constitution-friendly approach to the text of the CCP, the TK decided to refrain from annulling its rule on the reopening of proceedings. Simultaneously, as if anticipating the SN's obstinacy (Hermeliński 2012, 15) the TK invited the legislature to enact a new rule, this time literally obliging the SN to reopen proceedings even if they ended with an 'order' and not a 'judgment' (2.3.2004, S 1/04), which the legislature later accomplished.

In the meantime, the SN did remain obstinate, and consequently refused to reopen proceedings upon request from litigants, whose cassations, filed under the old rules, had been summarily dismissed by the SN in violation of TK's case-law. When litigants, having attempted in vain to have proceedings reopened, complained once again to the TK against the CCP rule invoked by the SN to their detriment, the TK decided that the time was ripe to declare the CCP rule in question unconstitutional instead of pronouncing yet another interpretive judgment which the SN would ignore (27.10.2004, SK 1/04).

6. Conclusions

The analysis has shown that the 'war of the courts' in Poland is not only a simple struggle for power between two judicial bodies, but also a clash of legal cultures. The stakes are therefore very high, and are crucial for the future of Polish legal culture – whether it will leave behind the simplistic and simultaneously intransparent hyperpositivist style of adjudication and embrace an open, pragmatic and transparent style, where all the actual interests and values involved can be openly weighed against each other. It seems from the case study, and more broadly from the 'war of the courts' the TK has been the champion of pragmatic adjudication in Poland, while the SN generally lagged behind, attached to the outdated clichés of hyperpositivism. I will now try to identify a number of factors which can be assumed to determine the choices of the two courts with regard to their argumentative strategies.

First of all, the two courts are staffed with persons having different experiences within the Polish legal community: the SN is dominated by high-level career judges with a minority of academics, whilst the TK is dominated by academics, with almost no career judges. Furthermore, academics at the SN tend to represent 'core' areas of private and criminal law, whilst academics at the TK represent, apart from the dominant practical disciplines (e.g. private law, financial law) also legal theory and history (Dębska 2013b, 188–189). Different backgrounds translate themselves into different argumentative habits. Whereas SN judges, originating from the community of career judges, represent its habits and values, TK Justices, recruited from academia, legal practice and often linked to the world of politics, do not share that professional experience and hence do not necessarily represent the habits and values of the ordinary judiciary.

Secondly, of importance is the issue of institutional role models. Whereas the SN, boasting an almost centennial tradition, does not need to look to foreign supreme courts for inspiration, the TK has been a novelty on the Polish legal scene. In building their institutional identity, TK Justices certainly looked up to Western European constitutional courts as their role models, thereby taking over ideas of judicial activism and pragmatist argumentation (Kühn 2011, 264–265). Other courts, to which the TK is prone to look up to in search of inspiration include the European Court of Justice ('ECJ') and the European Court of Human Rights ('ECtHR'), both of which have a proven track-record of pragmatist adjudication, very far from the hyperpositivist ultra-formalism.

Thirdly, it is possible to argue that the two courts speak to slightly different audiences. Although, in general, it can be said that their decisions are addressed to the Polish legal community and, to a smaller extent, to society at large, it seems plausible to put forward a more nuanced picture. It seems that owing to its strict institutional and genetic ties with the ordinary judiciary, and its relatively greater separation from the world of politics, the SN addresses its decisions mainly to judges of the ordinary judiciary. Therefore, regardless of the personal preferences of SN judges, they are inclined to formulate their arguments in a way which will persuade not a politician or academic, but a typical Polish career judge. Therefore, if career judges demonstrate a preference for hyperpositivist simplified adjudication, the SN does what it can to cater to their unrefined taste. The TK is in a different position. Owing to its closer ties with the world of politics and greater media focus upon its judicial activity, it must formulate its arguments in a more pragmatic fashion, assuming that it will be more persuasive. Furthermore, on account of its close bonds with the academia, TK Justices certainly write their opinions with the academic auditorium of constitutionalists and legal theorists in mind. Finally, the TK, which publishes its landmark cases in English on its own website, seems to be more concerned with its own perception by Western judiciaries and scholars, rather than the SN is. This strengthens the trend towards emulating the pragmatic style of Western constitutional courts.

Fourthly, the general institutional setting should also be mentioned as a factor. Whilst the SN enjoys, within the judiciary, an authority and prestige based on tradition and continuity, and can influence the case-law of the lower courts *via* a number of procedures which allow it directly to quash or modify a lower court's judgment, the TK's situation is much more difficult. Not only is its history much more recent, its Justices accused of being politicians in gowns, but also, for want of a direct complaint against a judgment, it cannot force the ordinary judiciary and the SN to obedience by quashing or modifying their decisions. The TK's insistence on persuasiveness and pragmatist style can be seen as a way of compensating for these weaknesses in comparison with the SN.

Finally, one should not underestimate the very nature of constitutional adjudication, as opposed to ordinary civil and criminal adjudication, which, on account of deliberate vagueness and open-textured character of constitutional instruments, invites and favours a more pragmatic style of adjudication, focused more on principles, values and legally protected interests, rather than detailed rules lending themselves to purely semantic analysis (Rytter 2007, 257–259; Kühn 2005, 7).

Acknowledgements

I would like to thank Hanna Dębska, Michael Hein, Siri Hummel, Jakub Łakomy and Paweł Snopek for reading and commenting on earlier versions of this chapter. All views presented in this chapter are exclusively those of the Author and should not be attributed to the European Union or any of its institutions, bodies or agencies.

References

Bereza, Arkadiusz. 2011. Sąd Najwyższy w Polsce Ludowej [The Supreme Court in People's Poland]. In *Sąd Najwyższy Rzeczypospolitej Polskiej: Historia i współczesność. Księga jubileuszowa 90-lecia Sądu Najwyższego 1917–2007* [The Supreme Court of the Republic of Poland: History and Modernity. A Jubilee Book of the 90th Anniversary of the Supreme Court 1917–2007]. Toruń: TNOiK, 191–297.

Cardozo, Benjamin N. 2010. *The Nature of the Judicial Process* [1921]. Milton Keynes: Universal Law Press.

Comella, Victor Ferreres. 2011. The rise of specialized constitutional courts. In *Comparative Constitutional Law.* Cheltenham-Northampton MA: Edward Elgar, 265–277.

Dębska, Hanna. 2013a. Legal Doxa as a Form of Neutralization in the Law: The Case of Constitutional Tribunal Judgments. In *Neutralization of Values in Law*, ed. Krzysztof Pałecki. Warszawa: Wolters Kluwer, 303–351.

Dębska, Hanna. 2013b. *Trybunał Konstytucyjny jako instytucja władzy symbolicznej* [The Constitutional Court as an Institution of Symbolic Power] PhD thesis, Jagiell. Univ.

Florczak-Wątor, Monika. 2006. *Orzeczenia Trybunału Konstytucyjnego i ich skutki prawne* [Decisions of the Constitutional Court and their Legal Effects]. Poznań: Ars Boni et Aequi.

Garlicki, Lech. 2007. Constitutional Court versus Supreme Court. *Int. J. of Const. L.* 5.1, 44–68.

Gray, Thomas C. 2003. Judicial Review and Legal Pragmatism. *Wake Forest L.R.* 38, 473–511.
Hein, Michael. 2011. Constitutional Conflicts between Politics and Law in Transition Societies: A Systems-Theoretical Approach. *Studies of Transition States and Societies* 3.1, 3–23.
Hermeliński, Wojciech. 2012. Dialog między Trybunałem Konstytucyjnym a Sądem Najwyższym. [The Dialogue Between the Constitutional Court and the Supreme Court] *Europejski Przegląd Sądowy* 12, 12–17.
Hesselink, Martijn. 2001. *The New European Legal Culture*, Deventer: Kluwer.
Heun, Werner. 2011. *The Constitution of Germany: A Contextual Analysis*, Oxford: Hart.
Izdebski, Hubert. 1986. Les sources du droit dans les pays socialistes européens (Histoire, théorie, pratique). *Rev. int. du dr. comp.* 38.1, 7–56.
Kozielewicz, Wiesław. 2011. Sąd Najwyższy Rzeczypospolitej Polskiej 1990–2007 [The Supreme Court of the Republic of Poland 1990–2007]. In *Sąd Najwyższy...*, 299–348.
KRS website. 2013. [http://www.krs.pl/pl/o-radzie/sklad-i-organizacja, accessed on 05.10.2013]
Kühn, Zdeněk. 2004. Worlds Apart: Western and Central European Judicial Culture at the Onset of the European Enlargement, *Am.J.Comp.L.* 52.3, 531–567.
Kühn, Zdeněk. 2005. Making a European Transnational Constitution: Some Central European Perspectives. [http://www.ecln.net/elements/conferences/book_prag/KuhnFinal.pdf, accessed on 06.10.2013].
Kühn, Zdeněk. 2011. *The Judiciary in Central and Eastern Europe: Mechanical Jurisprudence in Transformation?* Leiden: Martinus Nijhoff.
Łętowska, Ewa. 1997. The Barriers of Polish Legal Thinking in the Perspective of European Integration. *Y. of Polish Eur. St.* 1, 55–72.
Łętowska, Ewa. 2002. Kilka uwag o praktyce wykładni [Some Remarks on the Practice of Interpretation]. *Kwartalnik Prawa Prywatnego* 11.1, 27–64.
Lityński, Adam. 2013. Historia Sądu Najwyższego [History of the Supreme Court]. [http://www.sn.pl/osadzienajwyzszym/SitePages/Historia.aspx, accessed on 05.10.2013]
Malec, Dorota. 2007. Sąd Najwyższy w latach 1917–1939 [The Supreme Court Between 1917 and 1939]. In *Sąd Najwyższy...*, 121–189.
Mańko, Rafał. 2005. The Culture of Private Law in Central Europe after Enlargement: A Polish Perspective. *European Law Journal* 11.5, 527–548.
Mańko, Rafał. 2013a. Weeds in the Gardens of Justice? The Survival of Hyperpositivism in Polish Legal Culture as a Symptom/Sinthome. *Pólemos* 7.2, 207–233.
Mańko, Rafał. 2013b. Survival of the Socialist Legal Tradition? A Polish Perspective. *Comp.L.R.* 3.2. [http://www.comparativelawreview.com/ojs/index.php/CoLR/article/view/55/59, accessed on 13.06.2014].
Matczak, Marcin. 2007. *Summa iniuira. O błędzie formalizmu w stosowaniu prawa* [Summa Iniuria: The Formalist Error in Applying the Law]. Warszawa: Scholar.
Mażewski, Lech. 2010. *Posttotalitarny autorytaryzm. PRL 1956–1989. Analiza ustrojowpolityczna* [Post-Totalitarian Authoritarianism: The Polish People's Republic 1956-1989. An Analysis of the Political System]. Warszawa: Arte.
Mażewski, Lech. 2011. *Długa dekada lat siedemdziesiątych (1968–1981). Rola nowelizacji z 10 lutego 1976 r. Konstytucji PRL z 22 lipca 1952 r. w ewolucji ustroju PRL na tle konstytucji europejskich państw socjalistycznych.* [The Long Decade of the Seventies (1968–1981). The Role of the Amendment of 10 February 1976 to the Constitution of the Polish People's Republic of 22 July 1952 in the Evolution of the Political System of the Polish People's Republic Against the Background of European Socialist Statres]. Toruń: Adam Marszałek.

Michelman, Frank. 2011. The interplay of constitutional and ordinary jurisdiction. In *Comparative Constitutional Law.* Cheltenham-Northampton MA: Edward Elgar, 278–297.
Milej, Tomasz. 2008. Europejska kultura prawna a kraje Europy Środkowej i Wschodniej [European Legal Culture and the Countries of Central and Eastern Europe]. *Przegląd Legislacyjny* 15.1, 60–74.
Rytter, Jens Leo. 2007. Constitutional Interpretation – Between Legalism and Law-Making. *Scandinavian Studies in Law* 52, 258–272.
Sadurski, Wojciech. 1984. Marxism and Legal Positivism: A case study on the impact of ideology upon legal theory. In *Essays in Legal Theory.* Melbourne: Melbourne UP, 187–211.
Sadurski, Wojciech. 2005. *Rights Before Courts: A Study of Constitutional Courts in Postcommunist States of Central and Eastern Europe*. Dordrecht: Springer.
Sadurski, Wojciech. 2009. Twenty Years after the Transition: Constitutional Review in Central and Eastern Europe. *Sydney Law School Research Paper* 09/69.
Sadurski, Wojciech. 2010. Judicial Review in Central and Eastern Europe: Rationales or Rationalizations? *Israel L.R.* 42.3, 500–527.
Safjan, Marek. 2008. Politics and Constitutional Courts: A Judge's Personal Perspective. *EUI Working Papers*, LAW 2008/10.
SN website. 2013. [http://www.sn.pl, accessed on 22.10.2013]
Stone Sweet, Alec. 2012. Constitutional Courts. In *Oxford Handbook of Comparative Constitutional Law.* Oxford: OUP, 816–830.
Sulikowski, Adam. 2008. Współczesny paradygmat sądownictwa konstytucyjnego wobec kryzysu nowoczesności. [The Contemporary Paradigm of Constitutional Justice and the Crisis of Modernity] Wrocław: WUWr
TK Website. 2013. [http://www.trybunal.gov.pl/trybunal/sklad/indexs.htm, accessed on 06.10.2013]
Turano, Leslie. 2006. Spain: Quis Custodiet Ipsos Custodes? The Struggle for Jurisdiction Between the Tribunal Constitucional and the Tribunal Supremo. *Int. J. of Const.L.* 4.1, 151–162.
Wieacker, Franz. 2000. *A History of Private Law in Europe with Particular Reference to Germany* [1967]. Oxford: Clarendon Press.
Zdziennicki, Bohdan (interviewed by Andrzej Dryszel). 2013. Piętnastu ważnych ludzi [Fifteen Important People]. *Przegląd* [http://www.przeglad-tygodnik.pl/pl/artykul/pietnastu-waznych-ludzi, accessed on 21.04.2013].
Zirk-Sadowski, Marek. 2006. Transformation and Integration of Legal Cultures and Discourses – Poland. In *Spreading Democracy and the Rule of Law? The Impact of EU Enlargement on the Rule of Law, Democracy and Constitutionalism in Post-Communist Legal Orders*, ed. Wojciech Sadurski et al. Dordrecht: Springer, 299–311.

Legislation

SN Act (2002). Ust. z 23.11.2002 o Sądzie Najwyższym [Act of 23 November 2002 on the Supreme Court], Dz.U. 2002.240.2052, 2013.499.
KRS Act. 2011. Ust. z 12.5.2011 o Krajowej Radzie Sądownictwa, Dz.U. 126.714; 203.1192.

Part III
Theorising the European Union: Constitution, Division of Power, and Sovereignty

Paul Ricœur's Thought as the Basis for a Political Theory of the European Union

Marcin Pieniążek

Abstract

This chapter introduces the political theory of the European Union, based upon Paul Ricœur's definition of ethical aspiration – 'the intention of achieving "a good life" with and for another man in just institutions.' This definition constitutes the basis for a conception of interrelations of a man with the community, discussed as interrelations between a citizen, democratic society and institutions of the European Union. It is the core basis of an undertaken argumentation which starts with the micro-scale of the entity whose characteristic feature is the intention of a good life; it then goes on to the 'meso' level, i.e. to an interpersonal relationship in broad terms; finally the argumentation aims to describe the macro-scale of just political institutions. Consequently, the chapter presents a homogeneous conception of social structures, interpersonal relationships and democracy, related to the concept of the subject (*ipse*), as defined by Ricœur in his work *Soi-même comme un autre*.

1. Introduction

Today, the question about the social and political future of the European Union takes various forms in the context of uncertainty, caused by a recurring wave of economic upheaval. Current complications arise the need for a new political theory embracing the whole range of European players: institutions, states, small countries, businesses, and individual citizens. Such restored theoretical reflection could breathe a new spirit into EU structures in which the particularism of strong players prevails over the spirit of community. The following chapter constitutes an attempt to provide a fresh answer to the above-mentioned need, enlightening some relevant aspects of the political theory outlined by Paul Ricœur.

The choice of Ricœurian theory is justified, *inter alia*, by accuracy of his concept of the political paradox to current EU problems. Following it, on the one hand, political authority is legitimised if it comes from the rational consent of the governed; on the other hand, political practice is inevitably coercive and violent, something to which individuals cannot consent in principle (see Kaplan 2003, 125). Also, in his essay 'Ethics and Politics', Ricœur developed another meaningful thesis, according to which politics must first be defined in relation to the economic and social realms, before being contrasted to ethics. Kaplan states that Ricœur followed Arendt and Weil in contrasting political rationality (governing, customs, and actions of historical communities) with socioeconomic rationality (governing the spheres of material reproduction, the organisation of labour, consumption, etc.) (ibid., 126). Kaplan also indicates that Ricœur emphasised the intersection of ethics and politics in order to guard against the cynicism and complacency that arises from and depends on the separation of the two. Furthermore, according to Kaplan, in Ricœur's theory politics extends the range of ethics to include considerations of the rights and freedoms of neutral third parties. This is why Ricœur wrote that the state of law regulates the freedom of individuals by ensuring their equal protection, access and opportunity. Considering this, the state of law is an ethical agency that establishes legal equality.[1] The richness of Ricœurian thought is visible in his numerous writings, conjoining issues of political philosophy with areas of linguistic, ethical and ontological research. The aspect of political theory reconstructed below was developed together with his onto-ethical considerations undertaken in the book *Soi-même comme un autre*, in the course of creating a comprehensive theory of narrative, action and command. Wall, Schweiker, and Hall underline that in *Soi-même comme un autre* Ricœur explores the human sense of self with respect to the capacities to act, speak, narrate and impute responsibility (see Wall, Schweiker, Hall 2002, 2). Doubtlessly, the above-mentioned theory can be referred to as a political one, since (just as in the case of major theories which belong to the realm of political philosophy, i.e., utilitarianism, communitarianism, liberalism, etc.) on the grounds of the undertaken 'moral argumentation', Ricœur formulates an ethically grounded theory of the person (the individual's being), harmonised with the theory of social relations. It should be noted that a coherent moral argumentation, according to Kymlicka, is the principal basis of a political philosophy (see Kymlicka, 2001, 15). Consequently, ethical aspiration is defined by Ricœur as 'the intention of achieving "a good life with and for another man in just institutions"' (see Ricœur 1990, 202).[2] I would like to treat this definition as the basis for presenting an ethically grounded political theory, emerging from Ricœur's work, namely a conception about the interrelations of a man with the human community, which may also be referred to as the interrelations between an individual and a democratic society. What in fact emerges from the analysed views is a homogeneous conception of social structures and of the interpersonal relationship, derived from a relational conception of a person, based on the dialectics of *idem* and *ipse* elements (selfness and self).

The quoted definition of ethical aspiration plays a dual role in the following analysis. On the one hand, it constitutes the core basis of the undertaken argumentation which starts with the micro-scale of the entity whose characteristic feature

1 The issue of equality and just institutions will be discussed below. See Kaplan 2003, 130.
2 All translations were made by the author of the chapter.

is the intention of a good life, and then goes on to a 'meso' level, i.e. to a interpersonal relationship in broad terms, and then to the macro-scale of just political institutions. On the other hand, this definition is considered as a definition of 'civil aspirations' as I assume that a citizen is one who is characterised by the ethically well-established intention to act in the public sphere, *inter alia*, in good, social, national, or European institutions. Therefore, the question of citizenship or civil attitude will be revisited in the forthcoming discussion.

I would like to indicate two important philosophical sources which served Ricœur as the inspiration for the theory at issue: Lévinas's concept of Otherness, as well as the Aristotelian concept of *philia* (friendship). According to Dauenhauer, Ricœur in his political writings developed a kind of interplay with other important contributors to the normative dimensions of 'contemporary political life', including J. Habermas, J. Rawls and M. Walzer. Dauenhauer also writes that Ricœur brings to this interlocution a 'distinctive voice' formed by his reflections on I. Kant and G.W.F. Hegel (see Dauenhauer 1998, 2).[3]

2. Relational conception of the individual

The analysis undertaken in this section shows the smallest, yet a constitutive component in the structure of interpersonal and institutional relationships that exist in the proposed political theory. The ontological-ethical profile of the individual defined as 'the one-who-is-himself' is treated as the leading motif of *Soi-même comme un autre*, and it remains in close correlation with the cited definition of ethical aspirations, understood as the definition of civil attitude and determining the framework for the reconstructed theory.

The concept of relational personal identity is a key issue in Ricœur's theory. Ricœur brings closer the issue of identity by means of a dialectic between two opposing concepts, namely *idem* and *ipse*. On the one hand, it is identity as being the same (Latin *idem*, English *sameness*; German *Gleichheit*), and on the other hand, identity as being oneself (Latin *ipse*, English: *selfhood*, German: *Selbstheit*) (see Kemp 2002, 35).[4] Ricœur states that being oneself does not equal being the same, and since this main distinction is not recognised, the solutions to the problem of personal identity, which are not grounded in the narrative dimension, are erroneous (see Ricœur 1990, 140). The author writes: 'To say: the one-who-is-himself

3 In his book, Bernard P. Dauenhauer provides a comprehensive analysis of the origins of Ricœur's political theory, developed, *inter alia*, in the dialogue with Marxism and Christianity.

4 Kemp indicates that the distinction between *idem* and *ipse* is decisive for the whole structure of *Soi-même comme un autre*.

does not mean to say "I"' (ibid., 212). Notably, the correlates of the concepts *idem* and *ipse* are, respectively, 'character' and 'the word kept.' What is crucial in this ontological-ethical perspective is the concept of self-preservation. According to Ricœur, the one-who-is-himself actively confirms (authenticates) himself, despite changes in the external world, and sometimes in spite of 'permanent dispositions', identical to the concept of 'character.' Therefore, Ricœur treats being oneself as an ethical postulate; in his theory, self-preservation is not something given, but something assigned. This is why Ricœur states that a promise serves as a paradigmatic pattern of self-identity (see Ricœur, 2004, 203). Most importantly, a promise is never an obligation only to oneself, but primarily *vis-à-vis* another human being (this is why Ricœur associates identity with reciprocity, as discussed below, as well as with society) (see Kowalska 2005, XXVII). It follows that for Ricœur, it is the Other who is the original source of the validity and performance of the assumed obligations.

One must concur with the suggestion that a just society is based on the moral structure of its constituent units. The characteristics of the one-who-is-himself have such features which can be interpreted as constitutive elements of a socially significant civil attitude. The conception of being oneself 'following the pattern of the word given', contrasted with the 'ontology of character', responds to the demand for a personal model of a responsible participant of the public sphere. In a culture focused on libertarian self-nurturing, a theory according to which the promise is a paradigmatic model of identity constitutes a satisfactory theory of the action of a judge, teacher, politician, or in fact anyone who intends to maintain harmonious social relations. As Ricœur holds, self-preservation in the case of a person is understood as such a conduct whereby another person can count on us. In such an ontology a dialogue prevails over the separation from another man (as discussed in the context of Lévinas's philosophy). What constitutes a crucial element of this ontology is the activity understood as a consistent development of auto-narrative which guarantees unity, namely the consequence of a life as a politician, social activist, father, spouse, etc. Another noteworthy observation made by Ricœur is that self-esteem results from fidelity to the assigned 'plan of oneself.' In this context, it can be argued that the conscious state of being accountable is a major source of human fulfilment as a social being who is aware of his accountability for his actions taken *vis-à-vis* other people.

2.1 Interpersonal relationships and the concept of care

As signalled above, Ricœur directly relates views on the 'individual' to interpersonal relationships, expressed in the definition of ethical aspirations in the phrase 'with the other and for the other.' Here, some crucial analysis Ricœur dedicates to the concept of care. Ricœur states: '...self-esteem and care cannot be experienced or considered without each other. [...] Care does not attach itself to self-esteem from the outside, but it develops its dialogic dimension' (Ricœur 1990, 212). Thus, Ricœur captures once again the essence of the bonds within civil society which cannot exist without a conscious being of 'one for the other.' The author deepens the issue of care analysing the case of ultimate asymmetry between the Other and the Same (or between the master of justice and the summoned one), described by E. Lévinas in *Totalité et infini* and *Autrement qu'être ou au-delà de l'essence* (see Lévinas 1961, 1974). As P.S. Anderson puts it, Ricœur plays the idea from the philosophy of Lévinas concerning the face of the Other (see Anderson 2002, 23). Contrary to appearances, Ricœur's conclusion is not oriented at rejecting Lévinas's asymmetrical theory, but rather at developing it, namely at recognising the reciprocity of a moral claim which the Other addresses to us 'from above.' It can be stated that the effect of mutually 'going higher' by the actors, namely the effect of the mutual recognition of moral claims, is a relationship in which, as Ricœur says, we treat 'ourselves as the other' and 'the other as ourselves.'

Therefore, the starting point of 'living in the other and for the other' in a civil society – at the level of interpersonal relations – is to recognise the meaning of the call that is transmitted from the Other man. In my opinion such an attitude is the determinant of mature citizenship understood as the spontaneous involvement in local communities, in charity, volunteering, etc.; in other words, such citizenship which constitutes the realisation of the intention for a good ethical life 'with others and for others in just institutions.' Lévinas's views can therefore be considered as a premise adopted by Ricœur for the basis of his definition of ethical aspirations and as a 'preliminary phase' of his political theory. The first step to reciprocity is to break with selfishness and abandon separation; then we get access to an interpersonal social area where the Aristotelian Golden Rule moderates the mutual recognition of claims, creating a fabric of civil society. Ultimately, Ricœur concludes that respecting another as oneself and respecting oneself as another become fundamentally equivalent (Ricœur 1990, 226). This statement is in strict compliance with the previously presented relational conception of a person, and leads to the third interesting component of the definition quoted at the beginning, namely to the concept of 'just institutions.'

2.2 Interpersonal relationships and the concept of philia

As mentioned above, the reference to Aristotle's philosophy is of particular importance at the 'meso' level of the definition of ethical aspirations. In Ricœur's belief, especially, the Aristotelian concept of *philia* adequately expresses the reciprocity rule, providing a transition between the desire for a good life, which is of an individual nature, and justice – 'the virtue of human multiplicity of a political nature' (ibid., 213). This characteristic raises close associations with 'brotherhood' as a constitutive feature of civil society.

According to Ricœur, reciprocity is one of the most basic terms of *philautia,* going so far as to 'living together' (*sýzen*), i.e. to intimacy. Ricœur concludes that regardless of the form of the participation of *philautia* in the formation of friendship, the latter shows up immediately as a reciprocal relationship. Consequently friendship in the above-mentioned meaning does not only belong indeed to ethics as the primary development of the desire of the good life, but it especially moves to the fore the issue of reciprocity (ibid. 214). Ricœur writes:

> The concept of reciprocity in fact has its own requirements, which will be overshadowed neither by the creation from the Same, as in Husserl, nor by the creation from the Other, as in Lévinas. According to the concept of reciprocity, each loves the other as who he is. It is not the case in a useful friendship when one loves the other because of the expected benefit, and to even a lesser extent in the event of a pleasant friendship (ibid., 215).

I will not analyse the issue – left aside by Ricœur – of the friendship on account of mutual benefit, although what should be emphasised are the particular merits of referring to this concept, e.g. in the case of formalised legal relations. (In the context of the latter, we should bear in mind Aristotle's observation which is as follows:

> Therefore, the people who are mutually friends due to the arising benefit do not feel friendship for one another (*kath'hautoûs*) on account of the friend, but only in so far as there arises some good for each of them (*autoís par állellôn*) [VIII, 3, 1156 a 10-12]).

Additionally, in the context of the Golden Rule, Ricœur indicates the core element of friendship, namely the balance between giving and receiving, i.e. the balance in the exchange, which is the essence of a perfect relation in mutual agreements in which each party is equally entitled and obliged. In particular, he stresses the importance of the concept of *allélous*, i.e. 'one another', whose meaning, as mentioned, comes close to 'brotherhood' as a feature of civil society.

The discussed level of definition of ethical aspirations, expressed by the phrase 'with the other and for the other', constitutes a very interesting point in reconstructed political theory. The philosopher makes the effort of developing the element that would connect the individual with the public sphere without a gap that could put these elements in opposition to each other. Instead, he goes smoothly from the ontology and ethics of the subject to the ontology and ethics of human relations, thus preparing the foundations for the complementary notion of just institutions. At the same time, what Ricœur proposes at the 'meso' level of his political theory is the model of interrelations crucial from the perspective of European civil society. It is primarily such a model of interpersonal relations which meets the idea of self-government, local community and small homelands; it is the idea according to which the state is ancillary in relation to the citizen, while a prominent role is played by interpersonal interactions, resulting in various forms of citizens' initiative. Reciprocity, fraternity, the substitutability of roles and non-substitutability of people, grounded in the Aristotelian virtue of friendship and in the Golden Rule – are understood as the concepts which support the European assumptions of sustainable development and social inclusion. The premise here is leaving the non-civil, selfish separation (within the meaning of Lévinas) and recognising the moral claims of the other man. Consequently, one should accept a thesis whereby the existence of the community, including the European one, is inseparably connected with the bond of interpersonal relations, resulting from the creation of the very subject who is faithful to the assumed civil obligations, including legal ones. It should be noted that a prominent place in the European philosophy of law is taken by views which include law in political theory, thus emphasising the symmetrical, reciprocal and horizontal nature of legal interactions. An example is the conception of law as a network, outlined by Belgian theorists F. Ost and M. van de Kerchove (see Ost, Van de Kerchove 2002). This model is constructed in opposition to the vertical vision of law as a pyramid, referring to Hobbesian political philosophy (see Hobbes 2009, 576).

3. Life in just institutions

As mentioned above, when it comes to the definition of ethical aspirations, the third and broadest range of its implementation constitutes the level of just institutions. This plane of political theory, a crucial element of which is institutionalised justice, is placed by Ricœur above the plane of reciprocity, related to *philia*. Ricœur indicates that friendship is not justice, to the extent that the latter governs institutions and the former interpersonal relations. For this reason, he states, justice involves many citizens, while friendship allows a small number of partners. Ricœur clarifies that in the case of justice, equality is primarily understood as proportional, given the inequality of contributions, while friendship can be found only among good people of equal rank; in this sense equality is a prerequisite of friendship, while in state institutions it remains a goal to achieve (see Ricœur 1990, 215-216). In Ricœur's view, the institution as a 'point of applying justice' and 'the structure of the coexistence of historical community' cannot be reduced to interpersonal relationships, and yet it is connected with them 'in a manner worthy of attention' (ibid., 215-216). Additionally, in the context of the above-mentioned 'political paradox' the idea of institutions should be characterised by 'common habits, rather than forced rules.' Ricœur reinforces this distinction with Arendt's differentiation between 'common sovereignty' and 'domination' (see Arendt 1970, 120). According to Arendt, the concept of a common power is more primordial. She indicates that a common power cannot be automatically reduced to the meaning of a 'state' one, as it reflects the primordial and political ability to act in concert. Thus, the concept of common power is marked by interpersonal 'plurality' and 'agreement.'

Ricœur explains the deeper complementation of the definition of ethical aspirations with a third element. He writes that the concept of multiplicity suggests extending interpersonal relationships on all relations which are left as if outside by direct contact between 'I' and 'you' as belonging to a third party. 'The third' is immediately included by the multiplicity that determines the authority. According to Ricœur, in this way one imposes a limit on any attempt to restore social bonds only on the grounds of a purely dyadic dialogical relationship. Perhaps in a commentary on a similar attempt undertaken by Lévinas, Ricœur states: 'The multiplicity includes third parties who will never become faces. The defence of anonymity in the literal sense of the term is therefore included in a wider-ranging intention to achieve real [i.e. good – MP] life.' This inclusion of the third, according to Ricœur, should not be limited to the instantaneous aspect of the will to cooperate, but should be divided in duration. Ricœur underlines that the power gains this temporal dimension only from the institution (see Ricœur 1990, 228). He describes this aspect of power in a beautiful way:

> Acting in its political dimension constitutes the most elaborate attempt to attribute impermanent things with immortality, in the absence of eternity. Certainly, the power has its own insignificance, because is exists as long as people interact, and it disappears once they scatter. […] However, the insignificance of power is no longer the primordial and bare instability of mortal beings as such, but the insignificance of the second degree, which is a feature of the institutions and all the issues concerning the latter (ibid., 229).

Not withstanding its weakness, common power enhances ethical aspiration (which is the subject of the definition) with 'a necessary third dimension' which Ricœur understands as justice. The concept of justice at the level of institutions is, the author believes, a correlate of the concept of care in interpersonal relations and – in the micro-scale – a correlate of the autogenous self-esteem of the one-who-is-himself.

Ricœur quotes Aristotle's famous definition according to which 'everybody seeks to call justice this permanent disposition (*héxis*) by means of which they are able to perform fair actions (*praxeis*), by means of which they act justly and they wish what is just' (see Aristotle 1999, 360). Considering this, Ricœur states that a constitutive feature of just institutions is the fact that the individual no longer has the position of the 'other there', as was the case in the relation of reciprocity, but of 'every other' who in the distribution of goods receives all that he rightly deserves. This is why, in order to characterise the institutions, Ricœur applies the Aristotelian concept of distributive justice, which presupposes the existence of the political community 'when it comes to the distribution of honours or money, or other things that may be subject to allocation between the participants of the national community' (ibid., 360). This step enforces the observation that justice is treated by Aristotle as an ethical virtue, while the foundation of just institutions – as Ricœur assumes – is *éthos*, i.e. 'a common habit', rather than coercive rules. Finally, Ricœur proves the necessity of introduction of the above-mentioned concept of distribution, in order to allow the transition between the interpersonal and the social level of the definition of ethical aspirations. He states that 'the meaning of the concept of distribution lies in the fact that it sends empty-handed the protagonists of the false dispute on the relationship between the individual and society' (see Ricœur 1990, 233).

In the context of the above comments, it is possible to eliminate the apparent opposition between the citizen and the institution (state or European) by which an individual implements his intention of a good life in the public sphere. Ricœur concludes that it is unnecessary to create the wall that stands between the individual and society, thus preventing any transition from the interpersonal plane to the social one. He summarises: 'A distributive interpretation of institutions contributes to a demolition of this wall and ensures consistency between the three components: individual, interpersonal and social features of our concept of ethical aspirations' (ibid., 234).

Ultimately, Ricœur, guided by Aristotle's heritage, indicates a common principle which binds the planes of political theory. As indicated above, according to Ricœur, the cohesive principle is 'equality', which should be the characteristic feature of all relationships. He states that an average measure and proportional equality are only a secondary means of philosophical and ethical rescue of equality as such (ibid., 235). The principle of equality therefore assumes the proportions of a formal rule, common at the interpersonal level, including the plane of legal obligations and socio-institutional level. Ricœur states that equality has the same relation *vis-à-vis* life in institutions, as care relates to interpersonal relations (when the above-mentioned concept of care is of a philosophical sense which refers to *philia*). 'Care poses the-one-who-is-himself in front of the other who is the face in the strong sense, as taught by Emmanuel Lévinas (see Lévinas 1961).[5] Equality

5 I.e. in the subjective sense.

puts me in front of another who is everyone' (see Ricœur 1990, 236). Therefore, according to Ricœur, the sense of justice does not diminish care in any way; it even assumes the latter to the extent that it considers people to be unique. Ricœur summarises that justice in its part increases care to an extent to which the whole of humanity constitutes the area of interest. If one assumes such a perspective, Ricœur's vision also starts to raise crucial meanings for the theory of European civil society.

4. Democracy

Some further remarks made by Ricœur on democracy and the state reveal far-reaching accuracy regarding the current, practical problems of the European Union. Democracy, constantly with the depicted political theory, is also described by the philosopher in ethical terms, considering issues of conflict and power. Kaplan writes that for Ricœur a democratic state is one that maintains procedures not so much to eliminate conflicts but to allow them to be openly discussed and negotiated (in other words, the democratic state is based on free discussions). Moreover, a democratic state is one that guarantees its citizens the right to participate in decision-making, i.e. to participate in power. Following Ricœur, such a state is the form of government that limits the separation between the rulers and the ruled (ibid., 130).

It should be emphasised that at the institutional level, the current problems of the European Union are related to the limited effectiveness of decision-making mechanisms in conflict situations, as well as to the limited participation of citizens in exercising power on a European scale. The case of the financial crisis in Greece shows that ordinary European citizens have a negligible impact both on the shape of the decision-making mechanisms themselves and on the final decisions to be taken. Thus, from the perspective of the outlined political theory, what can be observed in the practice of the European Union is the lack of coherence at least between the interpersonal ('meso') level and the institutional ('macro') level. A failure of the decision-making mechanisms, as well as the detachment of citizens from real participation in 'the European power', is the essential prerequisite of the crisis of the European community, as indicated in the introduction. According to Ricœur, if the state is an organisation capable of effective decision-making, the question then is how it organises the community and for what reason or how it makes decisions (ibid., 130). In Ricœur's opinion, what defines the state is its ability to make decisions that help a historical community endure, survive, and create its own history while being protected from internal threats. Thus, as Kaplan underlines, the central issue for the state is the survival of the historical community (ibid., 128). Such an opinion, as expressed by Ricœur, goes into the essence of the problems and the tasks of the European Union perceived as a social and political community. The lack of participation on the part of citizens in decision-making mechanisms, as well as low transparency and efficiency of these mechanisms, may in fact lead to the political decomposition of the Union, and thus to the impossibility of reaching its basic objective, namely the survival of the continent's community.

As indicated above, in light of the theory at issue, the task set before the righteous European institutions has an important ethical dimension. Summing up, according to Ricœur, the ethical character of the state (and, let me add, the European Union) is a matter of prudence exercised by governments and the participation of the citizens in a democratic process geared towards negotiating conflicts and distributing power (ibid., 130). Democracy, as Ricœur emphasises, is closely related to equality realised in just institutions. It is debatable whether it is indeed equality that has to be the regulative idea of developing European political theory, i.e. equality which is manifested in treating the Other as oneself and treating oneself as the Other, in the substitutability of roles and non-substitutability of people, in conscious care for interpersonal relations, or in proportional equality as the method of distributing goods by public institutions. Yet, it is hard to deny that the theory developed by Ricœur is a coherent and complete conception which, at the same time, opens the doors to a discussion on the multi-faceted model of the European community of citizens.

This is the case as Ricœur maintains that the tie of citizenship is presupposed before we belong to any society, and thus it unifies the political realm. Kaplan underlines that in Ricœur's theory, membership of a political body is superior to our membership in any of the other many spheres that define our roles, advantages, obligations and responsibilities. Consequently, Ricœur describes the tie of citizenship as an 'encompassing – encompassed' relationship (ibid., 134). The above perspective manifests a peculiar relevance for the European Union's political theory. It allows one to capture the close relationship between a single European citizen and the level of the political community, moderated – eventually – by just European institutions. The presented political theory permits the level of individual citizens, small homelands, as well as nation-states to be embraced and unified. It should be noted that the basis of the above unification, in accordance with Ricœur's views, consists of values which determine the identity of European culture, including those values that belong to the realm of ethics. According to Ricœur, the sphere of ethics and politics overlap, but they are not coextensive. As Kaplan indicates, the ethical basis of a political community is comprised of values about which there is consensus (ibid., 131). Therefore, the presented political theory, based on the definition of ethical aspirations, can be regarded as a political theory of a united Europe only on the basis of consensus on the common European values. Following Ricœur, Kaplan writes that advanced Western democracies are the result of numerous traditions; thus (also in the body of the European Union), it would be impossible for citizens to reach consensus unless each bracketed the particular tradition – based on motivations that justify common values. Consequently, as Kaplan states, the values of society have an abstract character 'severed from their roots' in the multiple tradition and sources of motivation and justification. This situation may bring considerable danger when the values of a society take on an ideological character, becoming empty stereotypes used for the sake of political rhetoric (ibid., 131).

The above finding on common values allows us to indicate a crucial source of current threats to united Europe. The lack of consent, or the ideologisation of the axiological foundation, constitutes an essential component of the current crisis as well as a potential prerequisite of the political decomposition of the European Union. As pointed out by Kaplan, 'political consensus is only the thinnest kind of ethical relationship among citizens' (ibid., 130). Dauenhauer writes that Ricœur's conception of self and its kind of identity is superior to those that underpin liberalism, on the one hand, and communitarianism, on the other (see Dauenhauer 2010, 102-121). It should be noted that from the perspective of the characteristics proposed by Kymlicka, the discussed theory is neither a liberal, a utilitarian, nor a communitarian one (see Kymlicka 2001, 512), although Ricœur draws on the third of these trends, as evidenced by frequent references in *Soi-même comme un autre* to the achievements of Alasdair MacIntyre and Charles Taylor (see MacIntyre 2007, 312; Taylor 1985, 45). Doubtlessly, the analysed theory constitutes the original output of the thinker who exceeds common schemes and oppositions; it is a considerably fresh work and thus worthy of interest in the era of a demand for a new European political theory, significant for the practice of citizenship in the public sphere.

5. Conclusion

Ricœur's project, with its foundations in the ethical and ontological theory of the entity (the individual), assumes at the level of political theory the features of universality that put it next to the achievements of Hobbes and Rawls. It should be emphasised that this complex theory would not be possible in the proposed form without consistent references to the achievements of Aristotle and Lévinas. What should be emphasised is the particular value of the theory which deems natural a combination between the individual ethical aspiration (as I assumed – civil aspirations), the rule of reciprocity and the theory of just institutions whose subject of application is the distribution of goods. In my opinion, this theory meets the need for creating a model of a good European political practice, since it allows one to take a uniform look at the problem of an individualised civil being, interpersonal relationships and the phenomena occurring in the public sphere. It is worth recalling that Ricœur criticises both the opposition between the individual and the interpersonal relationship and that between the interpersonal relation and the institutional sphere, treating them as different manifestations of implementing the same intention of a good life. In this context, the European concepts of social responsibility, sustainability, and social inclusion gain a deeper meaning. According to Ricœur, there is a significant interconnection between just institutions and democracy. The latter is defined in terms of the institutions and practices that allow the conflicts to be negotiated in accordance with fair rules of arbitration. Something that seems to be especially accurate for the practice of the European community is that the main feature of the democratic society is its acceptance of contradictions as well as institutionalisation of its internal conflicts (see Kaplan 2003, 133). Finally, I would like to inculcate the belief that interpersonal care for a fair shape of public institutions – shared by everyone-who-is-himself – constitutes a measure of citizenship in the European community.

References

Anderson, Pamela Sue. 2002. *Ricœur's Reclamation of Autonomy. Unity, Plurality and Totality*. in: *Paul Ricœur and Contemporary Moral Thought*, edited by J. Wall, W. Schweiker, W.D. Hall. New York: Routledge.

Arendt, Hannah. 1970. *On Violence*. San Diego – New York: Mariner Books.

Aristotle. 1999. *Nicomachean Ethics*. Indianapolis: Hackett Publishing Co.

Dauenhauer, Bernard P. 1998. *Ricœur. The Promise and Risk of Politics*. Oxford: Rowman & Littlefield Publishers, Inc.

Dauenhauer, Bernard P. 2010. Ricœur and Political Theory: Liberalism and Communitarianism. In *Ricœur across the Disciplines*, edited by S. Davidson, New York: The Continuum International Publishing Group Inc.

Hobbes, Thomas. 2009. *Leviathan*. Oxford: Oxford University Press.

Kaplan, David M. 2003. *Ricœur's Critical Theory*. New York: State University of New York Press.

Kemp, Peter. 2002. *Narrative Ethics and Moral Law in Ricœur*, in: *Paul Ricœur and Contemporary Moral Thought*, edited by J. Wall, W. Schweiker, W.D. Hall. New York: Routledge.

Kowalska, Małgorzata. 2005. 'Introduction', in: P. Ricœur, *O sobie samym jako innym*. Warszawa: Wydawnictwo Naukowe PWN.

Kymlicka, Will. 2001. *Contemporary Political Philosophy: An Introduction*. New York: Oxford University Press.

Lévinas, Emmanuel. 1961. *Totalité et infini: Essai sur l'extériorité*. The Hague: Martinus Nijhoff.

Lévinas, Emmanuel. 1974. *Autrement qu'être ou au-delà de l'essence*. The Hague: Martinus Nijhoff.

MacIntyre, Alasdair. 2007. *After Virtue: A Study in Moral Theory*, Indiana: University of Notre Dame Press.

Ost, François, Van de Kerchove, Michel. 2002. *De la pyramide au réseau? Pour une théorie dialectique du droit*. Bruxelles: Publications des Facultés universitaires Saint-Louis.

Ricœur, Paul. 1990. *Soi-même comme un autre*: L'Ordre Philosophique. Paris: Editions du Seuil.

Ricœur, Paul. 2004. *Parcours de la reconnaissance. Trios etudes.* Paris: Éditions Stock.

Taylor, Charles. 1985. *Philosophical Papers*. Cambridge: Cambridge University Press.

Wall, John, Schweiker, William, Hall, W. David. 2002. *Paul Ricœur and Contemporary Moral Thought, Introduction: Human Capability and Contemporary Moral Though*t. New York: Routledge.

Vertical Division of Powers from the Perspective of the Member States – Police Power in the Context of European Union Constitutionalism?

Balázs Fekete

Abstract

This chapter argues that some recent developments of EU constitutionalism may be better understood by relying on a classic term of US federalism. This term is police power that was widely used in the 18th–19th century US constitutional discourse. In the first part, in order to point out the relationship between the actual EU developments and the concept of police power the chapter presents and discusses its various meanings in US constitutional law. In the second part, the study critically examines whether Article 4 paras (1) and (2) TEU incorporated into the founding treaties following the Lisbon reforms may be interpreted as the emergence of the concept of police power in this context. In sum, the chapter submits that the first judgments of the ECJ touching upon these Articles will answer the question if the concept of police power is really relevant in the EU constitutional discourse, but the use of term of police power can considerably contribute to the conceptual understanding.

1. The *sui generis* legal nature of the EU

When attempting to clarify the nature of the European Union, legal scholarship seems very reluctant to apply federal terms. On the contrary, it has developed various *sui generis* concepts to describe the unique nature of both the post-World War II European integration and the European Union itself (Schütze 2009, 1–10).

On the one hand, it is easy to understand the main reasons behind this line of thinking. The first forms of integration had already been unique political and legal constructions, alloying intergovernmental, federative and supranational components from the very outset. The institutional system of the European Coal and Steel Community serves as a good example (Alter-Steinberg 2007, 13). The High Authority had certain regulatory competences of supranational nature, while the Council provided considerable room for inter-state bargaining. In addition, the Assembly may be regarded as the seminal stage of a representative body as it had certain consultative competences in the early institutional setting.[1] The

1 See Article 14 TECSC empowering the High Authority to make binding decisions in order to carry out its tasks; Article 27 TECSC requiring member states to delegate one member

developments of the decades that followed have rendered this picture even more complicated with the appearance of both novel institutions and inter-institutional mechanisms (see Bitsch-Loth 2009). Furthermore, the emergence of a supranational legal order aiming to provide direct legal guarantees for the citizens of the member states also added a new element into this complexity. (Weiler 1990–1991, 2405–2431). In sum, the very nature of European integration called for non-conventional interpretation, which did not necessarily follow the existing patterns of public law or international law scholarship.[2]

On the other hand, the birth of this line of thought was also due to the special characteristics of the post-World War II European political scene. Although the vision of a unified Europe had already been elaborated by Richard Coundehove-Kalergi and others during the interwar period or even earlier (see Prettenthaler-Ziegerhofer 2012), sovereignty remained a prominent concern of European politics (Harpaz 2011, 77–78). Thus, European politics regarded sovereignty as an eminent value, and it determined its general attitude toward any supranational integration plans. The designation of the emerging European Communities as a federal entity would have raised serious criticism in both politics and academia. Therefore, in order to avoid these pitfalls, a non-federal understanding of European integration dominated the legal and political discussions from the 1960s. This facilitated the emergence of a broad academic discussion without forcing it to deal with very sensitive issues such as the future of sovereignty or the prospects of national interest. The study of Community law, therefore, has gradually become a narrow professional segment of legal scholarship developing its own conceptual tools – losing, however, almost all ambitions to address general questions of political nature.

The late Walter van Gerven's thesis on the nature of the European Union is a typical example of this line of legal scholarship. As for the nature of the EU, the former Advocate General argues that the EU is certainly not a state in the Westphalian sense. Although some of its features are comparable to conventional states – i.e. it exercises certain competences over a specific territory or it is recognized by

---

from their governments to the Council; Article 24 TECSC empowering the Assembly to have an open discussion about the High Authority's general, yearly report.

2 A vehement critique of these theories is formulated by Robert Schütze when advocating a federal understanding of the European Union: 'In the absence of a theory of federalism beyond the State, European thought invented a new word – supranationalism – and proudly announced the European Union to be sui generic. The belief that Europe was incomparable ushered in the dark ages of European constitutional theory. (…) In any event, the sui generis theory only ever provided a thin veneer in times of constitutional times.' (Schütze 2009, 3).

other states as an actor on the international plane – it lacks basic competences that would be necessary for exercising a real power of coercion. Without being able to exercise competences in the field of foreign, security and defense policy autonomously, that is, independently from the will and interests of the member states, the EU cannot fulfill the criteria of independent statehood (van Gerven 2005, 36–39). Therefore, it is argued by van Gerven, that the EU should be perceived as a political system or a body politic. This is the case, since there is a specific EU institutional setting; the EU has governmental powers through which political aims can be realized; the EU also has a certain impact on the distribution of resources; and, lastly, a continuous interaction exists among the various actors involved (ibid. 38).

What is very telling in van Gerven's otherwise well-founded concept is that he explicitly rejects the federal understanding. Even though this body politic clearly resembles federal systems on many points, it cannot be regarded as a federal entity yet. In van Gerven's eyes, the non-federal nature of the EU is due to the lack of the powers of internal and external coercion, the tensions between the supranational and member state levels of government, and the unsupportive attitudes of member states' populations (ibid. 60). In sum, the EU is a multi-layered political system, but not a real federation.

One should admit that van Gerven's anti-federal concerns are all valid points in the context of the current European political scene; however, they are not decisive factors with regard to the legal understanding of the EU's constitutional nature. In many European and non-European federations one can also point out similar tensions between the central and member state levels of government, and there are some groups or peoples with clear separationist attitudes in most of them. It is apparent that the EU has no comprehensive coercive power compared to a 'traditional state'; however, this does not at all mean that it has no chance to promote its own interests through other, sophisticated legal, means.[3] Thus, the constitutional mechanisms of the Treaties enable the EU to enforce the Community interests against the member states without a clear transfer of coercive power to it. That being said, although van Gerven raises important doubts on the federal nature of the EU, his theses fail to convincingly prove why a federalist understanding of the EU is unsuitable *ab ovo*. On the contrary, they mostly point out how fragile these 'non-federal but *sui generis*' approaches are if one compares their explicatory value to that of the federal theories.

3 The most important mechanism is the action for infringement of community law by a member state, that can be started by the European Commission and it may be ended in front of the European Court of Justice (Article 258 TFEU).

Yet, contrary to this influential line of thinking, some scholars have intentionally applied federal terms in the discussion of the EC's or EU's nature in the last decades. These scholarly attempts illustrated how fruitfully the federal approach can be applied in this context. These efforts focus primarily, albeit not exclusively, on analogies to the US federal doctrine. The best examples may be the works of J.H.H. Weiler, Koen Lenaerts or Robert Schütze. For instance, in his influential article highlighting the major trends of the early development of Community law, Weiler relied on core federal terms – i.e. enumerated powers or preemption – and argued for a clear federal understanding of the European Community (Weiler 1990–1991). Koen Lenaerts – the current Vice-President of the European Court of Justice – also applied federal tenets and discussed the main federal features of the European Community on a comparative basis (Lenaerts 1998). Recently, from the next generation of European scholars, Robert Schütze advocated for a federal-oriented approach of European integration. In doing so, he directly linked some provisions of the founding treaties to their US counterparts in order to demonstrate the applicability and relevance of this approach. For instance, he repeatedly referred to Article 235 of the Treaty establishing the European Economic Community (TEEC)[4] and its successors as the 'necessary and proper clause'[5] of European integration (Schütze 2009, 133–143).

One may conclude that it is certainly not impossible to discuss EU constitutional evolution with the language of federalism even if European public opinion is still reluctant to accept the federal scenario. Essentially, it may offer a more suitable conceptual framework than the *sui generis* theories since it makes it possible to learn from the century old federal experiences. By contrast, *sui generis* approaches may only rely on their own, post-modern conceptual framework lacking similar historical underpinning.

The present study intends to assess the development of EU law through federal lenses. In essence, it discusses how a main tenet of US federalism – police power[6] – can contribute to the ongoing discussion of the latest developments in EU constitutionalism.

---

4 'If action by the Community should prove necessary to attain, in the course of the operation of the common market, one of the objectives of the Community, and this Treaty has not provided the necessary powers, the Council shall, acting unanimously on a proposal from the Commission and after consulting the European Parliament, take the appropriate measures.'

5 The Constitution of the United States of America Art. 1 Sec. 8. 18.

6 Police power is a unique concept originating from the 18th century English legal thinking (Legarre 2007, 748 – 761). Its meaning is much broader than the simple indication of a

2. Police power as both a symbol and a cluster of competences

Police power had certainly been one of the key concepts of US constitutional law. It was frequently cited in 19th century American jurisprudence (Freund 1904), also resurfacing in contemporary US constitutional adjudication and thinking. However, contemporary US constitutional law scholarship is rather sceptical about its applicability; indeed, it does not refer to it frequently (Nowak-Rotunda 2010, 139). One may argue that state police power has lost its relevance in general because of the pervasive influence of constitutional rights on state competences. The impact of constitutional rights has considerably reduced the room for autonomous state action in the post-World War II period, contributing to the gradual fading of its importance.[7] Further, certain recent developments in Supreme Court case law have treated the idea of police power unfavourably, since the states' right to interfere with public morality has also been pushed into the background by constitutional concerns.[8]

However, police power – although its actual legal value has manifestly been reduced during the last century – as a concept of federal constitutional law may still be relevant from the aspect of comparative federalism. This is because it can help achieve a better understanding of federal structures. That is, the concept of police power may make it possible to shed light on the logic of member states' competences from their own point of view. Indeed, it can provide a different view on a question that was traditionally and prominently discussed from the perspective of federal governments.

Nonetheless, one problematic point should be taken into account. An inherent difficulty of police power is its rather broad and, therefore, imprecise meaning. In sum, throughout the last two centuries US legal scholarship has applied the concept in various contexts, and, therefore, diverse interpretations have been associated with it. Because of this broad penumbral meaning, as a first step of our study, two meanings of police power shall be contrasted.

---

government regulatory power of basic offenses, but encompasses governmental competences necessary to protect domestic order (for a detailed discussion see Freund 1904, 1–23).

7 For example: In 1927, the Supreme Court acknowledged that to punish those who abuse freedom of speech is a part of state police power (Whitney v. California), however, it overruled this interpretation in judgments dealing with the freedom of speech from the 1950's (Brandenburg v. Ohio).

8 For example: In 2003, the Supreme Court banned a Texas bill that made homosexual sodomy a crime on public morality basis by relying on the Fourteenth Amendment (Lawrence v. Texas).

2.1 Police power as a symbol of states' internal regulatory autonomy

The idea that is described by the term police power in constitutional law scholarship had already been an important component of the discourse that inspired the US Constitution of 1787. During the wide-reaching discussions surrounding the US constitution-making process, no one denied that British colonies had their own power to ensure 'peace, order and good government' on their territory (Legarre 2007, 770–771). Furthermore, the participants of these public debates regarded this power as a cornerstone of states' political existence. That is, the idea of inalienable self-government was among the major components of US constitutional thinking (ibid. 771–774). Thus, the constitutional system for the emerging United States of America was only conceivable if a certain degree of autonomy for the States was guaranteed. The Articles of Confederation (1777), predecessor to the US Constitution, afforded a prominent place for such a commitment to self-government. Article 2 set forth that: 'Each State retains its sovereignty, freedom and independence, and every power, jurisdiction and right, which is not by this confederation expressly delegated to the United States, in Congress assembled.'

That being said, the internal legislative autonomy of the states in the emerging Union was a undisputed point of the US constitutional thinking. During the Federal Convention in 1787, a Connecticut representative – Roger Sherman – even proposed the incorporation of an article explicitly referring to police power into the text of the new constitution in order to protect this idea. Sherman argued that the federal government should not 'interfered with the government of individual States in any matters of internal police' (ibid. 776). That is, police competences, whatever this term might have meant at the time, should have remained with the States. However, this proposition was rejected, and therefore the original text of the US Constitution did not mention the police power of states.

Yet, it should be borne in mind that the rejection of the above proposal did not at all mean that the existence of police powers was not later confirmed by corresponding constitutional practice. It simply meant that the original text of the US constitution did not include it – but police power, and the idea of self-government, has seriously influenced the public discourse on the limits of federal power from the birth of the US constitution (ibid. 777). This line of thinking was incorporated into the text of the constitution in 1789 since the Tenth Amendment was designed to emphasize the importance of internal state competences. This amendment declared that: 'The powers not delegated to the United States by the Constitution, nor prohibited by it to the States, are reserved to the States respectively, or to the people.'

The Tenth Amendment finalized the federal structure of the United States since it pointed out the fundamental limits of federal legislation (see Casto 1948–1949). The classic principle of the enumerated powers receives special emphasis here since the consequence of this clause is that those competences that are not explicitly delegated to the federal level remain with the states. That is, all other power, essentially competences that are manifest components of internal government and administration, are reserved to the states. And, these powers can be conceived of as police power in general. In this understanding, indeed, police power is the sum of those competences that remain with the states, under their autonomous legislative authority.

2.2 Police power as a cluster of competences protecting public interests

Besides the earlier, self-government oriented understanding of police power, another interpretation has emerged from the end of 19th century. This understanding is associated with specific state powers and competences. Because of the constantly increasing pressure of federal legislation, states tried to justify their local rules by relying on the concept of police power in order to defend public goods on their territory. The federal government intended to justify its jurisdiction from two directions. Firstly, a part of these federal regulations was based on the Commerce Clause allowing for the regulation of inter-state commerce by the Congress (Cushman 2000). Secondly, the due process clause of the Fourteenth Amendment and its substantive corollaries, such as the protection of property or the principle of the liberty of contract, also served as a justification for challenging state acts and regulations in the field of public interest (Harrison 1997). In defending their internal regulatory autonomy, states argued that their local rules were necessary to protect public health, public safety and public morals. Moreover, they also claimed that the protection of these public concerns was an essential component of the states' police power (Legarre 2007, 787). That is, states wanted to thwart the effects of the growing federal legislation by using the concept of police power as a cluster of those state competences that cannot be interfered with by the federal government.

The Supreme Court did not elaborate a consistent case law in relation to this approach of police power. That is, the case law of the Supreme Court has never defined its precise scope. This might be due to the sensitivity of the problem, with special regard to its very political nature and the constantly changing historical circumstances. However, two cases may illustrate the constraints among which the court had to find a proper balance. The *Mugler* case (Mugler v. Kansas) summarizes the early attitude of the Supreme Court, while the *Lochner* judgment (Lochner v. New York) points out the role of the Fourteenth Amendment when police power conflicts with the principles of federal constitutional law.

In 1887, a dispute between the state of Kansas and a brewery owner raised essential questions on the very nature of the states' legislative power. Peter Mugler, who started operating a brewery in 1877, had to shut down the business in 1881 when Kansas enacted certain new legal provisions in order to combat alcoholism in its territory. On the one hand, the constitution of Kansas was amended with an article generally prohibiting the production of alcoholic drinks. On the other hand, the local legislator also enacted a statute that linked the production of alcoholic beverages to holding a special license and ordered the fining of those producers who did not obtain such a permit. Muglers' attorney challenged the constitutionality of these regulations and argued that Kansas had no proper authority to pass them because of the due process clause of the Fourteenth Amendment.

First of all, the Supreme Court emphasized that its settled case law fully acknowledged the states' competence to regulate purely internal problems being connected to their 'moral and political welfare' (Mugler v. Kansas, 658). Further, the court argued that this amendment focusing on – inter alia – the requirement of due process of law did not overrule these powers, as constitutional amendments were generally not about interfering with states' internal regulatory autonomy. That is, states possess an internal legislative autonomy in general, although the Supreme Court stressed that in exercising this autonomy, they must respect the authority of the Constitution with special regard to citizens' rights and the competences of the national government (ibid. 663). As for Mugler's case, the court affirmed the judgment of the Supreme Court of Kansas and did not find the contested act providing a legal basis for fining Mugler unconstitutional.

Later, this decision became authority since it acknowledged and declared the existence of state police power. Some parts of the decision attempted to define the major components of police power, contributing thereby to the clarification of this complex and blurry concept. It must be noted, however, that the Supreme Court was inconsistent in the explanation because it associated a certain range of different definitions to police power (ibid. 658). Interpreted through the lens of *Mugler*, police power is basically about the protection of public health, public safety and public morals by state legislation. That is, if a state regulates a segment of life that falls into these areas and respects the general constitutional framework, its act in question can likely be justified as a valid exercise of state police power.

This understanding of police power was seriously challenged by the controversial and vehemently debated *Lochner* judgment in 1905 (see Sunstein 1987). The major question of the case was if New York had the authority to regulate the working conditions of bakers, especially the maximum number of working hours in a week, in order to protect their health and safety. That is, the state of New York wanted to justify its labour conditions regulation by claiming that it pertained to the exercise of police powers. However, the Supreme Court substantially curtailed the potential totality of police power since it argued in favor of liberty of contract against the states' legitimate authority to legislate on general labour conditions prevailing in their territory. As Justice Peckham pointed out, if state regulations on labour conditions interfere with the liberty of contract as provided by the due process clause of the Fourteenth Amendment, the individual liberty had to prevail unless such rules are related to very special and peculiar working conditions, as for instance underground mining which was seemingly not the case here (Lochner v. New York, 57).

Hence, this decision put general economic purposes in a prominent place and state public interests only came in second. Needless to say, it considerably decreased importance of police power on a state level by giving prominence to general economic interests. Following *Lochner,* to exercise state police power in a 'fair, reasonable and appropriate' manner, the state has to act in a way that is directly linked to public goods. A far and remote relationship, as was the case with the New York bakery working conditions regulation, was, in the eyes of the court, simply inadequate.

Following the *Lochner* decision, the scope of general state police power has been reduced even further, since both substantive due process arguments (Lawrence v. Texas) and the influence of constitutional rights have eroded it (e.g. Brandenburg v. Ohio). However, the existence of police power as such has never been questioned, and states' internal regulatory autonomy in respect to public goods is still a value of US constitutional architecture.

2.3 Summary: multiple, but intertwined layers of meaning

In conclusion, police power is mostly associated with two meanings in US constitutional history – a broader concept and a narrower one (Legarre 2007, 785–793). The broad concept is a cornerstone of federalism, since it reaffirms that federal power has its own internal limits posed by the jurisdiction of states and their residual sovereignty. In this sense, police power does have a symbolical meaning as it exposes an inherent limitation of Congress's powers. At this point, not the precise components and parts of police power that are important, but its message: federal power cannot be unlimited, but as to be balanced with the fact that states retained a part of their original sovereignty which they will never give up since a part of public goods can only be protected this way.

The narrow concept reflects a different approach. It sheds light on the fact that states' jurisdiction in a federal system comprises at least three important areas: the protection of public health, public safety and public morals. Thus, it points out some components of states' residuary sovereignty by putting emphasis on the public good. Obviously, these competences have been under a strong pressure from the beginning of the 19th century stemming from various sources, e.g. the Fourteenth Amendment's due process clause, or the pervasive effect of constitutional rights. But, their existence could never be denied; it was merely their proper scope that has been up for discussion.

3. Police power in the Post-Lisbon constitutional architecture?

3.1 Article 4 (1) and (2) TEU: a European approach to police power

The Lisbon Treaty that, among other objectives, aimed to restructure the system of Union competences by simplifying the pre-Lisbon setting (see: von Bogdandy-Bast 2002, 229–251) introduced qualitatively new provisions setting forth precise rules for delimiting the competences between the Union and the member state levels of government. Both the TEU and the Treaty on the Functioning of the European Union (TFEU) contain relevant provisions,[9] but Article 4 paras (1) and (2) TEU may have a prominent role to play in this discussion.

As for these articles, the first point that should be emphasized is the lack of any antecedents in the earlier treaty versions. It can generally be stated that the Lisbon articles on the division of competences originate from either some earlier articles or the case law of the European Court of Justice (ECJ) (Lenaerts-Van Nuffel 2011, 125–126). However, these two articles do not exhibit such a close connection to the constitutional past of the EU, and it makes their appearance in the corpus of the TEU even more surprising. Generally, it can be argued that Article 4 paras (1) and (2) TEU indicate a clear shift in the constitutional philosophy of the EU with respect to the vertical division of powers. It is so because both of paragraphs are devoted to the protection of member state powers. That is, they are centered on the legislative activities of member states.

One should not forget that prior to the Maastricht Treaty there were no provisions in the founding treaties dealing either with the existence of member state powers or their precise scope. They rather focused on the exercise of the Community powers, then later on Union competences.[10] Following the adoption of the Maastricht Treaty, the concept of subsidiarity appeared in the corpus of EU

9 Interestingly the EU constitutional order has no single competence clause that would regulate the division of competences in a single chapter. Actually, Articles 4 and 5 TEU, Articles 2 to 6 TFEU and Article 352 TFEU contain relevant provisions and their entirety can be conceived of as the 'competence clause' of the EU.

10 It should be mentioned that those provisions that enlisted certain exceptions under the principle of free movement of goods on the basis of – inter alia – public morality, public policy, public security and protection of health and life cannot be regarded as antecedents since they

constitutional law, but it constituted much more of a political response to the fears of certain member states regarding an emerging federative union than a real and functioning legal remedy against the potential misuse of Community powers (Davies 2006). Therefore, these articles illustrate to what extent the constitutional philosophy of the EU has changed in relation to the question of federalism. The nature and scope of member state competences have to be emphasized only in federal structures; in other, fundamentally non-federal constitutional orders it is simply unnecessary.

Moreover – and this is the most striking feature from the aspect of the present study – one can easily recognize that both articles reflect an understanding of member state powers that is almost identical to the US interpretation of police power. One may even conclude that they are intended to be the "police power clauses" of the EU treaties.

First of all, Article 4 para (1) TEU must be analysed in detail. It declares that: 'In accordance with Article 5, competences not conferred upon the Union in the Treaties remain with the Member States.' It can hardly be denied that this provision shares the same federal commitment that the Tenth Amendment to the US Constitution exemplifies. Obviously there are apparent differences between the two provisions. Firstly, the phrasing of Article 4 para (1) TEU is not as sophisticated as in the case of the US Amendment, since it is nothing more than a simple statement on the position of powers not conferred upon the EU. Secondly, as compared to its US counterpart, this Article does not contain any reference to the people, but merely mentions the member states as depositaries of these powers.

Yet, the meaning is definitely the same in a constitutional sense. A part of the EU member states' competences is not transferred to the supranational level, to the EU government. Thus, EU member states retain a part of their sovereignty irrespective of the strengthening of the supranational level of government. Put another way, one can find a clear reference to a basic tenet of federalism as determined by the symbolical meaning of police power. In the eyes of the European constitution-maker, the powers of the Union level are certainly not unlimited, but rather they are restricted by the residuary sovereignty of member states. That being said, contrary to the manifest differences on the surface, this conviction on the limited nature of the powers of the supranational level is a common point in both the US and the post-Lisbon EU constitutionalism. Basically, the symbolical understanding of police power earlier analysed is reflected in this new article.

---

did not deal with the competences of member states but they provided general grounds to justify those member state measures that may infringe this principle. (see Article 36 TFEU).

Article 4 para (2) TEU implies even more surprising conclusions when compared to the narrower approach of US police power. Indeed, this provision delimits the core of the political and constitutional existence of the member states; that is, it defines those competences that cannot be overruled by acts of the Union. In terms of the present analysis, the second sentence of this Article may gain particular importance. It obliges the EU to respect the member states (i.) essential state functions in general, and it mentions (ii.) the ensuring of territorial integrity, (iii.) the maintenance of law and order and (iv.) the safeguarding of national interest as major components. Although the constitution-maker did not specify the exact scope of these powers, these are the basic state competences necessary for territorial administration.

It is worth mentioning that Working Group V of the European Constitutional Convention originally had a different, essentially broader vision when drafting this provision. It argued that national identity as a constitutional concept consists of two main components. The first one focuses on 'the fundamental structures and essential functions' of a member state, whereas the second one concentrates on 'basic public policy choices and social values' (Final Report 2002, 11). However, perhaps as a sign of European *realpolitik*, the final draft entirely neglected the public policy choices and social values components in the text, and it only contained references to the essential state functions.

It is striking again to what extent the second sentence of Article 4 para (2) TEU echoes or mirrors police power when conceived of in a narrow sense – that is, as a cluster of state powers related to the protection of public goods in its territory. Essentially, no one can deny that the aim of this Article is to define, as broadly as possible, those legislative areas that cannot be dissociated from the member states in this configuration of power sharing. That is, the EU constitution-maker followed the same approach as the US constitutional discourse when trying to specify which state powers are needed to protect public health, public safety and public morals. Basically, the terms of 'essential state functions' and the 'maintenance of law and order' may comprise all those competences that have been identified as police powers in front of the US Supreme Court from the second half of the 19th century. A direct reference to public morals is actually missing from text of this article, but, theoretically, the word 'order' could be interpreted in this sense by the ECJ if necessary.

3.2 The ECJ and the individual, country-specific constitutional identity: opening the door for police power in EU context?

Today, it is impossible to say whether or not Article 4 paras (1) and (2) play a similar role in the future of EU constitutionalism that police power had played on the other side of the Atlantic. One may direct attention to the apparent similarities, but the judicial interpretation of these articles is still an open question. That is, the ECJ will play a prominent role in shaping the understanding of the exclusive member state competences, in establishing a fair balance between the Union and member state interests in order to create a fair and efficient system of division of powers.

The attitude of the ECJ toward member state competences as they are conceived in these two articles cannot be foreseen due to many reasons. Chief among these reasons is the actual uncertainty of the European political scene, as the ongoing European debt crisis profoundly changed the general attitude towards integration. And, this transformation may have a serious effect on the assessment of basic constitutional problems, such as member states' inalienable powers. However, in examining the settled case law of the ECJ, there is one decision that may yield some insights for predicting the ECJ's future approach in this field.

As regards state police powers, the most important decision of the ECJ may be the *Omega Spielhallen*. While this case had many implications, only one aspect has to be mentioned in the present context. The case, which started in Germany and gained particular importance, explicitly raised the question whether the principle of freedom to provide services can be restricted by referring to specific fundamental constitutional values – human dignity in this case – as a public policy choice. Human dignity has a prominent place in German constitutionalism, and its protection is one of the basic goals of the entire legal order. Therefore, it plays a special role beyond comparison with other member states.

In other words, the main dilemma of this case can be reformulated by using the term of police power. Does the Federal Republic of Germany have the right to provide a special, high-level protection to human dignity in order to protect a prominent value of German constitutionalism, even against the principles of the European Union? Essentially, the police powers of Germany in the field of public morals had to be weighed against EU basic principles. The ECJ answered the question affirmatively, declaring:

> that the specific circumstances which may justify recourse to the concept of public policy may vary from one country to another and from one era to another. The competent national authorities must therefore be allowed a margin of discretion within the limits imposed by the Treaty […]' (Omega-Spielhallen, para 31).

That is, in the *Omega Spielhallen* the ECJ theoretically acknowledged the existence of public policy objectives varying from one country to another. Moreover, it even accepted that these can be protected by country-specific restrictions, and if these do not conflict with some general principles of EU law – such as non-discrimination and proportionality (Omega-Spielhallen, paras 29 and 38) – they may even be valid under EU law.

Essentially, the argumentation of the ECJ in *Omega Spielhallen* certainly indicates one point. The ECJ is open to accept the existence of police powers if they are justified under the strict scrutiny of substantive and procedural requirements. Of course, this argumentation remains silent about the future interpretation of Article 4 paras (1) and (2) TEU, it only points out the starting position of the ECJ that may obviously change due to other relevant considerations.

4. Conclusion

In conclusion, two theses can be formulated at the end of this analysis that discussed the reception of police power in EU constitutional law. First of all, no one can seriously question the usefulness of this federal concept in the better understanding of EU law. The idea of police power is very useful for highlighting the broad, so to say comparative, context of Article 4 paras (1) and (2) TEU, and, therefore it contributes to their in-depth understanding.

Moreover, the more than two hundred years of constitutional history regarding police power, be it a symbol of residuary sovereignty or a cluster of specific powers, can also help in projecting the prospects of EU member states within the conditions of an emerging federal polity. Comparative constitutional history teaches us that the real room for member states to exercise their own competences in a federal system is determined by a case-by-case approach. That is, it is the field of a never-ending constitutional controversy between the supranational and member state levels of government, in which both sides try to preserve, and if it is possible, broaden and strengthen their powers. And, obviously, federal supreme courts have always been key actors in this process.

Therefore, we may conclude that the question of what kind of constitutional future the EU member states are looking ahead to in a more-and-more federalized EU can only be answered in the longer run by analysing the relevant case-law of the ECJ. Thus, we are looking forward to the first judgments of the ECJ interpreting Article 4 paras (1) and (2) TEU. Until such time, all legal literature regarding this problem is nothing more than a simple, but fascinating speculation.

References

Alter, Karen J. and Steinberg, David. 2007. The Theory and Reality of European Coal and Steel Community. *Buffett Center for International and Comparative Studies Working Paper*

No. 07-001. [http://www.bcics.northwestern.edu/documents/workingpapers/Buffett_07-001_Alter_Steinberg.pdf, accessed on 24.04.2014.]
Bitsch, Marie-Thérèse and Loth, Wilfried. 2009. European Institutions and Political Integration. In *Experiencing Europe. 50 Years of European Construction 1957–2007*, edited by Wilfried Loth, 103–123. Baden-Baden: Nomos.
Casto, Dayton C. Jr. 1948–1949. The Doctrinal Development of the Tenth Amendment. *West Virgina Law Quarterly* 51: 227–249.
Cushman, Barry. 2000. Formalism and Realism in Commerce Clause Jurisprudence. *The University of Chicago Law Review* 67: 1089–1050.
Davies, Gareth. 2006. Subsidiarity: The wrong idea, in the wrong place, at the wrong time. *Common Market Law Review* 43: 63–84.
Final Report of Working Group V, Brussels, 4 November 2002. CONV 375/1/02 WG V 14.
Freund, Ernst. 1904. *Police Power: Public Policy and Constitutional Rights*. Chicago: Callaghan and Company.
Harpaz, Guy. 2011. European Integration in the Aftermath of the Ratification of Lisbon: Quo vadis? *European Public Law* 11: 73–89.
Harrison, John. 1997. Substantive Due Process and the Constitutional Text. *Virginia Law Review* 83: 493–558.
Legarre, Santiago. 2007. The Historical Background of Police Power. *University of Pennsylvania Journal of Constitutional Law* 9: 745–796.
Lenaerts, Koen. 1998. Federalism: Essential Concepts in Evolution – The Case of the European Union. *Fordham International Law Journal* 21: 746–798.
Lenaerts, Koen and Van Nuffel, Piet. 2011. *European Union Law*. London: Sweet & Maxwell.
Nowak, John E. and Rotunda, Ronald D. 2010. *Constitutional law.* St. Paul (Minn.): Thomson-West.
Prettenthaler-Ziegerhofer, Anita. 2012. Richard Nikolaus Coudenhove-Kalergi, Founder of the Pan-European Union, and the Birth of a 'New' Europe. In *Europe in Crisis. Intellectuals and the European Idea 1917–1957*, edited by Mark Hewitson and Matthew D'Auria, 89 – 109. New York, Oxford: Berghahn Books.
Schütze, Robert. 2009. *From dual to cooperative federalism: the changing structure of European law*. Oxford: Oxford University Press.
Sunstein, Cass R. 1987. Lochner's Legacy. *Columbia Law Review* 87: 873–919.
Van Gerven, Walter. 2005. *The European Union: A Polity of States and People*. Oxford: Hart.
Von Bogdandy, Armin and Bast, Jürgen. 2002. The European Union's Vertical Order of Competences: The Current Law and Proposals for its Reform. Common Market law Review 39: 227–268.
Weiler, Joseph H. H. 1990–1991. The Transformation of Europe. *Yale Law Journal* 100: 2403–2484.

Treaties

Treaty establishing the European Coal and Steel Community (TECSC)
Treaty establishing the European Economic Community (TEEC)
Treaty on the European Union (TEU)
Treaty on the Functioning of the European Union (TFEU)

Court rulings
US Supreme Court

Brandenburg v. Ohio 395 U.S. 444 (1969)
Lawrence v. Texas 539 U.S. 558 (2003)
Lochner v. New York 198 U.S. 45 (1905)
Mugler v. Kansas 123 U.S. 623 (1887)
Whitney v. California 274 U.S. 357 (1927)

European Court of Justice

C-36/02 *Omega Spielhallen- und Automatenaufstellungs-Gmbh v Oberbürgermeisterin der Bundesstadt Bonn* [2004] E.C.R. I-9609

'Solange, Chapter 5?' The Law of the European Union and the Sovereignty in Rulings of the Constitutional Courts in Central Europe

Mariusz Jerzy Golecki

Abstract

Recent developments in the law of European Union raised the question concerning the scope of application and the meaning of the principle of primacy within the context of judicial rulings. The enactment of the Treaty on Functioning of the European Union resulted in many judgements of constitutional courts in some member states in which the concept of sovereignty and the doctrine of sovereign powers play an important role. The application of this concept seems to be significant not in national legal discourses pertaining to the constitutional law, but also for the prospective development of the European legal order. The chapter will thus concentrate on two issues, namely on the difference between the meaning of the concept of sovereignty and its application by different constitutional courts in different member states, and on the theoretical foundations of the potential solution to the problem of comprehensive application of the primacy principle throughout the member states.

1. Introduction

Recent developments in the EU law have raised the question concerning the scope of application and meaning of the principle of superiority within the context of judicial rulings. The enactment of the Treaty on Functioning of the European Union resulted in many judgements of national courts in some member states in which the concept of sovereignty plays an important role. The application of this concept seems to be significant in national legal discourses pertaining to the constitutional law. This chapter will thus concentrate on two issues: first, the difference in the meaning and the content of the concept of sovereignty, and second, its application by different constitutional or supreme courts in different member states. From the perspective of the theory of judicial discourse it seems that the supremacy principle of the EU law remains a double-blade sword. On the one hand, there is a view on the primacy of the EU law from the perspective of the European Court of Justice (ECJ), and on the other hand, the reception of that principle by national courts in the member states. Additionally it seems that there is no unanimous understanding of the principle of sovereignty.

First, the question arises whether the interactive character of the EU law and the EU as an intergovernmental and multilevel structure leads to any deviation from the traditional doctrine of sovereignty. Two models will be analysed within this chapter. According to the traditional meaning of sovereignty as offered by John Austin in jurisprudence or by Carl Schmitt in political and legal theory, sovereignty is to be based on the idea of autonomy, exclusivity and independence (external aspect). Additionally, sovereignty is traditionally associated with superiority and concentration of undivided power (internal aspect). The second issue concerns the relationship between the legal and constitutional meaning of sovereignty within the EU law context. I will thus concentrate on the investigation of the most fundamental judgements of both the ECJ and the constitutional and supreme courts in some Central European member states, particularly in Germany, Austria, Poland, Hungary and the Czech Republic. The research question is therefore of double nature, since it pertains to both the concept of sovereignty referred to the EU and to the relationship between the member states and the EU itself. It seems that the ECJ adopted in its judgements the concept of exclusive sovereignty, whereas the jurisprudence of some constitutional courts adopted a more refined concept of sovereignty based on a multilevel and multi-centric character of law in Europe. This conclusion seems to be paradoxical, however it could well be explained by the very nature of judicial dialogue in the EU. Some potential advantages and disadvantages or limits of these strategies will be investigated in a final part of this chapter.

2. A tale of two sovereigns

The autonomous character of the EU law has been established based on a judicial understanding of the autonomy of the European Communities and later on the European Union as a separate legal order. This autonomy has been understood in two ways.

First, the *autonomy* could be understood as the *internal* one. In a series of cases the ECJ established the doctrine of superiority of the EC law over the legal systems of the member states. In two benchmark cases the ECJ introduced this concept, stating in case 26/62 *Van Gend en Loos* (1963), that the EC law had created 'a new legal order', and reaffirming this in later case 6/64 *Costa v. ENEL* (1964), where it emphasised that the Communities in reality are governed by an 'own legal system.' These developments gave rise to the assertion that the EC law must be superior over the legal systems of the member states. The content of this doctrine has albeit never been clear.

As a consequence, the question arises how to solve the potential conflict between the EC law and the constitutions of the member state. This question seemed to be pressing, since many member states, especially in Central Europe, had adopted the doctrine of superiority of their constitution over any other legal norms, including international or the EC/EU law. One potential solution to this problem was offered by the authors of the Treaty establishing a Constitution for Europe (2004), whose Art. I-6 contained an explicit statement concerning the superiority of the EU legal order. Additionally, this article has been supported by a political declaration of the member states, according to which the explicit statement on superiority of the EU law should not be understood as creating a new legal principle. In contrast, the principle of primacy is rather a declaratory one, based on the long-standing doctrine established by the European Courts, since Declaration 1 reads as follows: 'The Conference notes that Article I-6 reflects existing case-law of the Court of Justice of the European Communities and of the Court of First Instance.'[1]

However, this attempt to insert the primacy claim into the system of quasi constitutional rules on the European level failed when the Constitution for Europe was doomed to failure by voters in France and in the Netherlands in 2005. Nevertheless, a different solution was found in the Lisbon Treaty (2007, in force since 2009): In the Treaty on the Functioning of the European Union the formal primacy claim of the former article I-6 was removed, but in Declaration 17 annexed to its Final Act, the member states laid down 'that, in accordance with well settled case law of the Court of Justice of the European Union, the Treaties and the law adopted by the Union on the basis of the Treaties have primacy over the law of Member States.'[2] Most interestingly, the member states have additionally decided to attach the Opinion of the Council Legal Service on the primacy of EC law.[3] The opinion explicitly refers to the well-established judicial practice. This solution creates a very interesting puzzle, where the policy principle is to be supported by the legal doctrine and judicial practice rather than other way around, as it is much more common in constitutional law.

Second, the position adopted by the Lisbon Treaty does not solve the problem of *external autonomy*, i.e. the autonomy concerning the relation between EU law and international law. This problem has been well articulated by the ECJ in the cases C-402/05P and C-415/05P *Kadi and Al Barakaat v Council*, where the ECJ emphasised the need of respect for the EU law as autonomous legal order even in case of conflict with the international law, for example created by the institutions

---

1 Final Act, 1st Declaration on Article I-6. In: *Treaty establishing a Constitution for Europe*. Official Journal of the European Union, 2004/C 310/01, 420.

2 Final Act, 17th Declaration. In: *Consolidated versions of the Treaty on European Union and the Treaty on the Functioning of the European Union*. Official Journal of the European Union, 2010/C 83/01, 344.

3 Ibid.

of United Nations like the Security Council. The legal acts of the UN which contradict the principles of the EU law should not be followed by the member states, which only means that the principle of primacy refers to international law. The scope of this principle is still limited by the fact, that it can be applied by the member states only. However the external aspect of the principle produces additional tensions and uncertainties regarding its scope of application, its meaning, and the results on the relationship between the EU and the European Convention on Human Rights.[4]

From the perspective of the theory of judicial discourse it seems that the principle of the supremacy of the EU law remains a double-blade sword. On the one hand, there is the perspective of the EU Court of Justice, and on the other hand, there is the reception by the national courts in the member states. Additionally it seems that there is no unanimous understanding of the principle of sovereignty. In many legal systems (British, French, German, Spanish, Polish) the concept of sovereignty sets out limits for the application of the principle of superiority. From the functional perspective the concept (or a constitutional principle) of sovereignty plays an important role, creating a ground for the so-institutionalised *Kompetenz-Kompetenz* dilemma.

It seems that the very nature of the EU as a complex and specific legal system creates an unresolved problem of competing claims for superiority. In the following, I will concentrate on two aspects. First, the question arises whether the interactive character of the EU law and the EU as an intergovernmental and multilevel structure leads to any deviation from the traditional doctrine of *exclusive sovereignty*. Two models will be analysed: According to the traditional meaning of sovereignty as offered by John Austin in jurisprudence (Austin 1832, 128–129) or by Carl Schmitt in political and legal theory (Schmitt 1922, 20), sovereignty is to be based on the idea of autonomy, exclusivity and independence (external aspect). Additionally sovereignty is traditionally associated with the superiority and concentration of undivided power (internal aspect), as it was emphasised by Jean Bodin (1583) or Thomas Hobbes (1651). This double-sided concept remains vivid as a point of reference for the discourse concerning the relationship between state, law and power. Its jurisprudential interpretations range from Herbert L.A. Hart (1964) and Hans Kelsen (1992) to different constitutional doctrines such as *ultra vires*

4 It seems that the relation between the EU and the European Court of Human Rights (ECHR) is based on relative autonomy and respect for the specific character of the EU law. See however the case C-299/95 *Kremzov* [1997] ECR I-2629; [1997] 3 C.M.L.R. 1289, where the ECJ did not take the liability for breach of the EC law into account, neglecting the view of the ECHR.

in British law or the principle of constitutional sovereignty in Germany, France, Poland and Spain. The question remains whether the development of the EU law in general and the content of the principle of superiority formally constructed in the judgements of the ECJ have added anything to this traditional picture.

In contrast, it is possible to refer to a competing concept of sovereignty based on the notion of inclusion and influence upon other states rather than on autonomy and exclusion. This concept seems to be an output of the concept of governance and governability and could be associated with authors as Ulrich Beck (1992), Giovanni Arrighi (1994), Beverly J. Silver (Arrighi and Silver 1999) or Jadwiga Staniszkis (2003). This concept is based on the opposition between the centre of political, economic or legal affairs and the peripheries. *Inclusive sovereignty* can be understood as an ability to maintain control over some pivotal parameters and at the same time to influence other agents (e.g. states) acting within a wider structure of governance or managerial framework such as: the global financial market, international relations, or regional and international organisations. Inclusive sovereignty is thus to be understood not in a negative but rather in a positive way as an ability to play an important role in a wider international or regional system. Additionally, the centres of such powers do not necessarily coincide with traditional states, since states seem to be understood as a nexus of different multilevel structures of governance. Therefore, the concept of inclusive sovereignty differs from exclusive sovereignty also in this respect and can thus successfully be integrated in the legal discourse pertaining to the problem of the superiority principle and the very nature of the EU law.

The second issue concerns the relationship between the legal and constitutional meaning of sovereignty within the EU law context. The research question seems to be of double nature, since it pertains to both, the concept of sovereignty referred to the EU legal order and to the relationship between the member states and the EU itself. It seems that in the judgements of the ECJ in cases such as case 26/62 *Van Gend en Loos* (1963), case 6/64 *Costa v. ENEL* (1964), case 11/70 *Internationale Handelsgesellschaft* (1970), case 106/77 *Amministrazione delle Finanze dello Stato v. Simmenthal SpA* (1978) and more recently cases C-402/05P and C-415/05P *Kadi and Al Barakaat v Council* (2008) the EU courts adopted the concept of exclusive sovereignty, whereas the jurisprudence of some national constitutional courts, e.g. the German, Polish and Spanish ones adopted a more refined concept of sovereignty based on a multilevel and multi-centric character of law in Europe. This conclusion seems to be paradoxical, however it could be well explained by the fact that the very nature of judicial dialogue in the EU has to lead to such juxtaposition of the two different concepts of sovereignty (inclusive vs. exclusive) even if they seem to be of inverted nature.

It should however be noted, that the solution to this problem might be found through the interactive process of judicial dialogue. This dialogue between member states and EU Courts seems to be a new and powerful tool for shaping a different concept of inclusive sovereignty, understood as the power of control and participation within a pan-European lawmaking process rather than a power to limit the application of the other systems. In a nutshell, inclusive sovereignty is about the influence upon institutional settings rather than the exclusion from this settings. Two approaches along these lines by the Polish and German Constitutional Courts call particular attention: In three judgements, the Polish Constitutional Tribunal established a refined doctrine of constitutional supremacy and its limits. In judgement P 1/05 of 27 April 2005, the court found the European Arrest Warrant Framework Decision (EAW) unconstitutional, since the Polish Constitution explicitly prohibited the extradition of Polish citizens, whereas the EAW was based on a cooperation requiring 'surrender' of the offender to other member states. The Tribunal however suspended the annulment of the European Arrest Warrant Framework Decision for an 18 months adjustment, thus giving the parliament the opportunity to amend the Polish Constitution in order to enable the operation of the EAW in Poland.[5]

In another decision concerning the constitutionality of the accession treaty between Poland and the EU, the Polish Constitutional Tribunal emphasised the need for cooperation and political participation, criticising the extension of the pro-European interpretation of legal acts in Polish law. Departing from a relatively traditional concept of supremacy as control over the interpretation of the Constitution, the court reached the conclusion, that the Constitution should be interpreted in a manner sympathetic to EU law, but '[i]n no event may it lead to results contradicting the explicit wording of constitutional norms' (judgement K 18/04 of 11 May 2005). Additionally, the court established its right to control the constitutionality of EU law:

> The supremacy of the Constitution finds its confirmation in the constitutionally regulated mechanism of control of constitutionality of the Accession Treaty and acts which form its integral parts. […] In such a situation other acts of primary law of the EC and EU being parts of the Accession Treaty, however indirectly, become subject to the control of constitutionality (ibid.).

At the same time, the court sketched the wider concept of a multi-centric legal order and inclusive sovereignty, stressing the need of cooperation and participation

5 In Contrast, the German Federal Constitutional Court immediately annulled the EAW as unconstitutional, which put Germany in a difficult situation within the European Union (Decision 2 BvR 2236/04 of 18 July 2005).

within the EU lawmaking process, since the application of the EU law is based on mutual cooperation and the 'coexistence of different legal rules produced by different law-making bodies and applied by various courts' structures' (ibid.).

Finally, the Polish Constitutional Tribunal established a doctrine of constitutional identity, constituting the claim for sovereignty in particular areas strictly limited to basic constitutional principles and the protection of human rights. Thus the source of sovereignty seems to be found in a sophisticated concept of rights rather than in political power and its monopoly over the territory. This problem loomed on the horizon together with the doubts concerning the constitutionality of the Lisbon Treaty. In its judgement referring to this question, the court clearly articulated the concept of constitutional identity as a source of sovereignty, enabling the state to participate in the EU within the constitutional limits. The Tribunal observed that:

> Article 90 of the Constitution, being a normative anchor to the state's sovereignty, determines the limits of conferring competences on the Union. This limit is constituted by the following factors determining constitutional identity of the Republic of Poland: the respect for the principles of Polish sovereign statehood, democracy, the principle of a state ruled by law, the principle of social justice, the principles determining the bases of the economic system, protection of human dignity and the constitutional rights and freedoms (judgement K 32/09 of 24 November 2010).

Similar reservations to the unlimited primacy of the EU law have been raised in the so called 'Lisbon Treaty decisions' of the constitutional courts of Germany (judgement 2 BvE 2/08 of 30 June 2009), the Czech Republic (Pl. ÚS 29/09 judgement of 3 November 2009), and Hungary (judgement 143/2010 of 12 July 2010). It has been suggested that the doctrine of sovereignty was primarily used by these Central Europe courts (including the Polish one) for domestic reasons. Wojciech Sadurski has pointed out that the constitutional courts' attempt at gaining recognition and legitimacy through the process of protection of its national systems against an exuberant, extensive application of the primacy principle of EU law was not invented in one of the post-communist countries (Sadurski 2006; 2012, 134–138). With their '*Solange 3*' decisions (as Sadurski has put it), the courts in Poland, Hungary and the Czech Republic simply adopted the scepticism concerning the superiority of the EC law as it was expressed many years earlier by the German Federal Constitutional Court in its so called '*Solange*' cases in 1974 and 1986 (*Solange 1* and *2*; Judgement of 29 May 1974, 37 BVerfGE 271, and Judgement of 22 October 1986, 73 BVerfGE 339).

However, the story of the '*Solange*' decisions has recently been supplemented by two more chapters, written by the German and the Austrian Constitutional

Courts, respectively: The German Constitutional Court has emphasised the need of constitutional control and protection of constitutional rights, concentrating on the relationship between the German Constitution and the development of the EC/EU law in a long series of cases, including the *Bruner case* (1994), the *Banana case* (1997) and the *Treaty of Lisbon case* (2009). The court cautiously avoided direct invalidation of the EC law, but setted out the potential limits of constitutionality in respect of the application of the EU law. It seems that the most recent case concerning the constitutionality of the Lisbon Treaty (which I would like to call '*Solange 4*'; judgement 2 BvE 2/08 of 30 June 2009, par. 33, 229 and 235) entails the complete doctrine of sovereignty based on the concept of *Staatenverbund*, i.e. the Sovereign Association of Sovereign States. The Court explicitly referred to the development of the primacy of the EU law, taking into account three fundamental issues: the inexplicit and vague character of the primacy principle of the EU law, the unlimited power vested upon the Constitutional Court in order to control and guard the constitutional order and the character of the EU as a purpose-oriented association of interdependent rather than independent, but nonetheless sovereign states. The Court expressed these concepts in the following three lucid passages:

1. 'The primacy of Union and Community law over national law is still not explicitly regulated' (par. 33).
2. 'The obligation under European law to respect the constituent power of the member states as the masters of the Treaties corresponds to the non-transferable identity of the constitution (Article 79.3 of the Basic Law), which is not open to integration in this respect. Within the boundaries of its competences, the Federal Constitutional Court must review, where necessary, whether these principles are adhered to' (par. 235).
3. 'Article 24.1 of the Basic Law underlines that the Federal Republic of Germany takes part in the development of a European Union designed as an association of sovereign states (*Staatenverbund*) to which sovereign powers are transferred. The concept of *Verbund* covers a close long-term association of states which remain sovereign' (par. 230).

The last sentence directly expresses the concept of internal sovereignty within a long-term association of states, taking into account that states can seize to participate in this endeavour. In a sense states remain sovereign as possessing control over the degree of participation, the content of participation or lack thereof in a similar way in which the Federal Constitutional Court possesses the control over constitutionality of the EU law in Germany, even if it represents an astonishing compliance with the EU law and only very rarely decides against the validity of the EU law or it's applicability in Germany. The control over the decision and the content of the decision remain two separate issues. This position has recently been reinforced in the provisional decision of the German Federal Constitutional Court pertaining to the validity of the Decision of the Governing Council of the European Central Bank of 6 September 2012 concerning Outright Monetary Transactions (OMT) and the continued purchases of government bonds on the basis of this decision and of the predecessor programme for Securities Markets (SMP). Here, the Court repeated that the protection of constitutional identity remains its exclusive prerogative and this doctrine has been commonly accepted by other EU member states (judgement 2 BvR 2728/13 of 14 January 2014). It seems that the German Federal Constitutional Court treats the doctrine of constitutional identity and a special concept of sovereignty in respect of the participation in the EU as a consolidated doctrine shared by many other constitutional courts and belonging to the common constitutional identity of these member states.[6] However, the Court decided to suspend the case and to refer questions for a preliminary ruling on the interpretation of various provisions of the EU law to the ECJ.

The same issue of controlling the application of the EU law has been raised by the Hungarian Constitutional Court at the very moment of accession. On 1 May 2004, the Hungarian Parliament enacted a law 'On measures concerning agricultural surplus stocks', which implemented the Commission Regulations (EC) No. 1972/2003 of 10 November 2003 and (EC) No. 60/2004 of 14 January 2004 and introduced some transitional measures in the sugar sector. In its judgement 17/2004 of 25 May 2004, the Constitutional Court considered the Surplus Act to be retroactive and therefore declared it unconstitutional. In a later decision the Hungarian Constitutional Court reaffirmed this legal argument and explained that the court limits its powers to control the constitutionality of domestic laws: 'Under Article 2/A of the Constitution community law applicable in Hungarian law is just as valid as is law adopted by Hungarian legislation' (judgement 61/B/2005 29 September 2008). This line of argument, reflecting the difference between international law, which is not controlled in respect of its constitutionality, and internal law (including implemented EU law), which constitutes a subject of control, was also reflected in the decision concerning the constitutionality of the Lisbon Treaty (judgement 143/2010 of 12 July 2010; see also Blutman and Chronowski 2011).

Here, the Hungarian Constitutional Court adopted two views: The first one concerns the formal aspect of the constitutional control, enabling the Court to control the scope of sovereignty transfer from the state to the EU institutions. While interpreting art. 2/A of the Hungarian Constitution[7] the court observed, that 'Article

6 A similar attitude has already been signalled by the Polish Constitutional Tribunal (see judgement SK 45/09 of 16 November 2011).

7 'In the interest of participating as a member state of the European Union on the basis of international treaties – to the extent required to exercise rights and to perform obligations

2/A had established a competence for the court to determine whether the transfer of further competences in amendments to the EU treaties is acceptable.' Obviously, this position should also be maintained under the new Fundamental Law of Hungary (in force since 1 January 2012), since art E essentially copied the so called 'European Clause' of the former art. 2/A. Second, the Court pointed out that the doctrine of sovereignty should still be treated as the source of constitutional identity. The Court expressed the view that the Constitution cannot be interpreted in a way that would deprive the constitutional provisions on sovereignty and the rule of law of their substance. Hence, the Court referred to the concept of sovereignty as the indirect albeit ultimate limitation of the principle of primacy of the EU law. Additionally, the principle of the rule of law limits the operation of the primacy principle of the EU law (judgement 143/2010 of 12 July 2010).

The participatory character of sovereignty was also emphasised by the Czech Constitutional Court. In the decision on the constitutionality of the European Arrest Warrant Framework Decision (decision Pl ÚS 50/04 of 8 March 2006) the Czech Court unlike its counterparts in Germany and Poland found that the requirement of cooperation is more important that the sole literal meaning of the legal act, and did not decide against the constitutionality. The doctrine elaborated in was based on the assumption that the Court plays an essential role in deciding on the scope of integration, since it preserves the constitutional doctrine of sovereignty:

> The delegation of a part of the powers of national organs may persist only as long as these powers are exercised in a manner that is compatible with the preservation of the foundations of state sovereignty of the Czech Republic [...]. In such determination the Constitutional Court is called upon to protect constitutionalism (ibid.).

Three years later, the Czech Constitutional Court also found the Treaty of Lisbon constitutional, albeit setting out limits for the transfer of powers from the state to the EU institutions. Thereby it referred to the famous *Kompetenz-Kompetenz* expression and the idea of participatory integration and inclusive sovereignty, since

> there would be a breach of the Czech Constitution if, on the basis of a transfer of powers, an international organisation could continue to change its powers at will, and independently of its members, i.e. if a constitutional competence (competence-competence) were transferred to it (decision Pl. ÚS 29/09 of 3 November 2009).

---

set forth in the basic treaties – Hungary may exercise some of its authorities stemming from the Constitution in conjunction with the other member states through the institutions of the European Union.'

In sum, it became obvious that in all examined jurisdictions the judicial understanding of the sovereignty doctrine is based on two fundamental assumptions: First, the European Union does not exert sovereign powers and thus the primacy principle of EU law should be limited to those cases, where the member states explicitly transferred power to the EU. Second, there are some 'inalienable' powers, namely the power to waive the power of transferring powers. Accordingly the whole process of transfer of powers should be controlled by the Constitutional Courts, since the courts control the constitutionality of the integration process understood as further, long-term association of cooperating sovereign states. Hence, judicial empowerment of Constitutional Courts seems to play an important if not pivotal role in this process.

However, this approach has been challenged by the Austrian Federal Constitutional Court. In its decision on the constitutionality of the Charter of Fundamental Rights (which I would like to call '*Solange 5*') the Court established an *a posteriori* review jurisdiction over the application of the Charter of Fundamental Rights of the European Union. The Court observed that

> the Constitutional Court, after having referred a matter for a preliminary ruling to the Court of Justice of the European Union according to Article 267 TFEU as appropriate, takes the Charter of Fundamental Rights in its scope of application as a standard for national law (Article 51(1) CFR) and sets aside contradicting general norms according to Article 139 and/or Article 140 Federal Constitutional Act (B-VG). In this manner, the Constitutional Court fulfils its obligation to remove from the domestic legal order provisions incompatible with Community law, which is also postulated by the Court of Justice of the European Union (judgement U 466/11-18 of 14 March 2013).

Certainly this challenge does not affect every other member state to the same degree, since the applicability of the Charter is to some extent limited e.g. in Poland and the Czech Republic.[8] Nevertheless, the emerging doctrine of sovereignty understood as the power to ultimate control over the constitutionality of legal acts will be seriously weakened by the prospect of harmonisation of the application of the EU Charter of Fundamental Rights through the member states. The Austrian Federal Constitutional Court has concluded that the Charter may be enforced in front of the Constitutional Court as if it contained 'constitutionally guaranteed rights', and, furthermore, that the Charter may serve as a standard of review of constitutionality of domestic law. This issue seems to play an important role in constructing the framework of the EU legal order. It seems that the application of Charter could at least to some extent bring more coherence

8 See Sadurski 2012, 4–13; for a different view see ibid., 76–78.

and participatory judicial dialogue into increasingly polarised conflict on the *competence-competence* issue. Alternatively it may predict the final chapter of this never-ending story, namely the chapter entitled the ultimate constitutionalisation of the European Union as federal legal order.

This conclusion leads to another problem, explicitly articulated by Neil MacCormick (1999), i.e. the feasibility of an attempt to build a hierarchical legal system in the EU or the possibility of an ultimate solution to the problem of sovereignty and the ultimate superiority of the EU or alternatively, the national legal systems. Two solutions, presented by the German and the Austrian constitutional courts seem to be available and to incorporate this problem. It seems that the distinction between inclusive and exclusive sovereignty may play an important role in finding a proper solution to this problem, and to become a kind of effective 'shock absorber.'

3. Inclusive sovereignty and the concept of a complex legal system

The theory of a complex legal system offers a peculiar description of the structure and functions of contemporary public institutions. The main characteristics of the systemic nature of law include a coexistence of various judicial bodies and institutional structures working on adjudication within a given jurisdiction. This kind of coexistence of adjudicating institutions leads to the evolution of their adjudicative functions and expansion of their jurisdiction due to a creative interpretation of existing constitutional and statutory laws. Since some courts of last instance have gained autonomous positions as institutions responsible for constitutional review of lawmaking process and for judicial control of the administration, the problem of interpretation and validity of existing legal rules becomes a crucial element. In other words, the institutional practice of judicial bodies leads to the creation of new legal concepts, principles and rules. This expansion of judicial power seems however to be diversified. In general, the transformation from simple to complex legal systems is discernible on two levels, internal and external.

Internally, the constitutionalisation of a legal order accompanied by the emancipation of judicial institutions inevitably leads to competition and conflict between higher courts. The tensions between judges of the Constitutional Tribunal, the Supreme Administrative Court and the Supreme Court in Poland may serve here as a good illustration of the evolution from a relatively simple hierarchical legal system to a complex system based on self-referring rules (see also Rafał Mańko's chapter in this volume). According to art. 8.2 of the Polish Constitution its provisions 'shall apply directly, unless the Constitution provides otherwise.' The question remains how to understand the scope and meaning of the very term *direct application.* According to the judges of the Polish Constitutional Tribunal, no other court is authorised to decide on the constitutionality of specific statutory rules. In case of doubt the court shall rather initiate a preliminary reference procedure before the Constitutional Tribunal.

Other high courts such as the Supreme Court and Supreme Administrative Court have been questioning this interpretation of art. 8.2 They claim that in some special cases the unconstitutionality could lead to an automatic invalidation of a given unconstitutional provision by the adjudicating court. In particular, the Supreme Administrative Court invented the doctrine of 'ostensible unconstitutionality' according to which it can declare unconstitutionality in some obvious cases. Additionally, the court claimed an exclusive power to review statutory regulations enacted by the government. A similar conflict between constitutional and ordinary courts took place in France, where during the 1980s the Constitutional Council initiated constitutional review in form of interpretative judgements (*réserves strictes d'interprétation*), whereas other courts sometimes ignored its verdicts. As Alec Stone Sweet (1992, 2007) observed, the French Court of Cassation gradually developed a rule that required judges to interpret statutory provisions in a way coherent with constitutional law. The Council of State finally adjusted general principles of administrative law such as 'individual liberty', 'equality before the law', and 'freedom of conscience' to equivalent constitutional rights (Stone Sweet 1992, 80–93).

Externally, the question arises whether the efficacy of EU law in the member states leads to the creation of a single complex legal system or to interacting legal systems. This problem can accurately be analysed with the theory of Joseph Raz, who distinguished two different situations: an integrity of legal orders leading to the creation of a single complex legal system, and the exceptional operation of one system within a jurisdiction over the other one, which does not lead to a creation of a single complex system. In discussing the issue of membership criteria of a legal system, Raz (1980, 102) assumes that a legal system contains norms which should be applied by norm applying institutions such as courts. His focus on law applying rather than on law making institutions results from the fact that judicial organs ultimately decide on the adopted criteria of validity and their institutionalised practice could be reconstructed in form of the rule of recognition adopted by a given legal system.

Additionally, Raz (1979, 87–88; 1980, 189–197) distinguishes two different situations or reasons for application of some legal rules within a legal system: First, some rules may belong to a given legal system and create a part of it. Second, some rules may operate within a legal system but do not necessarily belong to it. The latter operation of legal rules is based on permission of a legal system in which those rules operate as effective but external norms. If rules could operate either as a part of a legal system or without becoming a part of a system, just due to the permission to operate as an external norm within a given system, than the question arises about the criteria or conditions for distinguishing between the internal and external efficacy of rules. Certainly the evidence justifying external or internal operation of a given legal rule should be referred to the practice of adjudicating bodies and the justifications provided by them.

4. Conclusion

A divergence between two rulings on the superiority of the EU law two member states means that the operation of EU law in these national legal systems is of different character. The divergent application of the superiority principle leads to the conclusion that the EU legal system as a whole could rightly be perceived as a complex one. Certainly such a legal system could remain a simple one, if the practice of the ECJ would constitute a single and sufficiently coherent rule of recognition. However, this is not the case at least at the present stage of European integration, although the most recent decision of the Austrian Constitutional Court may pave a way to this kind of unification through constitutionalisation. The question remains how a complex legal system like the European one would be changed in the long run if there exist many courts formally independent from the ECJ and at the same time belonging to different judicial structures.

Acknowledgement

This research was supported in the framework of TÁMOP 4.2.4. A/2-11-1-2012-0001 „National Excellence Program – Elaborating and operating an inland student and researcher personal support system' key project. The project was subsidised by the European Union and co-financed by the European Social Fund.

References

Arrighi, Giovanni. 1994. *The Long Twentieth Century: Money, Power and the Origin of Our Times*. London, New York: Verso.

Arrighi, Giovanni, Silver, Beverly J. 1999. *Chaos and Governance in the Modern World System*. Minneapolis et al.: University of Minnesota Press.

Austin, John. 1832. *The Province of Jurisprudence Determined.* Cambridge et al.: Cambridge University Press 1995.
Beck, Ulrich. 1992. *Risk Society: Towards a New Modernity*. London et al.: Sage.
Blutman, László, and Chronowski, Nora. 2011. Hungarian Constitutional Court: Keeping Aloof from European Union Law. *Vienna Journal on International Constitutional Law* 5: 329–348.
Bodin, Jean. 1583. *Les six livres de la republique*. Aalen: Scientia 1961.
Hart, Herbert L.A. 1964. Self-Referring Laws. In *Festskrift tillägnad Professor, Juris Doktor, Karl Olivecrona vid hans avgang fran professorsämbetet den 30 juni 1964 av kolleger, lärjungar och vänner*, edited by Fritjof Lejman, 307–316. Stockholm: Norstedt & Söner.
Hobbes Thomas. 1651. *Leviathan*. London: Penguin 1985.
Kelsen Hans. 1992. *Introduction to the Problems of Legal Theory.* Oxford: Clarendon Press.
MacCormick, Neil. 1999. *Questioning Sovereignty: Law, State and Nation in the European Commonwealth*. Oxford: Oxford University Press.
Raz, Joseph. 1980. *The Concept of a Legal System: An Introduction to the Theory of Legal System*. Oxford: Oxford University Press, 2nd ed.
Raz, Joseph. 1979. *The Authority of Law*. Oxford: Oxford University Press.
Sadurski, Wojciech. 2006. 'Solange, Chapter 3': Constitutional Courts in Central Europe – Democracy – European Union. *EUI LAW Working Paper*, 2006/40.
Sadurski, Wojciech. 2012. *Constitutionalism and the Enlargement of Europe*. Oxford et al.: Oxford University Press.
Schmitt, Carl. 1922. *Politische Theologie. Vier Kapitel zur Lehre von der Souveränität*. Berlin: Duncker & Humblot 1996, 7th ed.
Staniszkis, Jadwiga. 2003. *Władza globalizacji [The Power of Globalisation]*. Warszawa: Scholar.
Stone Sweet, Alec. 1992. *The Birth of Judicial Politics in France*. New York: Oxford University Press.
Stone Sweet, Alec. 2007. The Juridical Coup d'État and the Problem of Authority. *German Law Journal* 8: 915–926.

Court Rulings
European Court of Justice

Case C-26/62 *Van Gend en Loos v Nederlandse Administratie der Belastingen*
Case C-6/64 *Flaminio Costa v ENEL*
Case 11/70 *Internationale Handelsgesellschaft v Einfuhr und Vorratsstelle Getreide*
Case 106/77 *Amministrazione delle Finanze dello Stato v. Simmenthal SpA*
Case C-299/95 *Friedrich Kremzow v Republik Österreich*
Joined Cases C-402/05 P and C-415/05 *P. Yassin Abdullah Kadi and Al Barakaat International Foundation v Council of the European Union and Commission of the European Communities*

Austrian Federal Constitutional Court

Judgement U 466/11-18 of 14 March 2013

Czech Constitutional Court

Judgement Pl ÚS 50/04 of 8 March 2006
Judgement Pl. ÚS 29/09 of 3 November 2009
Judgement Pl. ÚS 5/12 of 31 January 2012

German Federal Constitutional Court

Judgement of 29 May 1974, 37 BVerfGE 271
Judgement of 22 October 1986, 73 BVerfGE 339
Judgement 2 BvR 2236/04 of 18 July 2005
Judgement 2 BvE 2/08 of 30 June 2009
Judgement 2 BvR 2728/13 of 14 January 2014

Hungarian Constitutional Court

Judgement 17/2004 of 25 May 2004
Judgement 61/B/2005 of 29 September 2008
Judgement 143/2010 of 12 July 2010

Polish Constitutional Tribunal

Judgement P 1/05 of 27 April 2005
Judgement K 18/04 of 11 May 2005
Judgement K 32/09 of 24 November 2010
Judgement SK 45/09 of 16 November 2011

The Balancing Role of National Parliaments in Transforming the European Union. Towards a Parliamentary Polity?

Karolina Ristova-Asterud

Abstract

The Lisbon Treaty of 2009 represents a serious step moving the EU away from the path of de-parliamentarisation, typical since its foundation, towards a path of re-parliamentarisation. This is done not only by strengthening the European Parliament, but also by providing national parliaments of the member states a more active role. This chapter aims to present how the recent treaty novelties regarding national parliaments affect the balance of power in the intergovernmental system of EU governance. On a more theoretical level, it explores how the shared European intellectual traditions on sovereignty have influenced these developments, and how they may further transform the EU from a dominantly intergovernmental into a parliamentary polity.

1. Introduction

Even before entering into force on 1 December 2009, the Lisbon Treaty had started to be commonly referred to as 'the Treaty on Parliaments.' One of the main reasons for this qualification was the inclusion of five articles (articles 3, 8.a, 8.c, 48 and 49) in the main treaty text referring to the national parliaments, with art. 8c as the most significant, for its central role in stipulating how 'national parliaments contribute actively to the good functioning of the Union' (now Art. 12 TEU).[1] Until then, in almost sixty years of the EC/EU existence, national parliaments were absent from the main texts of the EC/EU treaties, and only implicitly referred to. In addition, for the first time, annexed to the Lisbon Treaty are two legally binding protocols that regulate the role of national parliaments in the EU: *the Protocol on the Role of National Parliaments in the European Union* (PRNP) and *the Protocol on the Application of the Principles of Subsidiarity and Proportionality* (PAPSP).[2]

1 In the *Consolidated versions of the Treaty on European Union* (TEU) *and the Treaty on the Functioning of the European Union* (TFEU). Official Journal of the European Union, 2010/C 83/01, the five articles are incorporated in articles 5, 10, 12, 48 and 49 TEU and articles 69, 70, 71, 81, 85, 88 and 352 TFEU.

2 Ibid., 203–209.

These treaty novelties are not mere nomotechnics, but rather indicate a significant shift in the conceptual premises of EU governance. As presented in section 2, these changes have been triggered by gradual developments in the political contexts of EU member states, only to culminate on EU's supranational level in the process of ratifying the Maastricht Treaty, and in a form of a wide-open debate about 'the democratic deficit in the EU' in the mid-1990s (see Majone 1998, 5–28; Moravcsik 2002, 603–634; Follesdall and Hix 2006, 533–562). The main criticism has boiled down to the claim that the EU's institutional design has not been set-up to meet the tenets of parliamentary democracy, has not reflected constitutionally embedded political values of the member states, and, consequently, has not claimed popular political legitimacy. Governmental ministers by 'flying to Brussels' transform into main legislators in the Council. The parliamentarians, though elected citizens' representatives, are side-lined into co-legislators, as those in the European Parliament (EP), and with little information and say in the European affairs.

In effect, the EU's democratic deficit has been, and still is, primarily perceived as 'parliamentary deficit.' As such, it must be dealt with treaty reforms. Sections 3 and 4 focus on the reforms that the Lisbon Treaty has introduced regarding national parliaments, in particular how they affect the balance of power in EU governance. In section 5 I turn to the theoretical aspects of the issue, and assert that these treaty novelties are rooted in the shared European intellectual traditions on sovereignty. I conclude with a proposition that the process of EU's re-parliamentarisation by way of strengthening the competences of both national parliaments and EP may prospectively transform the EU from a predominantly intergovernmental to a parliamentary polity.

2. Defining and positioning of national parliaments in the EU's political system

There are 28 national parliaments in the EU, out of which 15 are unicameral and 13 bicameral. As a matter of constitutional autonomy, each member state defines what constitutes the 'national parliament' in its own constitutional order. Despite the differences (see Kiiver 2006, 4), it seems that the term is used as a catch-all denomination on EU level. National parliaments are treated as self-explaining and uniform institutions, common to the European traditions of the separation of powers concept, in which parliaments are the representative bodies in charge of certain common functions: ratification of EU treaties, transposition of EU legislature into national legal orders, and scrutiny over their governments in EU affairs.

The principle of constitutional autonomy is also crucial for understanding the process of positioning national parliaments in the EU. Its prevalent feature is the *bottom-up approach*: novelties usually first emerge in parliamentary practices and national constitutions, and then finding verification in the EU treaty framework. Three phases can be identified:

Initially, the EC/EU affairs were treated as foreign affairs (mid 1950s–mid 1980s), and dealt with through established bodies and procedures commonly used for parliamentary competences in international relations (see Norton 1996; Maurer and Wessels 2001). Specialised European affairs committees (EAC) were established only in the German *Bundesrat* in 1957 and in the Belgian national parliament in 1962. Only in these two member states the ratification instruments of EC treaties contained an explicit government's obligation to inform national parliaments about EC legislature. In practice, however, EC legislation would quite often come up for debate only after it had been decided on EC level (see Bulmer 1986, 225; de Winter 1996, 77). The Italian national parliament went further by adopting periodical omnibus laws that delegated legislative competences to the government to deal with the 'international obligations' from Brussels (see Furlong 1996, 38–39).

In the next period (mid 1980s–mid 1990s), national parliaments started to make institutional adjustments to cope with the European integration. This was triggered by the first EC enlargement that brought Denmark and the United Kingdom into membership, two countries with history of strong parliaments. Both national parliaments from the very start tied the EC membership to establishing strong EACs and special procedures for scrutinising EC's political and legislative decision-making process. In 1974, the Danish EAC had established *de facto* procedure by which the government was politically obliged to obtain parliamentary mandate prior to each EC decision of greater political significance, while the British House of Commons adopted to similar effect the so-called *Scrutiny Reserve Resolution* in 1980. In addition, the *Act concerning the Elections of the Representatives of the Assembly by Direct Universal Suffrage* of 1976 introduced direct elections to the EP, thus ending the 'dual mandate' of national parliamentarians. Finally, the *Single European Act* in 1987 increased the EC's legislative competences in areas that had not been perceived as 'foreign affairs' (health, environment, economic and social cohesion).

These events triggered the formation of EACs in each national parliament, accompanied with procedural reforms for *ex-ante* information and decisional influence in EU affairs (European Parliament 1989). The cutting-off of the ties with the EP had led national parliaments to find other forms of inter-parliamentary co-operation on European level. First such form was the *Conference of Speakers of*

National Parliaments of the EC that had first assembled in 1963. It has been regularly functioning as a semi-annual forum since 1975. A more ambitious project was the formation of the *Conference of Parliamentary Committees for EC Affairs* (COSAC) in 1989.

The third phase covers the period between the Maastricht Treaty of 1993 and the Lisbon Treaty of 2009, when the role of national parliaments in EU affairs have started to be constitutionalised, both in national constitutions and in the EU's treaty framework. *Declaration No. 13 on the role of national parliaments in the European Union* attached to the TEU for the first time declared the importance of greater involvement of national parliaments in EU's activities and that the governments must ensure that national parliaments receive Commission's legislative proposals 'in good time for information or possible examination.' TEU's referendum failures in Denmark and France in 1992, as well as the growing debate on 'the democratic deficit in the EU' turned this declarative consideration into a legally binding one with the *Protocol on the role of national parliaments in the European Union* attached to the Amsterdam Treaty of 1997. The Protocol went further and specified which Commission's documents must be made available 'in good time' to the national parliaments by their governments. Subsequently, the *Laeken Declaration on the future of the European Union* (2001) mandated the Convention of the Future of Europe of 2002–2003 to concretely define the role of national parliaments in the EU treaty framework. This indeed was reflected in the *Treaty on the Constitution of Europe* of 2004, which, however, failed to enter into force because of the negative referenda in France and the Netherlands in 2005. Nevertheless, all its novelties on national parliaments subsequently were included in the Lisbon Treaty.

On the member states level, pioneering amendments to the constitutions of France (art. 88-4) and Germany (articles 23 and 45) were introduced in 1992, by which national parliaments, their EACs, and the relations with their governments in the EU affairs have become a constitutional matter. In Germany, this was followed by implementing laws regulating parliament-government relations in the EU affairs. This constitutional approach was followed in all subsequent EU enlargements since then (1995, 2004, 2007 and 2013). Finally, the Lisbon Treaty gave national parliaments a treaty status by including articles on their position and roles in the EU in the main treaty text. TEU and TFEU now provide for a better legal logistics for the roles that national parliaments have already on the 'horizontal level' of the member states, especially to those previously left to national constitutional autonomy. The real novelties consist of some new 'vertical powers' that enable national parliaments to influence the EU's supranational level more directly.

3. The horizontal balancing role of national parliaments *vis-a-vis* national governments after Lisbon

3.1 Stronger position in the revision and ratification of EU treaties

In EU's historical context of solidarity and cooperation, treaty ratification has traditionally been the weakest parliamentary function. With hardly any prior information, national parliaments have almost always obediently ratified all treaties that their governments arranged, with only two cases of refusal to ratify.[3] After Lisbon, art. 12.d TEU provides for an early notification and involvement of national parliaments in both ordinary and simplified treaty revision procedures in accordance with art. 48 TEU, including a veto power in the case of the *passerelle clauses* that allow the European Council to change certain treaty voting procedures or legislative procedures. Similarly, when it comes to accession treaties, national parliaments must be notified of every accession applications in the same time as the EP (art. 12.e TEU). The notifications of intended treaty revisions have to come to national parliaments directly from the EU supranational level at the same time as to their governments, which should enable national parliaments to influence the process much earlier than the 'take it or leave it' moment of treaty ratification so far.

3.2 Stronger position in the transposition of EU legislation on national level

National parliaments have never had much leverage in the transposition of EU directives. They are legally binding in their aim, and the only legal discretion that national parliaments are left with is the manner of their transposition in the national legal order. Prior to Lisbon, national parliaments depended on the information received and the transposition laws prepared by their governments, accepting them as *fait accompli*. The problem was worsened by the slow adaption of national parliaments in terms of specialised parliamentary bodies and procedures, as well as inadequate capacity of expert parliamentary staff to deal with the transposition.[4] The legislative role of national parliaments was also weakened by the fact that most directives were transposed with governmental by-laws or acts of independent regulatory bodies. Now, art. 12a TEU obliges EU institutions to forward all draft legislative acts to national parliaments in accordance with the

3 In 1954 the French Assembly refused to ratify the *Treaty establishing the European Defence Community*, while in 1986 the Danish Folketing refused to ratify the *Single European Act*, but only to be ratified the same year on a referendum.

4 For comparative study of the role of national parliaments in the European legislative process prior Lisbon Treaty see Maurer and Wessels 2001.

PRNP. On its part, the Protocol provides for an elaborate procedure for forwarding draft legislative acts and other EU documents, including Commission's annual legislative programmes, to the national parliaments *at the same time as* to the EU's co-legislators, i.e. the EP and the Council. In effect, the dominance of national governments over the European legislative process by monopolising EU legislative information has ended.

3.3 Improved parliamentary scrutiny over national governments in the EU affairs

Parliamentary scrutiny over national governments in the EU affairs is one of the original functions of national parliaments in EU's political system. However, it found a treaty expression not before the Maastricht Treaty. Art. 10.2 TEU now stipulates that member states are represented in the European Council by their heads of state or government and in the Council by their governments, themselves *democratically accountable either to their national Parliaments* or their citizens. Because of the intergovernmental nature of these particular EU institutions, much of the efforts for eliminating EU's parliamentary deficit has concerned the scrutiny role of national parliaments – better scrutiny over the governments, greater, though indirect, parliamentary influence in EU governance. Before the First Enlargement in the 1970s, national parliaments' scrutiny powers in EU affairs were characteristically *ex-post*. Only by following the models of parliamentary mandates and scrutiny reserve resolutions in the British and Danish parliaments, national parliaments had started to move towards developing an *ex-ante* scrutiny in the 1980s. However, that scrutiny for many years had largely remained in the area of EU's first pillar. As Maurer and Wessels (2001, 444–445) have pointed out, when it came to EU's second and third pillar, national parliaments continued to face an information deficit. The problem was worsened by the 'pure' intergovernmental nature of these pillars, set-up to function less transparently, with intergovernmental negotiations and voting procedures 'behind closed doors.' Still, COSAC research has shown that by 2007 most member states had developed distinct systems of parliamentary scrutiny in the EU affairs differentiated as: 'document- based system' (scrutiny of the content of individual legislative and other EU documents), 'procedural system' (scrutiny focused on the EU decision-making process, accompanied with parliamentary mandate prior to EU legislative or other decision) and 'hybrid system' (scrutiny that combines elements of the previous two; see COSAC 2007, 7–19).

Post-Lisbon, art. 12c TEU provides for national parliaments' involvement in the evaluation mechanisms for implementation of EU policies in the areas of freedom, security and justice, as well as for political monitoring of Europol and Eurojust activities. The ratification process of the Lisbon Treaty was also used by national parliaments as leverage *vis-a-vis* their governments to introduce new scrutiny mechanisms. A recent example for this is Austria's *EU Information Law* of 2012 that has enhanced the scrutiny powers of both federal parliamentary chambers by allowing them access to the Council's extranet, and introducing an obligation for the federal government to inform the chambers about 'future EU projects' on a semi-annual basis. Other member states have introduced internal parliament-government electronic databases for EU affairs.[5]

3.4 Influencing national nominations for EU posts

In 1994, Austria became a pioneering member state by introducing a constitutional basis for parliamentary involvement in the national nominations for EU posts. Art. 23c of the Austrian Constitution obliges the federal government to seek approval of the national parliament regarding nominations for members in the Commission, judges in the EU courts and members of the Management Committee of the European Investment Bank. The Austrian example may be followed by other member states also as a reflection of the new power of the EP to elect the President and approve the other members of the Commission (art. 17.7 TEU). It seems to be almost certain that national parliaments will mimic the 'politicisation' of this process on a national level.

4. The vertical balancing role of national parliaments on EU's supranational level after Lisbon

4.1 Participation in the 'convention method' of the EU treaty revision process

The Lisbon Treaty makes national parliaments direct treaty-making players on EU's supranational level. In ordinary treaty revision procedure, national parliaments are not only notified of the amending proposals but also participate at a convention called upon by the President of the European Council, where representatives of national parliaments deliberate on treaty revisions on equal footing with their governments, heads of state, the EP and the Commission. Only after the convention's consensual recommendation can an intergovernmental conference be convened to determine the revisions by common accord and submit them to ratification process in the member states (art. 48.3–48.5 TEU). This 'convention method' is not quite a new experience. It is only a treaty verification of a previous

5 For more on parliamentary changes after Lisbon, see COSAC 2012.

one, which has already been used for the *Charter of Fundamental Rights of the European Union* (1999–2000) and for the European Constitution of 2004. In both cases, the convention's composition was dominated by national parliaments' representatives, who were much organised, active and influential in shaping the documents (see Kijljunen 2004, 191–195). Most probably, national parliaments will make most of this new competences to further strengthen their scrutiny powers.

4.2 Direct participation in the supranational legislative process (the early warning system)

Art. 12b TEU gives national parliaments competence to guard the legislative border between the member states and the EU level by giving them scrutiny powers over the application of the subsidiarity principle in accordance with PAPSP. In effect, with respect to the Commission's legislative proposals that are not in the areas of the Union's exclusive competences, each *individual* national parliament has eight weeks to object on grounds of a subsidiarity breach by sending a reasoned opinion directly to the Commission (art. 6 PAPSP). National parliaments can also act *collectively* to protect the subsidiarity through the 'yellow' and 'orange' card procedures. In the former, if reasoned opinion is submitted by one-third of the votes allocated to national parliaments (each national parliaments has two), the Commission is obliged to give national parliaments a reasoned explanation why it keeps, changes or withdraws its proposal (art. 7.2 PAPSP). The latter refers only to the legislative proposals in the co-decision procedure and is almost identical with the 'yellow card.' However, if the Commission wants to keep the proposal, it must send a reasoned opinion to both EP and Council, which as Union's co-legislators have the final say (art. 7.3 PAPSP).

The most recent COSAC and Commission reports indicate that after four years of implementation, the role of national parliaments in protecting the subsidiarity has proven to be a success: The timeframe of eight weeks has proven to be generally sufficient and the Commission has been responsive on a satisfactory level (COSAC 2013, 26–34). Moreover, the early warning system has stimulated an unprecedented direct political communication between the Commission and national parliaments, both in the preparation of legislative proposals, and in obtaining timely responses to national parliaments' reasoned opinions, which amount to 663 only in 2012.[6] This may be the reason why the 'orange card' has not been used yet,

---

6 See *Annual Report 2012 on Relations between the European Commission and the National Parliaments* [http://ec.europa.eu/dgs/secretariat_general/relations/relations_other/national parliamentso/docs/ar_2012_en.pdf, accessed on 17.09.2013].

and the 'yellow card' has been triggered only once. This relative success can also be explained by the great preparatory efforts in terms of strengthening national parliaments' legal, institutional, procedural and administrative capacity to deal with the subsidiarity scrutiny role (see COSAC 2011, 26–61). In fact, since the introduction of the principle in the Maastricht Treaty in 1993 until 2005, almost half of the national parliaments have embraced the role (see COSAC 2005, 77–79), and have only upgraded it ever since. Depending on the overall performance, in future treaty reforms national parliaments may extend their ambitions for an *ex-ante* subsidiarity scrutiny in the area of Union's exclusive competences, and demand a 'red card,' i.e. a real veto power to block legislative proposals in the co-decision procedure.

4.3 Action for annulment of EU legislation by the Court of Justice of EU (ECJ)

National parliaments (or their chambers) have also gained power to protect subsidiarity *ex post* by initiating an action for annulment of EU legislation on grounds of subsidiarity breach before the ECJ. However, in accordance with the rules laid down in art. 230 TFEU, national parliaments can submit such an action only via their governments. That is why constitutional amendments have been introduced in some member states (like France, Germany or Austria), whereby governments are obliged to submit the annulment action on the behalf of their national parliaments to the ECJ. In other member states, the dominant view is that their constitutional regimes of parliamentary democracy oblige the government for such an action (COSAC 2010, 29), which remains to be tested because no national parliament has initiated such an action yet.

4.4 Institutionalised inter-parliamentary cooperation and influence

Art. 10 PRNP institutionalises COSAC as part of the EU's political system and enumerates its roles as submitting contributions it deems appropriate to the attention of EP, the Council and the Commission; exchanging information and best practices between national parliaments and EP; and organising inter-parliamentary conferences on specific topics, in particular on the matters of foreign, defence and security policies. Again, the Lisbon Treaty only incorporates established practices that COSAC has developed since its formation in 1989. Its semi-annual reports on the best parliamentary practices and procedures in the EU affairs have been playing a crucial role in developing a more uniform institutional functioning across the national parliaments. Its contributions have influenced the shaping of treaty provisions regarding national parliaments in the treaties of Amsterdam, Nice and Lisbon. Its pilot projects and working groups during the Convention on the Future of Europe (2002–2003) have enabled national parliaments to better prepare for the early warning system, as well as changing the initial proposal of six to eight weeks for national parliaments' reasoned opinions. Moreover, these pilot projects had given the initial indications that the optimal application of the yellow and orange cards might be hindered in practice by differing parliamentary interest for certain legislative proposals, and that it would be hard to mobilise their votes (see Kiiver 2006, 158–161), as it has proved to be so with the so-called 'Monti II' regulation in 2012 as the only case of 'yellow card' so far.

5. EU re-parliamentarisation and the paradigmatic influence of the shared European intellectual traditions on sovereignty

The outlined strengthening of the competences and balancing roles of national parliaments, taken together with the strengthening of the EP, represent a definitive process of re-parliamentarisation of EU governance post-Lisbon. From a more theoretical view, this marks an important shift in the normative narrative on the *telos* of European integration and the meaning of democracy in the EU. I suggest that with the Lisbon Treaty, the shared European intellectual traditions on sovereignty are finally catching up in shaping the EU's political and institutional design. I also suggest that the long-term ignorance of these traditions is one of the reasons that had caused the problem of the EU's 'democratic deficit.'

In the many decades of the EU polity's institutional evolution, the powerful legacy of the so-called 'Westphalian paradigm' had been ignored. Ever since the Treaty of Westphalia of 1648, the modern idea of European statehood was understood as a stable political formation with an unchallenged, uniform, and one-dimensional *imperium* over defined territory and population. The political reality of this concept was intertwined with the intellectual legacy of the 16th–17th centuries' political philosophy of Bodin, Hobbes, later followed by Hegel, John Austin and Carl Schmitt, and staying viable deep into the 20th century. In terms of the internal state sovereignty, liberal political philosophy (Locke, Rousseau, Kant, Bentham, John Stuart Mill, Weber), reinforced with the American and French revolutions of the 18th century, have been shaping the concept of popular sovereignty, variably centred in the individual, the *demos* or the nation, but always embodied in its representative institution – the parliament (see Prokhovnik 2008).

It is this particular legacy that still dominates the political culture and the constitutional systems of EU member states, but in the same time that had not been embedded in the foundations of the EC/EU. So far, the EU has not been perceived as a 'state polity' on which the standards of a parliamentary state should or could be applied, but rather as an intergovernmental organisation, more so because its member states had been and remain to be the 'masters of the treaties.' The core of this political and doctrinal approach has remained to be dominant, despite of the growing transfer of competences to the EC/EU over the decades. It has remained basically unchanged even after the EU's legal order had been declared *sui generis* by the ECJ's jurisprudence, and even after the ECJ additionally had developed state-like concepts, such as the principle of direct effect of EU law and the principle of supremacy of EU law (all in the early 1960s).

The best explanation for the refusal to project the Westphalian paradigm on EU can be found in the reasoning of Giandomenico Majone (1998, 5–28). He has famously asserted that the de-politicisation and de-parliamentarisation of the EU had been the price to be paid to go ahead with deeper economic integration without sacrificing the state sovereignty, or creating a 'European super-state' to which a majority of European citizens were opposed. Moreover, those EU democratic and parliamentary deficits were and still are 'democratically justified', and any analogy with the parliamentary democracy on state level unfounded. Additionally, he argued that the EU as a polity has technocratic competences over 'efficiency oriented policies' on Union level, and consequently the standards for evaluating its institutions should move away from 'majoritarian' political standards of decisions towards technocratic 'non-majoritarian' standards of results. In effect, this means accepting the EU as an intergovernmental technocratic polity based on functional legitimacy, as well as on derivative parliamentary legitimacy provided by national parliaments' support of the national ministers who also serve in EU's Council of ministers.

However, as presented earlier, the derivative parliamentary legitimacy of EU's institutions, did not have such a sparkling record in practice as in the Majone's theory. Furthermore, as Follessdal and Hix (2006, 533–562) pointed out, the EU's competences over the years have expanded, and most are not 'efficiency oriented', but have a redistributive nature, and, as such, have to be decided in a democratic political process. Consequently, an analogous model of parliamentary democracy is necessary for the EU's institutional design and legitimisation. As it had become painfully obvious in the mid-1990s, European citizens tended to agree more with the position expressed by Follessdal and Hix than with the one of Majone.

What the governmental 'masters of the treaties' seem to have underestimated is that the Westphalian paradigm over the years has become part of the jurisprudence of both ECJ and national constitutional courts. In the ECJ's *Van Gend* decision, the principle of direct effect was judicially reasoned out from the preambles of the EC/EU treaties that clearly refer not only to the member states, but also to their 'peoples.' On member states level, it was the German Federal Constitutional Court that first reinstated the Westphalian paradigm in its interpretation of the nature of the EU polity in its famous *Brunner* decision on TEU of 1994. According to this judgement, the EU is in essence a union of sovereign states (*Staatenverbund*), and as such it does not have competences to decide over its competences (*Kompetenz-Kompetenz*). That power remains in the hands of the member states' sovereign, institutionally embodied in the national parliaments. The most controversial part of that decision was the Court's elaboration that the EU may aspire to such powers only if it transforms into a state, and that it can transform into a state only if it develops a *demos* in a socio-cultural sense (shared history, language, cultural traditions, etc.).

The same legal reasoning was restated by the German court in its *Lisbon case* of 2009, when it struck down the *Act extending* and *strengthening the rights of the Bundestag and the Bundesrat in European Union matters* accompanying the ratification of the Lisbon Treaty, as it had found it violating the parliamentary rights enshrined in the German Basic Law. Both the ECJ and the German Federal Constitutional Court subscribe to the unitary, hierarchical and one-dimensional legacy of the Westphalian paradigm on sovereignty, where the difference lies in that the ECJ, although implicitly, ties it to the new *sui generis* EU polity and its supranational parliamentarism, and the German court ties it to national statehood and national parliamentarism (see also Mariusz Jerzy Golecki's chapter in this volume).

6. Conclusion: The EU as a prospective parliamentary polity?

Four years since the implementation of the Lisbon Treaty, the trial period of the actual effects of national parliaments' new powers is still going on and somewhat inconclusive. Despite the new mechanisms to change the balance of power *vis-a-vis* national governments, there are grounds for some scepticism whether national parliaments are up to the task, especially when it comes to their political and administrative capacity to deal with the new competences. With respect to the vertical powers, one can also doubt whether parliamentary majorities, with strong coordination and scrutinising powers over their governments, would be prepared to show political discord on the supranational level.

However, the initial experiences are encouraging in terms of the potential of national parliaments' new competences to affect the balance of power and to decrease the democratic deficit in the EU. National parliaments are much better informed about the EU affairs, especially about the main legislative and policy proposals, and, for the most part, simultaneously with their governments. Their *ex-ante* and *ex-post* scrutiny powers over their governments (and, indirectly, over the Council and the Commission) are becoming more effective and efficient, set on the way to satisfy in the EU context the analogue standards of parliamentary governance of the member states. These powers are also definitely reinforced with the new vertical powers of national parliaments, most notably the power to *ex-ante* influence the primary law of the EU ('the Convention method') and the powers to protect the subsidiarity in the European legislative process (the early warning system and the action before ECJ). Moreover, for the first time in the EU history, these new vertical powers make the national parliaments players in the balancing of power on the supranational level. Not less important is the fact that the competences of national parliaments are not anymore primarily a matter of parliamentary practices and culture on national level, but very much a matter of constitutionalisation, both in national constitutions and the EU treaty framework.

What I would like to point out as most important tendency in the aftermath of the Lisbon Treaty is that the EU is a on an irreversible path of transforming its nature towards a parliamentary polity. As of now, the very influential *Brunner* and *Lisbon* jurisprudence of the German constitutional court suggests the contrary, i.e. that a full-fledged supranational parliamentary system 'beyond the state' is not possible, at least not without turning the EU into a federal state, and not without the formation of a *demos* in a socio-cultural sense. Although still as a matter of theoretical debate, I agree with the view that it is indeed unlikely that EU will ever turn into a federal state as its *sui generis* nature is deeply embedded in its institutional design and a widely accepted norm. Nevertheless, I also assert that that this does not necessarily imply that the model of parliamentary democracy cannot be projected unto the future development of the EU polity. The current re-parliamentarisation attests to the strong and open-ended influence of the Westphalian parliamentary paradigm in the EU governance, separate and without its accompanying legacy of one-dimensional and uniform state sovereignty.

In fact, the concept of 'state sovereignty' is going through a reconfiguration 'beyond national statehood' in the EU context. Alternative normative paradigms of multidimensional, heterarchical and pluralistic sovereignty are being developed, such as the concept of 'shared sovereignty' (Stephen D. Krasner) and 'post-sovereignty' (Neil MacCormick; see Walker 2006). In these novel concepts, the EU is seen as polity that could be functioning as a *sui generis* multi-level parliamentary democracy, very much modelled on the German federalist and parliamentary principles. I subscribe to the view that in such a polity it could be possible to have a co-existence between the *national demos* of the *Brunner* jurisprudence on the member states level, embodied in the national parliaments, with an upgraded version of competences as acquired with the Lisbon Treaty, and the *civic demos* derived from the European citizenship, with 'constitutional patriotism' towards the EU treaties, embodied in the EP (see Habermas 2001, 89–112; Weiler 1995). The EP, on its part, would turn into a full-fledged parliament, composed of two chambers (the current EP and the Council), similarly like the German federal parliament, while the Commission would completely take over the role of supranational executive branch of power.

References

Bulmer, Simon. 1986. *The Domestic Structure of European Policy-Making in West Germany.* New York and London: Garland.

Conference of Community and European Affairs Committees of Parliaments of the European Union (COSAC). 2005. *Fifth bi-annual report: Developments in European Union Procedures and Practices Relevant to Parliamentary Scrutiny.* Brussels: COSAC.

Conference of Community and European Affairs Committees of Parliaments of the European Union (COSAC). 2007. *Eighth bi-annual report: Developments in European Union Procedures and Practices Relevant to Parliamentary Scrutiny.* Brussels: COSAC.

Conference of Community and European Affairs Committees of Parliaments of the European Union (COSAC). 2010. *Thirteenth bi-annual report: Developments in European Union Procedures and Practices Relevant to Parliamentary Scrutiny.* Brussels: COSAC.

Conference of Community and European Affairs Committees of Parliaments of the European Union (COSAC). 2011. *Sixteenth bi-annual report: Developments in European Union Procedures and Practices Relevant to Parliamentary Scrutiny.* Brussels: COSAC.

Conference of Community and European Affairs Committees of Parliaments of the European Union (COSAC). 2012. *Seventeenth bi-annual report: Developments in European Union Procedures and Practices Relevant to Parliamentary Scrutiny.* Brussels: COSAC.

Conference of Community and European Affairs Committees of Parliaments of the European Union (COSAC). 2013. *Nineteenth bi-annual report: Developments in European Union Procedures and Practices Relevant to Parliamentary Scrutiny.* Brussels: COSAC.

de Winter, Lieven, and Laurent, Thierry. 1996. The Belgian Parliament and European Integration. In *National Parliaments and the European Union*, edited by Philip Norton, 75–91. London: Cass.

European Parliament. 1989. *Bodies within National Parliaments specializing in European Community affairs.* Luxembourg: European Centre for Parliamentary Research and Documentation.

Follesdal, Adreas, and Hix, Simon. 2006. Why There is a Democratic Deficit in the EU: A Response to Majone and Moravcsik. *Journal of Common Market Studies* 44: 533–562.

Furlong, Paul. 1996. The Italian Parliament and European Integration: Responsibilities, Failures and Successes. In *National Parliaments and the European Union*, edited by Philip Norton, 35–45. London: Cass.

Habermas, Jürgen. 2001. *The Postnational Constellation. Political essays.* Cambridge, MA: MIT Press.

Kiiver, Philipp. 2006. *The National Parliaments in the European Union: A Critical View on EU Constitution Building.* The Hague: Kluwer Law International.

Kijljunen, Kimmo. 2004. *The EU Constitution – A Finn at the Convention*. Helsinki: Eduskunnan Kanslian Julkaisu.
Norton, Paul. (ed.) 1996. *National Parliaments and the European Union*. London: Cass.
Majone, Giandomenico. 1998. Europe's 'Democratic Deficit': The Question of Standards. *European Law Journal* 4: 5–28.
Maurer, Andreas, and Wessels, Wolfgang (eds.) 2001. *National Parliaments on their Ways to Europe: Losers or Latecomers?* Baden-Baden: Nomos.
Moravcsik, Andrew. 2002. In Defence of the 'Democratic Deficit': Reassessing the Legitimacy of the European Union. *Journal of Common Market Studies* 40: 603–634.
Prokhovnik, Raia. 2008. *Sovereignties, Contemporary Theory and Practice*. Exeter: Imprint Academic.
Walker, Neil (ed.) 2006. *Sovereignty in Transition*. Portland, OR: Hurt.
Weiler, J.H.H. 1995. *The state 'über alles': Demos, Telos and the German Maastricht decision* [http://www.jeanmonnetprogram.org/archive/papers/95/9506ind.html, accessed on 21.03.2014].

Part IV
The Common Good, Constitutional Rights and Individual Obligations

The Common Good and Individual Rights

Szilárd Tattay

Abstract

Paradoxically, even though starting from a markedly individualist approach, the modern counterparts of the classical idea of public good, the Rousseauian concept of '*volonté générale*' and the utilitarian notion of 'public interest' both tend to supersede and neglect the individual's will, interest and rights. To be sure, the original Aristotelian understanding of the common good also implies that in case of conflict the good of the community should take precedence over that of the individual. Nevertheless, in the classical way of thinking the public and the private good are seen as typically existing in harmony with one another rather than in a state of conflict. In this chapter I seek to elucidate the ontological presuppositions and conceptual premises underlying the classical theory of the common good which, in my view, allow to avoid both the reduction and the opposition of the common good to individual goods and rights.

1. Introduction

In this chapter I will present, albeit in a tentative and sketchy way, the essential outlines of a concept of the common good which is meaningful, coherent, viable and at the same time compatible with the idea of individual rights. In doing so I will use the more comprehensive and traditional term 'good' rather than that of 'right', and I will rely mainly on the thoughtful analysis of 'atomist' and holist ontologies offered by Charles Taylor (see esp. Taylor 1985, Taylor 1997a, Taylor 1997b), and on the now classic essay of Péter Takács (1998) on the common good.[1]

In his critical discussion of 'Atomism', the communitarian political philosopher Charles Taylor describes atomism (or methodological individualism) as 'a vision of society as in some sense constituted by individuals' for the fulfilment of primarily individual ends, or as a class of political doctrines 'which try to defend in some sense the priority of the individual and his rights over society, or which present a purely instrumental view of society' (Taylor 1985, 187). From the atomist point of view, all goods are – at least 'in the last analysis' or 'in the last resort' – individual (Taylor 1997a, 128–129). Taylor does not define here holism, but it is not difficult to see that holism, on the contrary, conceives of society as a whole and gives priority to the community over the individual. Furthermore, in the holist perspective, there exist certain 'irreducibly social goods' (Taylor 1997a, 134ff.).

1 Henceforth I will refer to the German version of this essay (Takács 2007).

In his later study entitled 'Cross-Purposes: The Liberal-Communitarian Debate', Taylor presents a slightly different definition of atomist ontology, and, what is more important, differentiates ontological questions related to the nature of society or social life from so-called 'advocacy issues' concerning moral and political standpoints. As regards the latter:

> Here there is a gamut of positions, which at one end give primacy to individual rights and freedom and, at the other, give higher priority to community life or the good of collectivities. We could describe the positions on this scale as more or less individualist and collectivist. (Taylor 1997b, 181)

It is a significant difference, first, that in the case of atomism and holism, Taylor does not speak of degrees. Secondly, it seems clear to me that Taylor deviates here from his original discussion of atomism which does not strictly distinguish between ontological and political-moral questions. I think these two types of questions are much more interrelated than Taylor allows in this later writing. Therefore I will also draw, with some important reservations, on the conceptual framework provided by Fred D. Miller in his book on Aristotle's *Politics* (Miller 1995, ch. 6). According to Miller, even though individualistic and holistic conceptions of society have profoundly different implications, one should not speak simply of holism and individualism but of a wide spectrum of possible positions ranging from extreme individualism to extreme holism, including the intermediate standpoints of moderate individualism and moderate holism; and the most crucial debates are to be found in this 'central' area. To this we can add that in all the divergent positions of the scale ontological views seem to be interwoven with moral and political stances.

2. The problem

Theories of the common good are usually considered as reflecting a holist understanding of society, whereas doctrines of individual rights are generally regarded as manifestations of the atomist view. This produces an apparent tension between the two types of theories, which seems to be supported by the historical fact that while on the one hand Aristotle, Cicero, Aquinas and other classical theoreticians of the common good did not have a doctrine of individual rights, modern natural rights theorists on the other had a strong tendency to reduce the public good to the sum of individual goods or rights. Hobbes, for instance, clearly rejected any idea of *summum bonum* (highest good),[2] and founded the state entirely on self-interest and

2 Hobbes categorically asserted (*Leviathan* ch. 11, 70): 'there is no such *Finis ultimus*, (utmost ayme,) nor *Summum Bonum*, (greatest Good,) as is spoken of in the Books of the Old Moral Philosophers.'

fear. Locke, in his turn, equated the public good with 'the good of every particular Member of that Society' (*Two Treatises of Government* bk. 1, ch. 9, § 92, 210). This ostensible opposition is overstated and formulated in an uncompromising fashion by certain contemporary political philosophers representing the two respective traditions of thought, most particularly by Alasdair MacIntyre and Robert Nozick. While for MacIntyre natural or human rights simply do not exist, and 'belief in them is one with belief in witches and in unicorns' (MacIntyre 1981, 69), in Nozick's view 'there is no *social entity* with a good that undergoes some sacrifice for its own good. There are only individual people, different individual people, with their own individual lives. [...] Nothing more' (Nozick 1974, 32–33).

2.1 Solution I

In seeking a common ground between the conception of public good and that of individual rights, it is common and it seems logical – at least at first sight – to start from two modern counterparts of the classical idea of common good, the Rousseauian concept of '*volonté générale*' and the utilitarian notion of 'public interest', considering that these ideas take an individualist view of political society. But paradoxically, even though proceeding from the individual, both tend to supersede and neglect the individual's will, interest and rights (Takács 2007, 534–536).

For Rousseau, the chief aim of the social contract is to find a 'form of association which will defend and protect with the whole common force the person and goods of each associate, and in which each, while uniting himself with all, may still obey himself alone, and remain as free as before' (*The Social Contract* bk. 1, ch. 6, 14). This markedly individualist approach notwithstanding, the 'general will', as understood by Rousseau, has become a common scarecrow against the idea of public good. This can be easily explained by the fact that it has virtually nothing to do with the actual will of either the individual or the people, still it 'is always right and tends to the public advantage' (ibid., bk. 2, ch. 3, 25); and, accordingly, 'whoever refuses to obey the general will shall be compelled to do so by the whole body. This means nothing less than that he will be forced to be free' (ibid., bk. 1, ch. 7, 18). Moreover, Rousseau emphatically insisted that each individual should be perfectly independent of other individuals, but at the same time totally dependent on the state, 'as the strength of the State can alone secure the liberty of its members' (ibid., bk. 2, ch. 12, 48).

Bentham, as is well known, identified the common interest with 'the greatest happiness of the greatest number.' He considered the axiom of utility maximization as 'the measure of right and wrong' (Bentham 1838b, Preface to the First Edition, 227), and described individual 'good' or 'happiness' as the predominance of pleasure over pain: 'Nature has placed mankind under the governance of two sovereign masters, *pain* and *pleasure*. It is for them alone to point out what we ought to do, as well as to determine what we shall do' (Bentham 1838a, ch. 1, 1). Bentham thought it possible to quantify happiness, and hence regarded 'public interest' as the simple aggregate of the interests of individuals, having no separate quality that would distinguish it from individual utility.[3] This, however, is not the sole problem with Bentham's theory. The utilitarian calculus does not take into account differences between persons. Consequently, it is indifferent as to how public goods are distributed among the members of society, and can thus permit the sacrifice of the goods or the limitation of the fundamental rights of certain individuals for the sake of general welfare (Takács 2007, 535–536).

2.2 Solution II

So this way seems to lead to an impasse. Another possible solution is to try to bring the classical, ancient idea of the common good closer to atomist or nominalist ontology. This is the essential goal of Fred Miller's reinterpretation of *The Politics*. Miller maintains that Aristotle's discussion of the common good or common advantage is open to different readings:

> One line of interpretation is *individualistic*: to promote the common advantage is to promote the end of its individual members. The polis is happy or flourishing provided that its individual citizens are happy. Hence, the best constitution must take seriously the fact that its members are distinct individuals and must respect the interests of each of them. Another line of interpretation is *holistic*: the polis resembles an organism in that it has an end which is distinct from, and superior to, the end of its individual members. (Miller 1995, 194)

Miller argues that the Aristotelian concept of common good rests not upon a holist but a 'moderate-individualistic' understanding of society, which does not differentiate between the political community's good and that of its members (Miller 1995, 204–205, 211–224). He claims, for instance, that Aristotle did not exactly say that the good of the city-state exceeds that of a single individual, but only that it is better to attain and preserve the good of the city-state (Miller 1995, 193).

However, this view does not seem convincing. First, this interpretation, as we will see later in detail, is far removed from Aristotle's original intentions and words. To take only one illustration, in Book One of *The Politics* (ch. 2, 1253a, 14) the Greek philosopher wrote: 'The proof that the state is a creation of nature and

3 See e.g. Bentham 1838c, pt. 1, ch. 15, 321: 'This public interest which you personify, is only an abstract term: it represents only the mass of the interests of individuals.'

prior to the individual is that the individual, when isolated, is not self-sufficing; and therefore he is like a part in relation to the whole.' Secondly, and more importantly, Miller's reading of Aristotle leads to the same problem of reductionism I have pointed out in the case of Hobbes, Locke and Bentham: in this perspective, the public good signifies no more than the sum of the goods of individuals and thereby inevitably loses its separate quality. Therefore, I think, it proves only that certain moderate forms of individualism are not incompatible with the notion of common good; e.g. one that holds that the individual's good and perfection includes other-regarding virtuous activities and hence requires participation in the political community (ibid., 200, 205).

2.3 Solution III

Consequently, taking everything into consideration, the only alternative that remains is to hark back to the original – ancient and medieval – Aristotelian conception of the common good. Above all, it should be stressed that the question whether to use the terms 'will' and 'interest' or the word 'good' is much more than a *lis de verbis*; it has real theoretical relevance. Although both Aristotle and Thomas Aquinas used the phrase 'common good' (*koinon agathon/bonum commune*) interchangeably with the expression 'common advantage' (*koinon sympheron/utilitas communis*), the primary concept of Aristotelian ethics is the 'good.' This is in sharp contrast to e.g. John Rawls's political philosophy which gives priority to the notion of right over that of the good (Rawls 1971, 31–32). Besides the fundamental significance of the fact that, in contrast to the diversity of connotations of the words 'will', 'interest', 'benefit', 'utility', etc., the notion of human 'good' self-evidently implies moral rightness, it also inherently involves some sort of dialectic between the good of the community and the individual's good, which seems to be an organic element of any theory of the common good.

At the beginning of the *Nicomachean Ethics*, Aristotle declared politics to be the 'highest master science' on the ground that

> even if the good is the same for an individual as for a city, that of the city is obviously a greater and more complete thing to obtain and preserve. For while the good of an individual is a desirable thing, what is good for a people or for cities is a nobler and more godlike thing. (*Nicomachean Ethics* bk. 1, ch. 2, 1094b, 4)

This argument combines what might otherwise be seen as mutually exclusive alternatives: the statement that the common good is the same as the individual good, and the principle that the common good is superior to the individual good (Kempshall 1999, 26). In asserting that happiness is the same for a single human being and for the entire polis, Aristotle meant that it is the *same in kind*, that is, the same standard should be used in evaluating whether an individual human being or a community of human beings is happy: the life of virtue (Miller 1995, 213–214). On the other hand, Aristotle maintained that the common good of the city-state is not only quantitatively but also *qualitatively different* from the individual good of one person, inasmuch as 'the state is by nature clearly prior to the family and to the individual, since the whole is of necessity prior to the part' (*The Politics* bk. 1, ch. 2, 1253a, 14).[4]

3. Ontology of the common good

If we approach Aristotle's above assertions and their implications from the perspective of ontology, we can arrive at the conclusion that it is probably more than a mere coincidence that the most influential theories of the common good have been developed on the philosophical basis of moderate realism. It is certain that a coherent doctrine of the common good must find a place on the spectrum of metaphysical views somewhere between extreme realism or holism and extreme nominalism or atomism. But where exactly? Let us have a closer look at it.

An extreme nominalist or atomist conception of society bases political and social cooperation exclusively on self-interest. Consequently, it acknowledges only 'convergent goods' (in Taylor's terminology), e.g. public safety, which are manifestations of collective instrumental action. These goods are merely convergent, because the fact that they are secured collectively does not in itself render them 'common' in the strict sense:

> It has nothing to do with what makes them goods. Security as a valued end is always security for A, and for B, and for C. It is in no wise a different good, let alone a more valued one, because it is in fact ensured collectively. (Taylor 1997b, 191)

Contrary to this, the authentic notion of common good makes sense only if we accept the existence of 'irreducibly social goods', which are not 'decomposable into' or 'reducible to' individual goods. The examples given by Taylor are language, culture, positive liberty as 'participatory self-rule', 'frank and equal relations', and so on (Taylor 1997a, 134 ff).

Arguably, a meaningful concept of common good requires not only the rejection of extreme atomism but also the accentuation of civic or political friendship, which Aristotle called 'the greatest good of states' (*The Politics* bk. 2, ch. 4, 1262b, 34).

4 For a similar argument in Thomas Aquinas, see *Summa theologiae* IIaIIae 58, a. 7, ad 2.

The Stagirite professed a thoroughly social view of human fulfilment. As MacIntyre points out, Aristotle thought that human beings can only achieve their proper end within the polis, and he believed that 'a community whose shared aim is the realization of the human good presupposes [...] a wide range of agreement in that community on goods and virtues' and necessitates a special bond between citizens (MacIntyre 1981, 146). As Aristotle himself put it:

> Friendship seems also to hold cities together, and lawgivers to care more about it than about justice; for concord seems to be something like friendship, and this is what they aim at most of all, while taking special pains to eliminate civil conflict as something hostile. (*Nicomachean Ethics* bk. 8, ch. 1, 1155a, 144)

This opinion seems evidently to imply, pace Miller (1995, 207–209), a moderate holist view of society.

On the other hand, a coherent concept of common good also excludes an extreme version of holism, as represented, for instance, by the idealism of Plato or Hegel, considering the state as the ultimate end of the individual, who exists for the sake of the whole. In reality, good citizens are supposed to like the community they belong to because the goal at which it aims – virtuous activity – is the ultimate good at which human beings should aim (Kraut 2002, 353). As it is well known, Aristotle overtly and vehemently opposed Plato's theory of the ideal state, especially the communistic tendencies inherent in it. In addition, he criticised the Platonist doctrine that there is only one single form of Good, thereby endorsing a certain degree of pluralism:

> Unity there should be, both of the family and of the state, but in some respects only. For there is a point at which a state may attain such a degree of unity as to be no longer a state, or at which, without actually ceasing to exist, it will become an inferior state, like harmony passing into unison, or rhythm which has been reduced to a single foot. (*The Politics* bk. 2, ch. 5, 1263b, 37)

This way, the moderate holist conception of the common good avoids the strict subordination of the individual to the body politic, and regards the good of the community as including the good of its individual members. Furthermore, it is important to stress that according to the classical theory of the public good, state power only acts as a *defensor pacis*; it safeguards, but does not itself determine or create the common good. As Péter Takács pertinently observes: 'Nicht der Gesetzgeber sagt es, worin dieses Gut besteht, denn das ist auch für ihn gegeben. Die Staatsgewalt ist weder Besitzer, noch Festleger oder Garantie des Gemeinwohls, sondern sein *Behüter* und den Möglichkeiten gemäß sein *Förderer*' (Takács 2007, 537).

But what if John Rawls is right in affirming that in modern democracies the pluralism of values is irreducible (Rawls 1987, 4) A tentative Aristotelian answer to this embarrassing question, proposed by Richard Kraut, might be that even if the members of a given society cannot achieve a consensus about what their good or well-being is, they can still manage to agree upon a conception of good citizenship as the common goal of the community:

> The solution to this problem consists in rejecting its assumption that citizens can agree that their city is pursuing the common good only if they achieve a consensus about what well-being is. Suppose they have no such consensus, but nonetheless agree that their city ought to promote the conditions that encourage each citizen to be a certain kind of person, namely a good citizen. That, according to Aristotle, would be a way of promoting the common good, and not merely what seems good. (Kraut 2002, 398)

The citizens of such a political community, not sharing a common conception of the good life, can take the good pursued through collective decisions to be one thing, and the good pursued individually to be another, but so long as their allegiance to the outcome of collective decisions is strong enough, the state will be stable, and by fostering the virtue of the good citizen as an approximation of the virtue of the good man, it will realise considerable value. (ibid., 399)

4. The common good and the individual good

It is a standard thesis of the classical doctrine of the common good that in case of conflict the good of the community should take precedence over that of the individual (Takács 2007, 531–533). As Cicero famously formulated this principle: ‘salus populi suprema lex esto’ (*De legibus* bk. 3, ch. 3, § 8, 91). Nevertheless, in the ancient and medieval Aristotelian way of thinking the common and the individual good were seen as typically existing in harmony with one another rather than in a state of conflict (Tierney 1997, 313). For, after all, these are but two different aspects or levels of the same good, and the boundary between the two is far from being impermeable. Accordingly, in this perspective the public good constitutes, on the one hand, the indispensable condition of the attainment of private good, and on the other hand, the good of the community presupposes that of the individual. As Takács underlines: ‘das Gemeinwohl von den Gesichtspunkten des Individuums nicht getrennt werden kann […] Ein Begriff des Gemeinwohls also, der dem Individualwohl gegenüber steht, ist unvorstellbar’ (Takács 2007, 531). Political goodness ultimately depends upon what is good for the individual members of the state: it can attain happiness and the good life only because, and to the extent that, its citizens are happy and live well (Miller 1995, 197).

In order to illustrate this point, I will quote here three relevant and revealing passages from three different representatives of the Aristotelian tradition. The first is Aristotle himself, followed by the statements of two scholastic Aristotelians, Thomas Aquinas and Francisco Suárez:

> Everyone approves of and praises those who take special trouble to act nobly. And if everyone strives for what is noble and strains to do the noblest actions, everything will be as it should be for the common interest, and individually each will have the greatest goods, since such is virtue. So the good person should be a self-lover, since he will help himself as well as benefit others by doing noble acts (*Nicomachean Ethics* bk. 9, ch. 8, 1169a, 176).
>
> Since therefore every man is a part of the State, it is impossible for any man to be good unless he is well adjusted to the common good; nor can the whole of anything be properly composed unless its parts are well adjusted to it. Hence it is impossible for the common good of the State to be secured unless the citizens are virtuous (*Summa theologiae* IaIIae 92, a. 1, ad 3, 98).
>
> For, in the first place, the good of private individuals [...] forms a part of the common good, when the former is not of a nature to exclude the latter good; being rather such that it is a necessary requisite in individuals [...] in order that the common good may result from this good enjoyed by private persons. (*On Laws and God the Lawgiver* bk. 1, ch. 7, sect. 3, 91)

5. Conclusion

As it seems to me, the texts cited above clearly show the harmonious relationship and interdependence of common and private good in Aristotelian political and legal philosophy. In direct contrast to this approach, modern thought tends to postulate their disharmony and conflict. And for the most part, the dichotomy between the public and private good is transcended by reducing the common good to the aggregate of individual goods. This way, the public good unavoidably loses its independent quality. In the course of my argumentation, I have tried to reconstruct, albeit in a sketchy and tentative manner, the ontological presuppositions and conceptual premises that underlie the classical theory of the common good. If these theoretical preconditions can be fulfilled, as I believe (and hope to have demonstrated) they can, then both the Scylla of reducing and the Charybdis of opposing the common good to individual goods and rights can be avoided.

Acknowledgements

This study is published in the framework of the project no. TÁMOP-4.2.1.B-11/2/KMR-2011-0002 at the Pázmány Péter Catholic University (the progress of scientific research at the PPCU).

References

Aquinas, Thomas. 1952–1956. *Summa theologiae*, edited by Pietro Caramello, 3 vols. Turin: Marietti.

Aquinas, Thomas. 2002. *Summa theologiae* IaIIae 92: The Effects of Law. In *Political Writings*, edited and translated by Robert W. Dyson, 95–100. Cambridge: Cambridge University Press.

Aristotle. 1996. *The Politics*, translated by Benjamin Jowett. In *The Politics and The Constitution of Athens*, edited by Stephen Everson, 9–207. Cambridge: Cambridge University Press.

Aristotle. 2004. *Nicomachean Ethics*, edited and translated by Roger Crisp. Cambridge: Cambridge University Press.

Bentham, Jeremy. 1838a. *An Introduction to the Principles of Morals and Legislation.* In *The Works of Jeremy Bentham*, vol. 1, edited by John Bowring, 1–154. Edinburgh: Tait.

Bentham, Jeremy. 1838b. *A Fragment on Government.* In *The Works of Jeremy Bentham*, vol. 1, edited by John Bowring, 221–295. Edinburgh: Tait.

Bentham, Jeremy. 1838c. *Principles of the Civil Code*. In *The Works of Jeremy Bentham*, vol. 1, edited by John Bowring, 297–364. Edinburgh: Tait.

Cicero, Marcus Tullius. 1950. *De legibus*, edited by Konrad Ziegler. Heidelberg: Kerle.

Hobbes, Thomas. 1996. *Leviathan*, edited by Richard Tuck. Cambridge: Cambridge University Press.

Kempshall, Matthew S. 1999. *The Common Good in Late Medieval Political Thought*. Oxford: Clarendon Press.

Kraut, Richard. 2002. *Aristotle: Political Philosophy*. Oxford: Oxford University Press.

Locke, John. 1988. *Two Treatises of Government*, edited by Peter Laslett. Cambridge: Cambridge University Press.

MacIntyre, Alasdair. 1981. *After Virtue: A Study in Moral Theory*. Notre Dame (Ind.): University of Notre Dame Press.

Miller, Fred D. 1995. *Nature, Justice, and Rights in Aristotle's Politics*. Oxford: Clarendon Press.

Nozick, Robert. 1974. *Anarchy, State and Utopia*. New York: Basic Books.

Rawls, John. 1971. *A Theory of Justice*. Cambridge (Mass.): Harvard University Press.

Rawls, John. 1987. The Idea of an Overlapping Consensus. *Oxford Journal of Legal Studies* 7: 1–25.

Rousseau, Jean-Jacques. 1923. *The Social Contract*. In *The Social Contract and Discourses*, edited and translated by G.D.H. Cole, 1–123. London: Dent.

Suárez, Francisco. 1944. *On Laws and God the Lawgiver* (excerpts), translated by Gwladys L. Williams et al. In *Selections from Three Works of Francisco Suárez, S.J.*, vol. 2, 1–646. Oxford: Clarendon Press.

Takács, Péter. 1998. A közjó [The Common Good]. In *Iustum, aequum, salutare: Emlékkönyv Zlinszky János tiszteletére: Festschrift in Honour of Professor János Zlinszky*, edited by Gábor Bánrévy, Gábor Jobbágyi and Csaba Varga, 269–276. Budapest: PPKE JÁK.

Takács, Péter. 2007. Der Begriff des Gemeinwohls. In *Theatrum Legale Mundi: Symbola Cs. Varga Oblata*, edited by Péter Cserne, István H. Szilágyi, Miklós Könczöl, Máté Paksy, Péter Takács and Szilárd Tattay, 527–537. Budapest: Szent István Társulat.

Taylor, Charles. 1985. Atomism. In *Philosophy and the Human Sciences: Philosophical Papers 2*, 187–210. Cambridge: Cambridge University Press.

Taylor, Charles. 1997a. Irreducibly Social Goods. In *Philosophical Arguments*, 127–145. Cambridge (Mass.): Harvard University Press.
Taylor, Charles. 1997b. Cross-Purposes: The Liberal-Communitarian Debate. In *Philosophical Arguments*, 181–203. Cambridge (Mass.): Harvard University Press.
Tierney, Brian. 1997. *The Idea of Natural Rights: Studies on Natural Rights, Natural Law and Church Law, 1150–1625*. Atlanta, Scholars Press.

Towards a 'Soft' Concept of the State Neutrality Principle

Wojciech Ciszewski

Abstract

This chapter considers a fundamental problem set against the backdrop of contemporary legal and political philosophy: that of the state neutrality principle – one of the most important standards of modern liberal democracies. The chapter aims at defining an adequate formula of state neutrality, starting with the most significant objection raised against the principle (to be referred to as 'sceptic's charge'). The purpose of the chapter is to elaborate a formula of state neutrality that is resistant to the objection. Possible elements of the conception of neutrality will be analysed by indicating three different questions concerning (1) the character of the principle, (2) its rationale and (3) its reference. In the concluding part, a formula for soft state neutrality is presented, that is, on the one hand, theoretically well-grounded and, on the other hand, functional and useful in practical discourses, especially in legal discourse.

1. Introduction

The neutrality principle is one of the main liberal constraints on the activities of public authorities. Similar to human rights, principles of proportionality or subsidiarity, the neutrality standard aims for protection from the arbitrary use of state power. The special esteem that is attributed to neutrality can be illustrated by a metaphor of Ronald Dworkin (1985, 181–204), who regards this principle as the nerve of contemporary liberalism. In fact, disputes about neutrality are much older than recent liberal ideas; as pioneers of such considerations, we may indicate Immanuel Kant and John Stuart Mill. The contemporary understanding of the neutrality principle, for the most part, was developed in discussions evoked by the publication of John Rawls' 'Theory of Justice', where the author offered, on theoretical grounds, an influential critique of the perfectionist vision of the state and politics.

In turn, on legal grounds, the reception of state neutrality took place in the second half of the twentieth century. The conception was at that time incorporated as a principle in many national legal systems and afterward, in supranational legal orders. The social background of this reception was constituted by the improvement of democracy as a political regime and international initiatives aimed at the global protection of human rights. Definitely, the most fundamental role was performed by the development of political liberties, which has generated deep social differentiations with respect to values that are held by citizens, their moral beliefs and their attitudes. The idea of neutrality imposes a duty on a state and its representatives to stand aside from ethical and religious disagreements, acknowledging that each citizen is entitled to decide such issues on his own. Predominantly, in the legal context, the neutrality principle has been used as a criterion for the settlement of cases concerning the place of religious considerations and religious symbols in the public sphere. Despite the fact that relations between church and state are still one of crucial issues concerning the application of the neutrality principle, currently, it seems to be beyond doubt that the standard should apply to a broader scope of worldviews, not solely to ideas that are religious in their essence.

In this chapter, I challenge one of the most important objections raised against the states neutrality principle. The criticism, which I call the 'sceptic's charge', maintains that it is not possible to fulfil the requirements of the principle with state institutions and public authorities. According to the charge, the essence of political and legal actions is at odds with the specificity of duties imposed by the neutrality standard. I claim that the understanding of the principle that is presupposed in the sceptic's argument is *too strong* and hence excludes as impermissible a very broad scope of actions performed by public servants. In other words, critics employ a very specific, narrow definition of the state neutrality principle and subsequently demonstrate that state policies very often cannot comply with such a demanding standard. In section two of this chapter, I first argue that the scope of political actions identified as non-neutral depends to a great extent on the understanding of the principle and secondly that a strong version of the neutrality principle is not the only possible depiction of it. In section three, I will emphasise and examine in detail the three most questionable assumptions of the strong definition, and in section four, I will reply to the sceptic's charge by introducing the idea of *soft* state neutrality, which admits a significantly wider range of actions as neutral and permissible. In my argument, I will make use of concepts and ideas that have been elaborated by contemporary political and legal philosophy. In my opinion, soft neutrality constitutes a coherent formula that is resistant to weaknesses attributable to the strong version of the principle. Therefore, the formula is also functional as a legality criterion and as a standard of the legitimacy of political actions.

The last necessary remark in this section aims at invoking one very important feature of the legal and political meanings of neutrality. The principle should contain a criterion that enables us to make a distinction between neutral actions and non-neutral ones. In particular, we should be able to differentiate between activities that fulfil the requirements of neutrality and those that fail to do so. Appealing to the Dworkinian distinction between rules and principles, we can conclude that the neutrality principle should be applied in an *all or nothing fashion*, which makes it closer to a rule in Dworkin's sense. Because of this fact, recognising the adequate criterion of neutrality becomes critical.

2. The sceptic's charge

The sceptic's charge points to the crucial feature that I have just attributed to the principle, namely the practical impossibility of differentiating between neutral actions and non-neutral ones. This criticism is based on the negation of the usefulness of the principle as a standard that can guide political and legal actions. In the most common version of the objection, the sceptic employs a particular understanding of the principle, which is based on the idea of epistemic scepticism. According to the sceptical rationale of neutrality, (1) in the world exist plenty of goods and values, and (2) we do not have any rational grounds for choosing among different visions of the good. Our cognition is limited and fallible. In the face of such a predicament, neutrality seems to be the most reasonable position to be adopted by a state. Because every possible choice is arbitrary, public authorities should refrain from making such choices.

The aforementioned reasoning constitutes the first premise of the sceptic's charge. The whole line of argumentation consists of two assertions and the conclusion (see Raz 1986, 120–124; Kraut 1999, 315–332; MacIntyre 1989, 344–348; Legutko 1998, 63–69):

(1) The neutrality principle based on the idea of epistemic scepticism requires refraining from actions aimed at realising values.
(2) Political and legal actions (actions performed by public authorities) are, in their essence, based on different values.

Hence: it is impossible to fulfil the requirements of the neutrality principle with regard to actions performed by public authorities.

It is clear that the second thesis (2) of the sceptic's charge is true; namely, it is beyond doubt that most political and legal actions are intended to realise and reinforce objectives that are significant from a moral perspective. Examples of such valuable public goals may include public security, public health protection, economic efficiency, the promotion of culture and the arts or environmental protection; in each case, actions are based on moral reasons. If it is true that the sceptical rationale for neutrality requires us to be indifferent with respect to such values, then the neutrality principle seems to be excluded as a standard that guides political and legal actions.

In my opinion, the weakness of the reasoning is located in the first premise (1), the one claiming that 'the neutrality principle based on the idea of epistemic scepticism requires restraint from actions aimed at realizing values.' This thesis is based on some disputable and contentious assumptions, which finally lead to a very distinct depiction of the principle, one that can be called 'strong neutrality' or 'neutrality in the strong sense.' Strong neutrality is characterised by the fact that its evaluation criteria are so demanding that almost no political actions may conform to them. Therefore, the principle excludes from the class of neutral activities a very broad scope of actions (any action aimed at realising any value). With respect to strong neutrality, almost all political actions seem to be illegitimate, even those that are not socially contested.

In the next section, I will challenge the three most questionable assumptions of the strong neutrality principle. Replacing answers given by a sceptic with other, better-justified, ones will enable us to formulate the content of soft neutrality. Soft neutrality corresponds very well with the character of political and legal actions, which makes it resistant to the charge.

3. Three contentious assumptions of strong neutrality

Three disputable claims that constitute the first premise according to the charge are answers to three different questions concerning the content of neutrality: (1) what is the character of the principle, (2) what is the rationale (justification) for its validity and (3) what is the reference of the principle? The conception of strong neutrality, which I find indefensible, replies to the first question that the essence of neutral actions are adequate (neutral) aims, as an answer to the second question, it indicates epistemic scepticism and it responds to the third one by invoking broadly understood values.

3.1 What is the character of the neutrality principle?

Contemporary political and legal philosophy gives three main answers to the question of the character of the principle. The requirement of neutrality may apply to the aims of the action, the effects of the action or the reasons for performing it (see Larmore 1996, 121–151; Kymlicka 1989, 883–905; Patten 2012, 249–272; De Marneffe 1990, 253–274).

The essence of the *neutrality of aim* is a prescription that actions performed by state representatives should be guided only by neutral intentions. The notion of intention is to be understood here as a state of affairs that one intends to realise by his activity. The intentional state of affairs is a practical goal of one's actions. For that reason, public authorities are not responsible for all effects that emerge as a consequence of their actions – the responsibility is limited only to those results that can be ascribed to the agent's will. In other words, we can conclude that an agent violates the neutrality of aim when he aims at improving (or worsening) the social situation of a concrete worldview conception relative to other such conceptions. Adequate legitimacy can be attributed only to modes of conduct that are impartial with regard to social conflicts of values. However, this conception is vulnerable to at least two serious charges.

First, it is difficult to clarify and maintain the notion of a 'neutral state of affairs.' We should be aware that differences, disagreements and value conflicts constitute the substance of contemporary politics in pluralistic democracies. It is difficult to imagine what an impartial solution is – a neutral state of affairs – with regard to conflicts concerning abortion or euthanasia, the legalisation of same-sex marriages or ritual slaughter. The position adopted by the state will always be seen as partial by all sides to the dispute. Second, problems of the conception may emerge in connection with the distinction of the intentional state of affairs, for which we can blame the agent, and other, non-intentional consequences for which the agent is not responsible. It seems that, in most practical situations, it is very difficult to determine the real content of the agent's aim and which consequences should be classified as not planned. There is also a significant problem with the effects of actions that were not purposeful but easily predictable.

Two other conceptions of the character of the principle aim at solving complications that emerge with regard to the neutrality of aim. The first posits abandoning the problematic distinction between intentional and unintentional states of affairs and consequently applying the criterion of neutrality to all effects of the agent's actions. The second answer, in the face of the same dilemma, resigns from judging actions as neutral or non-neutral on the basis of their consequences and admits that the legitimacy of one's action reflects its adequate justification (reasons that speak in favour of one's act).

Pursuant to the *neutrality of effect*, actions performed by the state fulfil the requirements of the neutrality principle if and only if any consequences of these actions provide greater assistance to some worldviews in comparison with others. In particular, the state should not do anything that has the effect (intended or not) of promoting or disapproving of any particular worldview. It is not the aims of the agent's actions but the social effects that are of importance here. S. Caney (1991, 463) claims that there are two basic interpretations of neutrality of effects: according to the first – equal-effects neutrality – the state is neutral if and only if its actions have an equal effect on all worldviews. The crux of the second interpretation – equally easy neutrality – is the assertion that the state is neutral if and only if it ensures that all worldviews do equally well (Caney 1991, 463).

Still, it should be noted that requirements that are put on public authorities' actions pursuant to this interpretation of neutrality are even more difficult to carry out than those postulated by the first idea. It is hard to imagine the possibility that a state's policies will always equally affect all worldview conceptions and distribute perfectly evenly social goods and duties between different conceptions of the good. The neutrality of effect becomes impossible to maintain in the circumstances of the contemporary welfare state, which pursues an active policy designed to promote economic and social development, for example, by imposing different tax rates on different products, stimulating some activities through subsidies and grants, providing tax relief, etc.

In my opinion, much more plausible is the answer given by the *neutrality of justification*. According to this proposition, we should definitely abandon judging actions through the lens of their consequences. An action fulfils the requirements of the neutrality principle if and only if it is properly justified, which means justification in neutral terms. The reason for acting (as opposed to an aim or the consequences) is the most important aspect of an action from the point of view of neutrality. No action performed by public authorities can be arbitrary; it should always be taken on the basis of good reasons. It is worth emphasising that, according to the third conception, neutral conduct may lead finally to non-neutral results (states of affairs) on the condition that it was justified neutrally.

The last conception recognises as permissible a significantly broader scope of actions. To fully explicate how the neutrality of justification works, it is necessary to consider the two following questions.

3.2 What is the rationale for the neutrality principle?

It is necessary to define the rationale that stands behind neutrality, not only for better theoretical grounding of the principle but also because the justification has a significant influence on its content. Its scope, strength and conditions of validity cannot be defined without invoking the values that justify the principle's validity. Nevertheless, it is important to note that there are several different reasons for the admission of neutrality, and as J. Waldron (1993, 143–149) claims, these different justificatory grounds support different visions of the standard, which may be impossible to reconcile. Distinct rationalisations may impose contrasting obligations and duties (compare Ackerman 1980, 10–12). The most important arguments usually given in defence of neutrality are as follows: (1) the idea of epistemic scepticism, (2) the liberty principle and (3) the principle of equal respect and concern.

As I indicated in the third section, strong neutrality is based on the idea of *epistemic scepticism*. The sceptical rationale of neutrality states that there are plenty of incomparable goods, values and beliefs in the world, and it is impossible to make rational choices among them because we do not have any common denominator (see Ackerman 1980, 362–369; Feinberg 1998, 310–311). Our knowledge about the good is inaccessible. Taking this circumstance into account, the most reasonable attitude (for a state) is to stay neutral toward different moral disagreements. The problem with this rationale is that it leads, on a practical level, to impossibility of taking any political or legal actions. This is the crux of the sceptic's charge. The fact that knowledge about the good is inaccessible successfully 'demolishes' every axiological basis for political and legal activities. This is the main reason that the epistemic rationale fails.

Since the epistemic rationale leads to evident complications, we should turn to other types of justification. The neutrality principle, contrary to what the sceptic claims, does not have to be based on a value-neutral path of argumentation. The validity of the principle may be derived from a value that is superior to neutrality. It seems that two 'value-entangled' justifications deserve our special attention.

The first rationale, which is embraced by many philosophers, states that the neutrality of public authorities is grounded in the *principle of liberty*. This version of justification assumes that people differ deeply in their beliefs, preferences and opinions, so universal pursuits of individual happiness do not exist. Each person is different and able to find his own road to happiness and satisfaction. This is the crux of the famous John Stuart Mill's *best-judge argument*. According to the author of 'On Liberty', each person should be treated as the best judge of what is good for him and for his interests. Everyone should search for his self-realisation by performing so-called *experiments in living* (Mill 1859, 261). From the assertion that people are the best judges of their interests, some theorists draw the conclusion that the state should be neutral toward such experiments (as long as one does not harm others). Only neutral legal order, founded on liberty, will bring people to the good.

The neutrality principle, based on the principle of liberty, can be called *anti-paternalistic*. We should note that this type of rationale does not disable political and legal actions; quite to the contrary, it imposes on public institutions a duty to act in favour of broadening the range of personal freedom and accordingly extending the sphere of individual choice. The anti-paternalistic state is neutral with regard to different conceptions of good life only if all conflicts that emerge between the autonomy of persons and acting for one's good are settled for the benefit of self-government.

In my opinion, the anti-paternalistic rationale first is theoretically unpersuasive and second seems to be inadequate as a justification for the neutrality principle in contemporary democracies. One can easily reach the conclusion that the Millian principle of freedom is based on overly optimistic assumptions concerning the rationality of people. The belief that an individual is always the best judge of his interests is patently false. Nobody has perfect knowledge about different ways of life, so in many situations, one cannot make right and responsible choices. It seems that even Mill was aware of this problem, which finally prompted him to permit some forms of paternalism as morally justified. For example, he rejects the possibility of voluntary servitude and postulates that slavery should be prohibited by law. An anti-paternalistic argument is not consistent in this respect. The second problem for the liberty-based justification is the discrepancy between the concept of freedom presupposed by the Millian argument and the meaning of the same term in contemporary legal discourse. In my opinion, if we agree that, according to the neutrality principle, we should settle every conflict between freedom and state paternalism in favour of the former, then we are forced to consider a very broad scope of state actions as non-neutral and impermissible. Some paternalistic regulations, such as compulsory social insurance, national health insurance or compulsory seat belts, seem to be commonly accepted and do not raise objections, especially in contemporary welfare states. Such regulations are not seen as a denial of state neutrality in the legal discourse.

Such complications do not concern the third rationale, which is constituted by the *moral principle of equal concern and respect* (see Dworkin 1971, 272; Larmore 2008, 196–220; Sadurski 1990, 117–119). According to this idea, the validity of state neutrality is a consequence of the recognition of the equal moral status of citizens. Public authorities are obliged to respect a citizen's dignity and fulfil the obligation only when they act for reasons that are commonly acceptable and intelligible for everyone. Actions performed by the state are legitimised and neutral only if they are aimed at values that every reasonable person can acknowledge, regardless of his professed religion or worldview. The fundamental concept of 'reasonable values' may be illustrated by an example. In my private life, I may have no respect for my own health (I may drink alcohol, eat only junk food, engage in risky activities, etc.) because being healthy is not an important goal in my life plan. However, as a reasonable citizen, I should understand that the protection of health constitutes a basis for moral claims of other persons. Similarly, Thomas Nagel (1983, 215–240) gives an example of practicing one's religion and religious freedom as neutral values (Nagel calls these values *impersonal*), as opposed to adherence to the Catholic faith, which is purely non-neutral. The former may be adhered to regardless of one's private set of goals and beliefs, and for this reason, the state may enforce the right to religious liberty.

As we can see, the principle of neutral justification does not postulate neutrality with regard to values in general; it explicitly affirms specific kinds of values, namely those that are acceptable by democratic citizens. It seems that the last interpretation, which may be referred to as *anti-perfectionist*, fits very well the demand of soft state neutrality.

3.3 The reference of the neutrality principle

The last doubt about a state neutrality principle concerns its point of reference. As mentioned above, according to strong neutrality, public authorities should be neutral in relation to *all moral values*. The sceptic claims that it is not fair to exclude from the political sphere only some values because such exclusion establishes an unjustified asymmetry between them; some values are legitimised and may constitute reasons for political and legal actions, and the rest are devoid of political significance. Soft neutrality may respond to this objection. The possibility of maintaining asymmetry between different moral premises for actions is a result of the acceptance of a non-neutral rationale. Definitely, the standard cannot be indifferent with respect to its justification. Nonetheless, the question concerning the reference of the principle is still in need of an answer. We should know what public authorities are required to be neutral about.

The first possible answer claims that they should stay neutral with regard to the *interests* of different worldviews and their supporters. According to some authors, neutrality necessarily presupposes a contest between two parties (worldviews, religions, ideals, etc.) and focuses our attention on a third party, whose actions or attitudes may be evaluated as neutral (see Waldron 1993, 145). What is important is the fact that actions performed by the third party influence the social positions of different sides. The demand for neutrality may be reduced to a kind of second-order rule that excludes some first-order reasons as impermissible – in particular, actions cannot be guided by the intention to benefit any party. Therefore, a state cannot aim at taking sides in any social conflict between moral, religious or philosophical worldviews. In my opinion, the answer invoking interests as the reference of the neutrality principle is too narrow and thus permits a number of non-neutral political and legal actions.

It is because of the fact that the neutrality principle is violated not only when a state's action is guided by an intention to benefit any side of the conflict but also when it imposes a controversial vision of the good by reason of its inherent moral superiority – for example, introducing a prohibition of homosexual relations because of their moral repugnancy may be seen as such a banned motivation or introducing religious education to schools (with explicitly moral aims) as a result of the recognition of the truth embedded in the doctrine. The intention behind such political actions is not the benefit of heterosexuals in relation to homosexuals or supporting the beliefs of religious people. It is not a matter of the benefit or the definite interest of any worldview. We can assume that in both situations that the legislator is guided by a certain vision of the common good – the problem exists in the fact that the imposed vision of moral good is based on non-neutral and thus impermissible reasons. In such situations, appealing to the neutrality principle is by no means desirable.

Therefore, in my opinion, the best possible answer to the question concerning the reference is that public authorities should be neutral concerning different controversial conceptions of the good. The concept of a good refers to individual ideals of life and includes beliefs about what gives value to life. It covers everything that makes one's life worth living. Very often, beliefs and values that constitute such conceptions are derived from so-called *comprehensive* moral, religious and philosophical doctrines (Rawls 1996, 58–65). An action should be seen as neutral only if it can be justified without appealing to the intrinsic superiority of any particular conception of the good life. As long as public authorities conform their decisions to this constraint, they act neutrally. This does not mean that all such conceptions are morally equal; it requires only the softer assumption that not the state but citizens themselves should decide whether certain beliefs or values are worth realising.

It should be emphasised that the reference does not cover all possible conceptions of the good but only those that are controversial; namely, they constitute a subject of social disagreement in a given society. Being *controversial* does not mean that the conception is a marginal phenomenon, so it is rejected by the majority. It rather constitutes a concept opposite to reasonable and common acceptance than majoritarian approval. Even a small minority can reject a given conception of the good and make it controversial in this sense (obviously, the rejection must be reasonable). In addition, we may recognise many state activities that promote uncontroversial (in a given society) goods such as, for example, protection of the environment, actions aimed at protecting public health or providing access to art and national heritage. According to George Klosko (2003, 177), such goods should be seen as so deeply ingrained in public culture and so commonly accepted that their validity as political reasons for action is beyond question. They should be regarded as a subject of wide social consensus. Only actions justified by a direct appeal to an inherent value of any controversial conception of good life should be recognised as violations of the neutrality principle.

4. A soft formula for the state neutrality principle

Considering answers to the three aforementioned issues concerning (1) the character of the principle, (2) its rationale and (3) the reference enables us to formulate the content of a soft concept of the state neutrality principle as *the political and legal standard that embodies the principle of equal concern and respect for persons by the prohibition of performing actions that are justified by an appeal to the inherent value of any controversial conception of the good.*

The soft definition of the state neutrality principle may be supplemented by a kind of thought experiment that helps us to differentiate neutral reasons from non-neutral ones. The essence of the test is a hypothetical image of the *reasonable democratic citizen* who is a model resident of a democratic regime. We have some information about him, but our knowledge (and his knowledge) on the subject is not full and precise (see Scanlon 1982, 103–128; Klosko 2003, 167–190). Above all, we know that he has a certain worldview and pursues a definite conception of the good, but we do not know which worldview and to exactly what conception he adheres. The hypothetical citizen has also certain characteristics and virtues (such as sex, nationality, social background and economic status); however, we also do not have precise information. In light of our test, we recognise a given value or reason for action as neutral if it is acceptable for such a roughly described citizen. It is highly probable that he would find plausible arguments appealing to fundamental democratic values (freedom, equality, the rule of law and human rights), rules of logical thinking and uncontroversial scientific evidence – generally, each inference that would be public, intelligible and repeatable. On the other hand, considerations that are non-neutral are vulnerable to rejection by a reasonable democratic citizen. It concerns, above all, arguments based on controversial metaphysical, epistemic or axiological assumptions but also cases when the factual basis, coherence or logic of inference raises serious doubts.

The formulation of a soft state neutrality principle constitutes a good answer to the sceptic's charge, which accuses neutrality of inconsistency and futility in the political and legal fields. We see that the objection, successful with regard to strong neutrality, does not strike at the soft definition of the principle because the definition is consistent with the claim that political actions are based on certain values. In this manner, the formula does not contradict the specificity of the public sphere. It allows, rather, a broad range of political activities, as pursuant to it, all actions performed for publicly accessible and commonly acceptable reasons should be recognised as permissible and neutral. This requirement is violated only by activities that are inadequately justified; namely, they are based on invoking any controversial conception of the good as inherently valuable or morally worthless.

5. Conclusion

In this chapter, I aimed at challenging one of the most significant objections advanced against the idea of state neutrality and subsequently at introducing a soft concept of the state neutrality principle as a reply to this objection. According to the complaint, the standard set by the concept of neutrality (with respect to actions performed by public servants) is incoherent and unattainable. The principle does not cohere with the peculiarity of political acting because it excludes too broad a scope of actions as impermissible. In my opinion, the range of excluded actions depends on the definition of the principle, so the sceptic's charge is persuasive, but only with respect to a strong depiction of state neutrality. This strong definition is based on some non-trivial claims concerning the character of neutrality, its rationale and its reference. The sceptic's objection remains in force as long as a defended principle: evaluates agent's aims or consequences of his actions, refers to epistemic skepticism as a sufficient justification for its validity and postulates all moral values as its point of reference. Nevertheless, the soft concept of state neutrality does not involve any of these questionable assumptions. It sets a duty of justifying political actions in neutral terms, it is established on a moral principle of equal concern and respect and it indicates only controversial conceptions of the good as its reference.

I claim that the advocated account of state neutrality is, at least in two respects, advantageous over other depictions of the principle. First, it is more consistent and coherent than the alternatives. As indicated in the chapter, it is resistant to weaknesses and imperfections attributable to the stronger version. In my opinion, it also fits accurately with our commonly held beliefs and intuitions concerning political justice. Second, I argue that soft neutrality may constitute a practical and functional standard of judging actions performed by public servants and authorities. An application of the principle in the political sphere will not lead to any unreasonable or paradoxical conclusions, as by employing it, we are able to draw a demarcation between neutral actions and those that do not fulfil the principle's requirements – the demarcation that is necessary to constitute the standard as a rule in the Dworkinian sense.

References

Ackerman, Bruce. 1980. *Social Justice in the Liberal State.* New Haven et al.: Yale University Press.

Caney, Simon. 1991. Consequentialist Defenses of Liberal Neutrality. *The Philosophical Quarterly* 41 (165): 457–477.

De Marneffe, Peter. 1990. Liberalism, Liberty and Neutrality. *Philosophy and Public Affairs* 19 (3): 253–274.

Dworkin, Ronald. 1971. *Taking Rights Seriously.* Cambridge (MA): Harvard University Press.

Dworkin, Ronald. 1985. Liberalism. In *A Matter of Principle*, edited by Richard Dworkin, 181–204. Cambridge (MA): Harvard University Press.

Feinberg, Joel. 1988. *The Moral Limits of the Criminal Law. Harmless Wrongdoing.* Oxford: Oxford University Press.

Klosko, George. 2003. Reasonable Rejection and Neutrality of Justification. In *Perfectionism and Neutrality. Essays in Liberal Theory*, edited by Steven Wall, George Klosko, 167–190, New York: Rowman and Littlefield Publishers, Inc.

Kraut, Richard. 1999. Politics, Neutrality and the Good. *Social Philosophy and Policy* 16 (1): 315–332.

Kymlicka, Will. 1989. Liberal Individualism and Liberal Neutrality. *Ethics* 99: 883–905.
Larmore, Charles. 1996. *The Morals of Modernity*. Cambridge et al.: Cambridge University Press.
Larmore, Charles. 2008. *The Autonomy of Morality*. Cambridge et al.: Cambridge University Press.
Legutko, Ryszard. 1998. Różne aspekty moralności światopoglądowej. In *Neutralność światopoglądowa państwa*, edited by Ewa Nowicka-Włodarczyk, 63–69, Fundacja Międzynarodowe Centrum Rozwoju Demokracji.
MacIntyre, Alasdair. 1989. *Whose Justice? Which Rationality?* Notre Dame (IN): University of Notre Dame Press.
Mill, John S. 1859. On Liberty. In *Essays on Politics and Society, Collected Works XVIII*, edited by John. M. Robson, 213–310. Toronto 1977.
Nagel, Thomas. 1983. Moral Conflict and Political Legitimacy. *Philosophy and Public Affairs* 16 (3): 215–240.
Patten, Allen. 2012. Liberal Neutrality: A Reinterpretation and Defense. *Journal of Political Philosophy* 20: 249–272.
Rawls, John. 1996. *Political Liberalism*. New York: Columbia University Press.
Raz, Joseph. 1986. *The Morality of Freedom.* Oxford: Oxford University Press.
Sadurski, Wojciech. 1990. *Moral Pluralism and Legal Neutrality*. Dordrecht, Boston, London: Kluwer Academic Publishers.
Scanlon, Thomas. 1982. Contractualism and Utilitarianism. In *Utilitarianism and Beyond*, edited by Amartya Sen and Bernard Williams, 103–128. Cambridge: Cambridge University Press.
Waldron, Jeremy. 1993. Legislation and Moral Neutrality. In *Liberal Rights. Collected Papers 1981–1991*, edited by Jeremy Waldron, 143–169. Cambridge: Cambridge University Press.

Another Brick in the Wall? A Libertarian Outlook on Constitutional Rights, Individual Obligations, and the Boundaries of Legal Consistency

Axelle Reiter

Abstract

This chapter analyses the interaction between constitutional rights and constitutional obligations from a libertarian standpoint. In this perspective, rights are conceived as choices and absolute side constraints on action and obligations are derived from pre-existing rights. This conception of rights allows to bypass the risks of utilitarian trade-offs and paternalist or moralist encroachments upon liberty, and rules out the balancing of conflicting rights and interests. The recognition of individual obligations in libertarian theories will be studied from three angles: the negative duty of non-interference; the acceptability of (limited) positive duties; and the co-possibility of the individual duties entrenched in a given constitution.

1. Introduction

From a libertarian standpoint, rights are conceived as choices and absolute side constraints on other laws and regulations, as well as on human interactions more generally, and obligations are derived from pre-existing rights rather than the other way around. Rights entitle individuals to veto interferences with the personal choices that they protect; hence, creating a corollary negative obligation of non-interference that binds all societal actors. Only the symmetric rights of others can limit individual freedoms and entitlements, in cases where these rights are abused for *liberticidal* purposes. Any departure from this general rule of liberty is unjustifiable. Yet, from an analytical viewpoint, a substantive theory needs to explain the entire range of legal rights generally enshrined in constitutions, including positive rights. Two questions must be raised in relation to the obligations generated by such rights: their accommodation in a libertarian theoretical framework and their reconcilability with the obligations that ensue from other rights. The recognition of individual obligations and their interaction with individual rights will be studied from three angles: the negative duty of non-interference; the acceptability of limited positive duties; and the co-possibility of the various duties entrenched in a given constitution.

2. Rights as side constraints on action and the negative duty of non-interference

Liberalism is ultimately founded on individualism. The methodological individualist analysis of social interactions in terms of the individual actions of the relevant agents leads to the ethical individualistic claim that 'all social, economic, legal, and political relations must be reconstructed in terms of agreements based on reciprocal consent or contract' (Chwaszcza 2007, 55–58 and 148). By default, sovereignty resides in the individual and not in the collective, the community or the state, which can only acquire it by delegation. The polity cannot validly claim any other competences than those which result from the aggregation of previously existing rights transferred to it by their individual holders (Nozick 1974, 89–90, 115, 118 and 133–134). Just institutions emerge from the antecedent rights of individuals. Basic rights are the perfect embodiment of philosophical individualism. Because of their consecration of the principle of self-sovereignty, right-based theories empower each and every individual with a veto over those acts and measures that interfere with her personal choices; which denotes an attachment to unanimity, rather than majority, as a requirement for social or political decisions (Nagel 1979, 114 and 116). In view of this, a general right to liberty knows no other limits than the liberty of others. Hence, the recognition of broad human rights eventually entails an adhesion to John Stuart Mill's 'principle of liberty' or 'harm principle' and to state neutrality (Mill 1859, chapter 1). More radically, this logically leads to the connection, exposed by Robert Nozick (1974, ix and 4), between the acknowledgement that 'individuals have rights, and there are things no person or group may do to them without violating their rights', and the question of philosophical anarchism. In such a conceptual frame, duties are only construed as the mirror image of pre-existing personal entitlements and derived from them; they are not recognised any intrinsic worth or conferred a basic place in the theoretical structure.

Right-based theories define justice through the elaboration of 'secondary' rules, which are content-free and deal solely with the boundaries of personal powers and the adjudication of competing claims. Basically, rights consist in the set of principles that sanction and legalise the appropriate allocation of freedom and control among individual human beings and its preservation. They are secondary norms in the Hartian sense of the term; that is, 'second order' rules that 'confer powers, public or private' (Hart 1961, 78–79, 91–92 and 237–238; Hart 1965, 1292; Hart 1994, 80–81, 94 and 283–284). They fit the definition of rules of competences and endorse a conception of justice that is empty of any other content than the respect and protection of a generalised freedom of action. They essentially organise the distribution and extent of the legal capacities of rival actors, and determine the scope of individual self-sovereignty. Hence, rights theories are not only deontological but also procedural, in the sense that they do not look at the outcomes of given acts and measures but rather at their historical record or pedigree. A pure procedural model of justice requires a complete absence of consequentialism at all levels of analysis. This means that a 'purer' theory of rights has to follow a historical entitlements' model, like the one developed by libertarians, and to conceive them as side constraints. Rival theories are typically partially forward-looking and fail thus to protect deontological rights adequately.

Analytically, to characterise rights as 'side constraints', 'trumps' or 'shields' implies that they are both privileged and personalised claims. Accordingly, 'rights are typically conceived of as *possessed* or *owned by* or *belonging to* individuals'; they form 'a kind of moral property of individuals to which they are as individuals entitled' (Hart 1955, 182). They are attached to the individual right-bearer and belong to her, in the sense that she owns them and can dispose of them as (and whenever) she wishes to. Conceiving rights as personalised claims implies that their holder retains the ultimate control over the enforceability and waiving of these claims. It entitles her to decide whether to bring a legal action in front of adjudicatory bodies and whether to put into effect the resultant judgement. In this vision, rights do not consist in mere interests, in need of public protection, to be forwarded by omnipotent authorities. They are the legal recognition of an individual's free will and autonomy, the perfect embodiment of the control she has over her own person and existence. In a word, they are legally protected choices (Hart 1954, 49; Hart 1955; Hart 1973; Hart 1982). The right-bearer has an unlimited power to exercise them, to hand them over, or to give them up. In consequence, 'the possessor of any right should be taken to be the claimant, not the beneficiary', and rights cannot be reduced to, derived from or defined 'in terms of duties' (Wellman 1997, 4).

Rights trace an unbridgeable frontier between the individual sphere of liberty and policy considerations of a utilitarian or otherwise instrumental nature, aimed at fostering particular interests, preferences or visions of the good. To be sure, 'there are some actions we would forbid even if a majority wanted them [and] if a utilitarian calculation supported these actions.' Hence, 'rights stand as barriers to maximising utility and, indeed, to satisfying the preferences of the people in a society' (Nozick 1977, 54). They are a safeguard against majoritarian and aggregative demands. They 'do not determine a social ordering but instead set the constraints within which a social choice is to be made' (Nozick 1974, 166). They impose, thus, limits on political legitimacy and the extent of acceptable public intervention. Essentially, legal rights are absolute side constraints on other laws and regulations. They bar all harmful interferences, regardless of their aims or overall outcomes, and paternalistic or moralistic encroachments on individual freedom and prerogatives. In such a model, 'it is not automatically true that the best act is the one with the best end state consequences.' This presupposes that 'what we choose among is not consequences, but rather doing various actions' (Nozick 1981, 497). In the words of Robert Nozick (1974, 30–33), 'side constraints upon action reflect the underlying Kantian principle that individuals are ends and not merely means; they may not be sacrificed or used for the achieving of other ends without their consent.'

3. Co-possibility of libertarian rights and obligations

Rights are *always* trumping non right-based considerations and they are never to be weighed, balanced, and traded off, in order to promote utility, the general welfare or majority preferences. Yet, the ensuing model still needs to be coherent and able to deal with concrete cases in an appropriate manner. A clear verdict of (il-)legitimacy, that derives directly from the application of the relevant rules of validity in a normative model, is required so that one can afford not to look at the consequences of given actions when assessing their acceptability. Only for absolute norms, because they are 'by definition infinitely stringent and cannot be overridden', is the simple fact of their applicability fully conclusive and 'action-determinative' (Schauer 1991, 115). This entails sufficiently precise rules that they do not clash one against the other and, thus, a logically coherent set of fundamental norms; here, a logically coherent set of basic human rights. In the event that basic rights collide with each other, the 'spectre of trade-offs' reappears from the usual checks and balances accompanying the evaluation of competing rights-claims (Waldron 1989, 508–509; Waldron 1993, 32). The weighing process deprives human rights from their normative character and downgrades their status to that of policy arguments, which can be quantified and tossed in the balance of costs and benefits with all other interests. This represents a serious problem for all rights-based theories that do not rule out, at the definitional stage, the practical occurrence of irreconcilable exigencies.

The first issue in hand is whether the emergence of such conflicts is inevitable or could be avoided altogether; namely, that of the co-possibility or 'compossibility' of any set of rights. The feasibility of this enterprise obviously depends largely on the way rights are conceptualised. This concern needs to be addressed both at a theoretical and more practical legal level. By definition, 'a possible set of rights is such that it is logically impossible for one individual's exercise of his rights within that set to constitute an interference with another individual's exercise of his rights within that same set.' Then, 'to establish the characteristics of the structure of a possible set of rights, we need a general description of the conditions under which two persons' exercises of their rights – two persons' actions – cannot be mutually obstructive.' To be logically possible, a set of rights needs to be 'title-based': rights ought to be indexed to the 'use of, and only of, objects belonging to the user' (Steiner 1977, 769–771). If one conceives of rights as choices and as absolute side constraints on the actions of each individual agent, 'rights are more or less incapable of conflicting with one another.' In fact, 'the negative and agent-relative structure of Nozick's theory more or less precludes such conflicts' (Waldron 1988, 74–75; Waldron 1989, 503–505). Nozick pictures rights as 'permissions to do something and obligation on others not to interfere.' In such a view, human rights are necessarily co-possible since 'each person may exercise his rights as he chooses'; nobody is entitled to hinder other people's actions, provided that they remain within their rights; and 'the particular rights over things fill the space of rights' (Nozick 1974, 92, 166 and 238).

Bearing in mind the libertarian deontological focus on the intrinsic moral quality of actions, it is difficult to imagine how conflicts could ever arise among the set of absolute entitlements pictured by Nozick. Since rights are simply drawing the limits of each person's individual sphere of freedom and decision, there is no place left for incompatibilities in their exercise unless one party trespasses on the self-sovereignty of another, thereby wrongfully infringing on her liberty; in which instance, there is no clash between competing entitlements but an unwarranted violation of fundamental rights. Defining rights as purely agent-relative constraints on one's conduct, which give rise to an obligation of non-interference and have no other conceptual link with the rest of the world, means that an individual agent is only concerned with her own personal respect of these rights, seen as a limitation of the existing options open to her. Agent-relative constraints of a negative nature merely limit a person's alternatives by preventing her from choosing some particular courses of action, which would otherwise be available to her. Once people refrain – as they should – from violating the individual entitlements protected by these constraints, there is no more possibility of disagreement about rights. The correlative duty is one of mere omission.

Nozick's analysis of rights as negative absolute side constraints on individual action allows building up a set of co-possible legal rights, of which all protected freedoms and entitlements can be enforced concomitantly. The usual mechanisms of checks and balances are purely redundant. Nothing needs to be balanced since individual rights are co-possible and the state has no legitimate public function, safe for that of protecting these rights. No other consideration needs to be taken into account at the level of adjudication than the existence of the claimed rights; and a verdict on the appropriateness of restricting people's liberty in a given case obtains from a strict application of this basic rule. This requires that rights be conceived as personal choices derived from a general entitlement to personal autonomy, whose only limits are those of the ban on aggression implied in Mill's harm principle. In such a thoroughly non-prudential perspective, rights do not need to be weighed or balanced, since they never clash, and the practical consequences of actions are disregarded as immaterial to the question of their legal validity. Yet, this all hangs on the internal consistency of the proposed rights matrix and the co-possibility of Nozick's set of absolute choice rights does not only depend on their being purely agent-relative but also on their mostly negative character.[1] In libertarian theories, all rights are construed negatively. They personify the reciprocal and symmetrical application of a general principle of non-interference in the sphere of freedom and self-sovereignty of other individuals and 'duties correlative to basic rights are all negative, refrainings rather than positive performances' (Lomasky 2007, 212).

4. Recognition of positive rights and obligations

It has been alleged that only negative rights can be universally enforced on all agents and in relation to all actions; precisely because they are correlated to a general principle of non-interference and merely impose 'omissions', rather than 'commissions' or the fulfillment of specific acts (Cranston 1973). More fundamentally, positive rights are hardly co-possible. This poses a problem since a substantive theory of rights needs to account for the entire range of rights enshrined in constitutional documents, which includes typically positive rights; chiefly, procedural rights and sometimes economic, social and cultural rights. The trouble does not lay so much in the difficulty to accommodate these rights in a libertarian framework, as in the irreconcilability of positive rights among themselves and their necessary restricting of negative rights; which eventually results in a theoretical deadlock. Nozick's theory opens up several avenues to the recognition of economic and social rights. Two pretty obvious candidates are the Lockean *proviso* to the original appropriation of natural resources and the need to rectify past injustices. In addition, the principle of compensation can be used to grant people further positive rights against the state or any other coercive structure whose existence violates people's autonomy.

1 The negative quality of the set of rights Nozick recognises needs to be somewhat qualified. He includes in the list of people's natural entitlements some procedural guarantees, which are essentially positive in character. As exposed below, this opens the way for the acceptance of other positive rights.

The Lockean *proviso* imposes limits on the appropriation of unowned resources. The original formulation of Locke's *proviso* required that there be 'enough and as good left in common for others' (Locke 1764, §§ 27, 33 and 37). Nozick interprets it as meaning that 'the situation of others is not worsened' (Nozick 1974, 174–182). David Gauthier further elaborates on Nozick's reading, from a rational choice perspective, in order to capture the idea of 'not taking advantage of others' (Gauthier 1986, 201–205 and 277–278; Gauthier 1993, 182). Nozick's reformulation of John Locke's *proviso* conditions the acquisition of previously unowned property to the exigency that it does not effectively worsen the situation of other individuals. Claiming original ownership in the absence of such a prerequisite would constitute an unjust appropriation, which would submit it to the rules of compensatory justice. In cases where the *proviso* is not respected, compensation is owed to the persons who experience thereby a net loss, whose amount is fixed so as to bring them back to a position on the same (or a higher) indifference curve as their baseline situation.[2] Besides, the *proviso* is not only construed as a restriction to the original appropriation of goods but also as a limited check on later transfers. Even though this is mostly incidental to its main function, it permits as well to avert results that would be catastrophic from a humane perspective. For example, it would proscribe the abusive use of monopolistically possessing the entire supply of a given natural resource like water, which is necessary for life (Hayek 1960; Nozick 1974, 180). This implies leaving at least a vital minimum for others; a set of survival rights must always be guaranteed (Waldron 1988, 281–283).

The introduction of a Lockean *proviso* into the initial acquisition of holdings only justifies the provision of people's critical needs, not a wide range of social rights, let alone a full-fledged scheme of redistribution. Corrective justice facilitates the validation of much more extensive positive rights. Nozick himself recognises the need for some form of redistribution, in today's real world, to compensate the victims of past injustices and palliate the impossibility of tracing historical misappropriations to their source. Since contemporary holdings are undeniably tainted with blood and corruption, he even suggests that a temporary application of Rawls' difference principle might serve as a plausible approximation for the legitimate rectification of ancient violations of rights (Nozick 1974, 230–231; Waldron 2002, 279). Some such type of reparation is clearly required by a purely procedural conception of justice. This results in the legitimacy of large

2 This means that they are either indifferent between which of the situations results or favour the latter and that they are left at least as well off after the appropriation and compensation have taken place than originally.

transfers both inside and (even more so) across contemporary societies to compensate for preceding misappropriations and for the historical subjugation of entire groups of people (Lyons 1977). Likewise, society's liability for creating part of the conditions for ill-health could justify compensatory positive rights to health care (Murray 2007, 51, 53 and 76–93). Independent of which particular solution is adopted as a rule of thumb, the rectification principle presents a pretty broad basis for the recognition of positive rights.

Furthermore, the granting of due process rights and of at least a nucleus of fundamental economic and social rights could be construed as a form of compensation for the existence of a coercive state system; either as an obligation of otherwise illegitimate institutions to provide for guarantees against their own abuses and for the basic needs of individuals in circumstances where they are not properly left free to fulfil them on their own; or, alternatively, as a sort of repayment for the loss of freedom inherent in the current institutional setting. The first option suggests the provision of a similar level of positive rights as the one guaranteed by the Lockean *proviso* in state-ruled societies, as a type of damages for the adverse economic consequences of the state's misappropriations and use of coercion. The second can be compared to the moral duty of Nozick's dominant protective agency to compensate independents, which it prevents from exercising their right to self-defence against its clients, by giving them free protection.[3] Thereby, Nozick would allegedly allow for some form of redistribution at the level of right-enforcement, due process and fair trial (Narveson 1977, 311); a mechanism which could be extended to fund economic and social rights. Indeed, 'people do not have

3 In Nozick's state of nature, individual rights are not purely negative. They also include some procedural entitlements, like the right to a fair trial. In this respect, a problem with the state of nature comes from the unreliability of the procedures some people might employ when exercising their right to self-defence and punishment, thereby breaching the right to a fair treatment by reliable and trustworthy procedures of the person under trial. As a result, most protection agencies will agree on the adoption of protective procedures to be applied by all in the settlement of claims involving their clients. Yet, independent actors who have not signed up with the said associations cannot be prevented from resorting to their own preferred techniques of adjudication without compensation, as this would impose on them illegitimate costs and disadvantages. As a form of compensation for the enforcement body's limitation of the exercise by unaligned individuals of their right to self-defence against its clients, the 'state-like entity' is then required to provide them with free services. The ensuing 'border crossing' morally justifies some sort of quasi-redistributive scheme in rights-enforcement, financed by the dominant protective agency and thus taken from the revenues it collects from its clients. This is considered to be the act of creation of the minimal state (Nozick 1974, 110-115).

a fundamental right to protection any more than to any [other] service people could supply.' Consequently, 'there has to be an argument why the state should do no more if it does anything at all' (Barry 1986, 140–144; Narveson 1988, 350 note 9; Shue 1985). Short of anarchism and a blanket prohibition on all forms of redistributive activities –namely, in the presence of any type of monopoly over the use of force, authority structure, or obligatory redistribution agency, however minimal –, social institutions are accountable to guarantee the respect of survival rights, aimed at protecting life and liberty.

Even bearing in mind that Nozick himself considers the compensatory justification lying behind the provision of those protective services to imply that it cannot be adequately termed 'redistributive' (Nozick 1974, 27 and 114), other positive rights could similarly be grounded on the need to compensate people for the curtailment in states' hands of their personal liberty and autonomy. Governmental institutions would then need to provide economic and social rights, as a form of repayment for the part of the power to control their own lives that they take away from individuals. Whether procedural rights are asserted as a matter of redistribution or of compensation, their acknowledgment opens the road to the recognition of additional positive rights. The latter alternative is clearly preferable to the former because it is more in keeping with Nozick's analysis and the nature of an historical theory of justice based on respect for individual entitlements. The delivery of rights protection as a public good necessarily involves an element of illegitimate redistribution. Since some people are compelled to provide for the welfare of others, liberal neutrality and the deontological separation of persons would be violated in the process. By opposition, corrective justice is not only consistent with the recognition of unrestricted rights but it is even contributing to their protection. It should be commended, independent of its convenience as an adequate basis on which to ground positive rights.

Of course, neither of these avenues would legitimise as such the original coercive structure, nor provide a basis for positive rights in its eventual absence or collapse. The discharge of the positive obligations correlative to these entitlements remains strictly the duty of public institutions and not that of private actors. Legally speaking, this is the way in which rights are normally conceived of: people are only bound to abstain from interference in the life of other individuals, while positive rights are mostly directed against the state apparatus (Donnelly 1985, 9 note 1). Nonetheless, reparation of past and present exploitation or violence permits to justify the global supply of certain limited social guarantees in the existing world. What concerns the transnational aspects of this question, compensatory justice obviously entails that, 'insofar as the policies of some states impose harms on the nationals of others, a legitimate claim for redress can be made' (Lomasky 2007, 218).

In view of the sheer mass and extent of the abuses committed, a cosmopolitan approach to rectification would impact widely on contemporary societal structures and international dynamics.

5. Co-possibility of positive rights and obligations

Positive rights of a procedural and social nature are accommodated within the libertarian frame of entitlements. Yet, this is not sufficient to escape the much more problematic issue of their logical co-possibility in the face of competing claims. To be sure, 'major difficulties are encountered by theories that claim that any right, other than a purely negative right to freedom of interference of various kinds, are always absolute' (Mc Closkey 1985, 129). Only in the presence of rules that do not conflict, one can afford not to look at the concrete consequences of actions. Basic norms have to be co-possible or their protection will necessarily entail some weighing or balancing of sorts. A conceivable avenue out of this quandary – or, more exactly, one that has been advocated as such – consists in identifying all recognised rights as negative.

Along such lines, Pogge (1989, 32) alleges that there exists 'a *negative* moral right, a claim the poor had against American citizens, specifically, who were collaborating in the imposition of an unjust economic scheme that tended to produce more severe poverty than is morally justifiable', based on a supposedly 'negative duty not to abuse just practices.' This is both confusing and analytically flawed. Aside from the contestability of the underlying ideological assumptions, a positive right and its corollary obligations do not suddenly become negative because they originate in the breach of a prior negative duty. Far from resolving the problem in hand, this stratagem futilely attempts to draw it out of the picture and obscures several typical features of fundamental rights in the process. Pogge's solution derives rights from pre-existing duties, misunderstanding the basic foundations of rights theories. It is grounded on a misconception of the nature of negative entitlements, which only give rise to an obligation of non-aggression against unwilling persons and of compensation for one's own *personal* interferences, and not to anything remotely close to a concept of collective responsibility in other people's misdeeds or those of society at large. It mischaracterises poverty as inevitably resulting from willful decisions of economic or social actors; missing both the moral neutrality of economics' laws (Nozick 1974, 250–253, 297–306 and 316–321) and the inherent decentralisation of a non-tampered market. Finally, it rests on an under-developed conception of what are justice, a 'just' economic scheme, a 'morally justifiable' level of poverty, and 'just practices'; which Pogge mostly assumes instead of arguing for it.

Renaming intrinsically positive rights 'negative' does not help turning their coexistence into a logical possibility. It ends up blurring completely unnecessarily the useful analytical distinction between negative and positive rights, with the result that so-called 'negative' rights lose the main advantage associated to this qualification; namely, their co-possibility. Hence, this type of stratagem should be resisted. The same criticism applies to the common believe that rights to a fair trial or due process are purely negative and to the allegation that there exists no difference between positive and negative entitlements. The distinction between positive and negatives rights is conceptually well-founded. It bears important consequences on the legal protection afforded to different types of rights and on the identification of the addressees of the resulting obligations. Negating it for instrumental reasons is pointless. In consequence, the issue of the coexistence of various positive rights and that of their impact on the respect due to negative freedoms and entitlements must be confronted head on. A study of this question should investigate the type of positive rights that derives from individual rights and from their identification with absolute side constraints on action. Once they have been adequately characterised, attention needs to be paid to the nature of the resulting duties they impose on other individuals and state authorities. The ensuing set of public and private obligations ought to be organised so that it holds logically and does not suffer from internal inconsistencies.

In a libertarian conception, the nature of economic and social rights is not so much to guarantee access to social services than to better secure individual freedom and democracy, itself defined in terms of rights. They should provide a basis not for a welfare-state but for a social state, where the conditions for effective freedom would be protected (Höffe 1988, 104). Two types of corollary obligations are derived from the recognition of positive rights. First, the fact that someone holds a right, be it of a negative or positive nature, implies that all other agents are bound not to interfere with and undermine her attempts to exercise that right or secure it for herself. They are obliged to refrain from infringing her rights, which is ultimately an expression of the negative duty not to harm other people. In contrast, the second type of duty ensuing from the existence of positive entitlements presents a purely positive aspect. This second variety of obligations is based on the idea that rights cannot be valued *per se* if they are not valuable to their holder or conducive of personal value (Lomasky 1987, 90, 93 and 128), which somehow leads to a partial collapse of the Rawlsian distinction between freedom and its exercise, value or worth (Rawls 1971, 204; Rawls 1999, 179). Accordingly, the necessary conditions for an effective exercise of their individual liberty ought to be guaranteed to each and every individual, which entails some positive actions.

In effect, 'to say that the valuable capacity to live a meaningful life is the *basis* of rights' implies that an adequate conception of rights must enable people 'to actually *live* meaningful lives.' Eventually, this means that core social rights to food, clothes, shelter, health care and education need to be provided for (Murray 2007, 94–133; Scheffler 1976, 64 and 69–70). Likewise, 'starting gate' libertarians claim that a sufficient amount of material resources is necessary for self-ownership to be effective (Cohen 1995, 94; Ingram 1994, 40 and 45; Otsuka 2003, chapter 1; Steiner 1994). Economic and social positive rights are designed to ensure to individuals the basic needs, without which they cannot exercise their negative rights or lead a meaningful life. Conversely, these subsistence rights cannot be equated with a full blown theory of redistributive justice or used as an argument to ground more ambitious political claims (Chwaszcza 2007, 150, 153 and 160). They do not have for object the provision of vaguely defined public goods or the bringing about of radical equalitarianism, and cannot serve to justify such attempts. One should never forget that the price paid for state-based social protection is extremely heavy. The more the state expands its interventionist powers, the smaller the sphere of privacy and competence left to individuals becomes. Today's paradigmatic welfare-state condones a generalised shrinking of the extent of all fundamental rights and not merely that of private property (Höffe 1988, 102). Last but not least, the public financing of any service entails a public budget, traditionally harvested through taxes. Although state authorities have always ignored them and preferred to resort to tax collection regardless of individual entitlements over private property, alternative avenues could be pursued.

In connection with the basic economic and social rights of the disabled, Michael Otsuka (2003, 41–53) suggests that universal taxation 'across the board' could be replaced by 'punitive taxation' through the imposition of a system of fines; as a form of legitimate punishment of the criminal activities of those 'individuals who have been properly convicted of performing justifiably criminalised acts', to whom he refers to as 'the unjust.' Peter Vallentyne (2007, 187 and 196–199) suggests the same type of financing by rights-offenders for procedural rights. Since the commission of the decried activities is voluntary but illegitimate, the proposed solution would allow circumventing the usual arguments against the coercive seizure of private property for redistributive purposes and the benefits of third parties; namely, that taxation constitutes at best theft, if not forced labour or slavery (Nozick 1974, 169–172). Even though the so-called 'unjust' clearly do not voluntarily contribute to the redistributive scheme, 'in the case of taxation of the unjust as opposed to universal taxation, one's forced contribution is the consequence of an unforced choice to do wrong', which should not have been exercised in the first place. It is acceptable as soon as one agrees to any type of retributive or deterrence-based sanction (Otsuka 2003, 47–49). Even in a mostly corrective model of criminal justice, like the one advanced by Nozick (1974, 62), nothing would prevent the state from employing the money left over after the victims have been fully compensated to fund its obligation to provide for positive human rights. Besides, the latent symbolic value of retribution (Nozick 1981, 370–380) entails that a contribution to the 'common good' of society, by participating in the provision of some social safety net, makes more sense as a form of punishment than the imposition of some purely gratuitous additional wrong on the offender.

In spite of the advantages of the proposed model, contemporary legal systems are unlikely to endorse such a radical change in their approach to criminal justice any time soon; leaving the conflict between positive rights and individual property unresolved in practice, if not in theory. In the absence of an internally coherent set of rights, the only way to escape unwanted trade-offs reside in an *a priori* hierarchisation of clashing entitlements (Gewirth 1981, 3; Nagel 1975, 141). The most primordial rights – the rights to life, physical integrity and personal liberty – could be entrenched unconditionally, while lesser ones would merely constitute trumps on competing claims and considerations that are not right-based and give way in inter-rights conflicts. Core rights protected as inalienable in international conventions, like *habeas corpus* and the ban on torture, should remain absolutely immune from any kind of bargaining and trade-offs; and the positive aspects of both procedural and social rights cannot be invoked for further restrictions than those encroachments on individual property that are strictly necessary to their financing. This solution might be criticised for its lack of neatness but it reduces the amount of legal uncertainty otherwise generated by the *ad hoc* balancing of competing claims.

6. Conclusion

To sum up, the recognition of negative rights conditions the legitimacy of all human actions and imposes, thus, a general duty of non-interference on all types of agents; be it individuals, other private actors or public officials. Conversely, the positive obligations that derive from the necessity to guarantee procedural and social rights only hold against states. The idea of rights as absolute side constraints, that is thereby established, has the merit to protect people from the perils of utilitarian policies. In effect, it is the sole paradigm that allows evading altogether the likelihood of state-promoted abuses, by conferring to individuals an unassailable sphere of self-sovereignty, a realm directed solely by their own choices and free will. The respect of its boundaries is, by right, absolute; insulated from majoritarian demands and shielded from utilitarian trade-offs. In this perspective, the only legitimate limit to individual liberty is that imposed by the need to respect the equal liberty of others and rights are ordered so as to avoid their balancing in the event of adjudication between competing irreconcilable claims.

References

Barry, Norman P. 1986. *On Classical Liberalism and Libertarianism*. Houndmills: Mc Millan.

Cohen, Gerald A. 1995. *Self-Ownership, Freedom, and Equality*. Cambridge: Cambridge University Press.

Cranston, Maurice W. 1973. *What Are Human Rights?* London: Bodley Head.

Chwaszcza, Christine. 2007. *Moral Responsibility and Global Justice*. Baden-Baden: Nomos.

Donnelly, Jack. 1985. *The Concept of Human Rights*. London: Croom Helm.

Gauthier, David. 1986. *Morals by Agreement*. Oxford: Oxford University Press.

Gauthier, David. 1993. Uniting Separate Persons. In *Rationality, Justice and the Social Contract: Themes from Morals by Agreement*, edited by David Gauthier and Robert Sugden, 176–192. London: Wheatsheaf.

Gewirth, Alan. 1981. Are There Any Absolute Rights? *Philosophical Quarterly*: 1–16.

Hart, Herbert L.A. 1954. Definition and Theory in Jurisprudence. *Law Quarterly Review*: 37–60.

Hart, Herbert L.A. 1955. Are There Any Natural Rights? *Philosophical Review*: 175–191.

Hart, Herbert L.A. 1961. *The Concept of Law*. Oxford: Clarendon.

Hart, Herbert L.A. 1965. Lon L. Fuller's The Morality of Law. *Harvard Law Review*: 1281–1296.

Hart, Herbert L.A. 1973. Bentham on Legal Rights. In *Oxford Essays in Jurisprudence (Second Series)*, edited by Alfred W.B. Simpson, 171–201. Oxford: Clarendon.

Hart, Herbert L.A. 1982. Legal Rights. In *Essays on Bentham: Studies in Jurisprudence and Political Theory*, 162–193. Oxford: Clarendon.

Hart, H.L.A. 1994. *The Concept of Law*, 2nd ed. Oxford: Clarendon.

Hayek, Friedrich A. 1960. *The Constitution of Liberty*. Chicago: University of Chicago Press.

Höffe, Otfried. 1988. *L'état et la justice: Les problèmes éthiques et politiques dans la philosophie anglo-saxonne; John Rawls et Robert Nozick*. Paris: Vrin.

Ingram, Attracta. 1994. *A Political Theory of Rights*. Oxford: Oxford University Press.

Locke, John. 1764. *Two Treatises of Government*. London: A. Millar et al.

Lomasky, Loren E. 1987. *Persons, Rights and the Moral Community*. Oxford: Oxford University Press.

Lomasky, Loren E. 2007. Liberalism beyond Borders. *Social Philosophy and Policy*: 206–233.

Lyons, David. 1977. The New Indian Claims and Original Rights to Land. *Social Theory and Practice*: 249–272.

Mc Closkey, H. J. 1985. Respect for Human Moral Rights *versus* Maximizing Good. In *Utility and Rights*, edited by R.G. Frey, 121–136. Oxford: Blackwell.

Mill, John S. 1859. *On Liberty*. In *Essays on Politics and Society, Collected Works XVIII*, edited by John. M. Robson, 213–310. Toronto 1977.

Murray, Dale F. 2007. *Nozick, Autonomy and Compensation*. London: Continuum.

Nagel, Thomas. 1975. Libertarianism without Foundations. *Yale Law Journal*: 136–149.

Nagel, Thomas. 1979. *Mortal Questions*. Cambridge: Cambridge University Press.

Narveson, Jan. 1977. Anarchy, State, and Utopica. *Dialogue*: 298–327.

Narveson, Jan. 1988. *The Libertarian Idea*. Philadelphia: Temple University Press.

Nozick, Robert. 1974. *Anarchy, State, and Utopia*. New York: Basic.
Nozick, Robert. 1977. Commentary on Symposium: Equality and Efficiency; What is the Optimum Equality in Incomes? In *Income Redistribution*, edited by Colin D. Campbell, 50–55. Washington: American Enterprise Institute for Public Policy Research.
Nozick, Robert. 1981. *Philosophical Explanations*. Oxford: Clarendon.
Otsuka, Michael. 2003. *Libertarianism without Inequality*. Oxford: Clarendon.
Pogge, Thomas W. M. 1989. *Realizing Rawls*. Ithaca: Cornell University Press.
Rawls, John. 1971. *A Theory of Justice*. Cambridge (MA): Harvard University Press.
Rawls, John. 1999. *A Theory of Justice*, revised ed. Cambridge (MA): Harvard University Press.
Schauer, Frederick. 1991. *Playing by the Rules: A Philosophical Examination of Rule-Based Decision-Making in Law and in Life*. Oxford: Clarendon.
Scheffler, Samuel. 1976. Natural Rights, Equality, and the Minimal State. *Canadian Journal of Philosophy*: 59–76.
Shue, Henry. 1985. The Bogus Distinction, 'Negative' and 'Positive' Rights. In *Making Ethical Decisions*, edited by Norman E. Bowie, 223–231. New York: Mc Graw.
Steiner, Hillel. 1977. The Structure of a Set of Compossible Rights. *Journal of Philosophy*: 767–775.
Steiner, Hillel. 1994. *An Essay on Rights*. Oxford: Blackwell.
Vallentyne, Peter. 2007. Libertarianism and the State. *Social Philosophy and Policy*: 187–205.
Waldron, Jeremy. 1988. *The Right to Private Property*. Oxford: Clarendon.
Waldron, Jeremy. 1989. Rights in Conflict. *Ethics*: 503–519.
Waldron, Jeremy. 1993. Liberal Rights: Two Sides of the Coin. In *Liberal Rights: Collected Papers (1981–1991)*, 1–34. Cambridge: Cambridge University Press.
Waldron, Jeremy. 2002. Justice. In *Political Science: State of the Discipline*, edited by Ira Katznelson and Helen V. Milner, 266–285. London: Norton.
Wellman, Carl H. 1997. *An Approach to Rights: Studies in the Philosophy of Law and Morals*. Dordrecht: Kluwer.

Ethnic Representation in National Legislatures – Normative Foundations and Challenges

Konstantin Sachariew

Abstract

In reports of minority rights groups as well as in the literature on democratic theory one can often find the claim that one of the criteria for a democratic parliament is that it should reflect the social diversity of the population in terms of gender, language, religion or ethnicity. Frequently this goes together with the demand for group representation through specialised measures and institutions that expand the traditional understanding of representative government and alter the electoral competition. These demands have been both supported and challenged by democratic theorists, governments and minority groups. This chapter reviews the current literature on group and descriptive representation and focuses especially on the normative debate that has formed around it.

1. Introduction

While reading about the political representation of ethnic minorities, one frequently finds demands for a stronger political participation of marginalised groups. These voices often advocate group representation and a mirroring of the constituency by the legislature in social and ethnic characteristics as means for enhancing the leverage of minority groups on policy outcomes. For example, Anders Johnsson (Secretary General of the Inter-Parliamentary Union) and Geraldine Fraser-Moleketi (Practice Director, Democratic Governance Group of the Bureau of Development Policy, UNDP) find that

> one of the ways in which they can exercise their right to development is for minorities and indigenous peoples to play a greater part in policy-making and decision-making. Yet until recently, this has seldom happened. The frequent absence of minorities and indigenous peoples from parliament and from parliamentary work in general is a striking example of their marginalization. (Powley 2010, 5)

They later establish that 'one of the criteria for a democratic parliament is that it should reflect the social diversity of the population in terms of gender, language, religion, ethnicity' (ibid.) Similar claims can be found in recent works on representation and democratic theory. Suzanne Dovi writes that 'democratic political institutions are often evaluated by the gender, ethnicity, and race of elected representatives [...]. Implicit in these evaluations is the assumption that democratic political institutions that lack any representatives from historically disadvantaged groups are unjust' (Dovi 2002, 729) and Mala Htun even finds that 'as the twentieth century progressed, [...] a consensus emerged in international society and within democratic polities that one social segment should not monopolize political power' (Htun 2004, 439). This consensus is questionable – we do not need to look too far to see examples of marginalised and politically excluded social groups even in established democracies. And we cannot ignore those authors who, for one reason or another, reject the notion of formalised group representation and the social mirroring in parliaments. Still, the concepts of *descriptive* and of *group representation* have left a mark on democratic theory and frame many of the contemporary writings on the political participation of ethnic and other minorities.

This chapter reviews the current literature on group and descriptive representation and focuses especially on the normative debate that has formed around it. It draws heavily on the literature on democratic representation and deliberation, on multiculturalism and group rights and on the political participation of disadvantaged social groups and minorities. The aim of this is to reach a better understanding of ethnic minority political representation and the norms and standards for its assessment. Thus, beginning with the thought that political participation is necessary in improving the lot of disadvantaged and discriminated groups, in raising the quality of the democratic process and in respecting the customary rights of native populations, the following questions shall guide the succeeding review: Is minority representation valuable at all? How can minorities be represented best in parliaments? Is representation by deputies resembling their minority constituencies (descriptive representation) valuable or necessary? Is there a need for a guaranteed and institutionalised representation of minorities (group representation)? In short – the aim of this chapter is to review some of the arguments in favour or against such measures as reserved seats for minority groups, racial redistricting, special constituencies and party list quotas.

2. The baseline – democratic equality and representation

Advocates of group representation and minority rights usually start their argument with a statement on the injustice of a persistent exclusion of certain groups from political participation. Permanent political exclusion can exist for many reasons even in established democracies that uphold legal guarantees of equal civic and political rights. But in most cases exclusion stems from two factors. The first is a natural result of the most common democratic way of decision making – majority rule. Where minority interests are distinct, persistent and conflicting with the interest of the majority this decision making rule tends to exclude their interests from the political process and the policy outcomes. The second stems from historical legacies of disenfranchisement and social and cultural marginalisation. When such marginalisation has created persistent social and status inequalities, disadvantaged groups do not have an equal chance of political participation, even if legally they are as much entitled to it as the dominant groups.

Such exclusion is a violation of the democratic ideal. If one accepts the general understanding of democracy as a political system in which all citizens are political *equals*, all are collectively sovereign and all possess the capacities, resources and institutions to govern themselves, then one cannot accept the permanent exclusion of citizens from political participation (Dahl 1989, 1). Equality is crucial. The foundation of democracy lies in the simple faith in some sort of equality between the citizens of a state in particular or generally between all mankind (Young 2000, 23). Therefore the exclusion of individuals or social groups from political participation violates the democratic ideal of political equality.

2.1 Democratic representation

Contemporary democracies are defined by the concept of representation. Advocating ethnic minority political participation is mostly advocating ethnic minority political representation. Political representation today is generally understood as the 'making present' of the interests and perspectives of citizens in the policy making process. Political representation takes place when elected representatives act in parliament in the interest of their constituency, in a manner responsive to it (Pitkin 1967, 209). But acting in the interest of someone else is a rather vague concept:

> And, despite the resulting potential for conflict between representative and represented about what is to be done, that conflict must not normally take place. The representative must act in such a way that there is no conflict, or if it occurs an explanation is called for. He must not be found persistently at odds with the wishes of the represented without good reason in terms of their interest, without a good explanation of why their wishes are not in accord with their interest. (ibid., 210)

This possible difference between the wishes and the interest of the represented as perceived by the representative is a cause for both blame and praise of democratic representation. If the wishes of the constituency are short-sighted and actually detrimental to it, a legislator who cares for the long-term interest of his electors, will ignore their wishes and decide in favour of their future welfare. This is a positive result of the liberty of democratic representatives. If on the other side the representative confuses the interest of his constituency or if he acts selfishly, the same liberty is clearly harmful.

The gap between the wishes and the interest of the constituency is not the only sphere where a representative has to weigh different demands and loyalties in fulfilling his duties. For example, how is his electors' interest to be balanced against a probably conflicting national interest? Is the will or the wishes of the majority of his voters binding? What about possible minorities inside his constituency that he should represent? If a deputy truly understands himself as a representative of a particular ethnic or cultural minority, how does he understand his role as a representative of an electoral district that in most cases will include citizens that are not part of the minority? Will he represent their interest, too?

The standard account of representation in democratic political philosophy has been defined by Urbinati and Warren as follows:

> First, representation is understood as a principal agent relationship, in which the principals – constituencies formed on a territorial basis – elect agents to stand for and act on their interests and opinions, thus separating the sources of legitimate power from those who exercise that power. Second, electoral representation identifies a space within which the sovereignty of the people is identified with state power. Third, electoral mechanisms ensure some measure of responsiveness to the people by representatives and political parties who speak and act in their name. Finally, the universal franchise endows electoral representation with an important element of political equality. (Urbinati and Warren 2008, 389)

This standard account has been challenged in the last two decades by two complementary processes.

2.2 The changing meaning of representation

The first process is characterised by the on-going change in the political landscape of western democracies that is driven by both the rise of 'identity politics' and the growing importance of transnational governance regimes. The ascent of 'identity politics' and 'multiculturalism' in the established western democracies but also in the post-communist world is the result of growing demands from civil rights movements and increasingly politically self-confident ethnic and cultural minority groups. Their demands for the recognition and preservation of cultural identities and for the introduction of group political participation have revealed some limits of the traditional understanding of political representation (Bird et al., 2011). So has the mushrooming of 'transnational, extraterritorial, and nonterritorial actors' ranging from formalised institutions, based on territorial units like the European Union, to a score of treaty organisations, nongovernmental associations and transnational movements, each claiming to represent universal or particular interests (Urbinati and Warren 2008, 390).

The second process that has altered the conception of democratic representation is the on-going work on the theory of deliberative democracy. Scholars of deliberation have changed the perspective of theorists of representative democracy from a rather simple concept of representative government as a mode of aggregation and representation of interest to a complex understanding of representation as one institution in a broader deliberative process of political decision making. Representation is now increasingly understood not as a weak substitute for real or direct democracy, like most classical critics and many supporters of representative government have held, but as a necessary means for indirectness and deliberation (Manin 1997, Urbinati 2006, Weymans 2005, Young 2000). Indirectness is understood as 'the representation of citizens' judgments to them by their representative and vice versa – through which the demos reflects on itself and judges its laws, institutions, and leaders' (Urbinati and Warren 2008, 401). Iris Marion Young describes this change as a shift from an aggregative model of democracy to a deliberative one:

> The first model interprets democracy as a process of aggregating the preferences of citizens in choosing public officials and policies. The goal of democratic decision-making is to decide what leaders, rules, and policies will best correspond to the most widely and strongly held preferences. [...] In the deliberative model democracy is a form of practical reason. Participants in the democratic process offer proposals for how best to solve problems or meet legitimate needs, and so on, and they present arguments through which they aim to persuade others to accept their proposals (Young 2000, 19, 22).

3. Group representation and its illiberal implications

Traditionally nation states grant and guarantee civic rights regardless of religious, class or ethnic membership. Every citizen is legally equal to all the others and is entitled to his civil rights as an individual, not as member of a cultural, religious or ethnic community. Multiculturalism or the *politics of identity* stays in this liberal domain, as it affirms the value and the rights of the individual. But it goes beyond the individualist approach to civic rights. A central demand of the multiculturalist programme is the introduction of certain *group rights* to certain minorities as a means of affirming their distinct identity and compensating for inequalities based on historic discrimination. Group rights are discussed and called for as a remedy for past injustice, a remedy that is necessary and more effective than the usual anti-discrimination policies.

The debate on multiculturalism and the implications of multiculturalist policies has been enormous. Of distinct interest here is the discussion on the dangers of granting special rights and exemptions to ethnic or cultural minorities, as it is highly informative for the evaluation of guaranteed minority representation through reserved seats, separate electoral districts and other similar means.

Multiculturalism as a political theory and movement has its roots in academic discussions and public policies of the late 1970s. It gained momentum in the 1980s and reached its greatest theoretical, political and social impact in the 1990s and early 2000s. Although the proponents of multiculturalism have been diverse in their sphere of action, in their scope, their aim and determination, one central belief unites most of them:

> Modern societies are said to be characterized by deep diversity and cultural pluralism. In the past, this diversity was ignored or stifled by models of the "normal" citizen, which were typically based on the attributes of the able-bodied, heterosexual white male. [...] Today, however, previously excluded groups are no longer willing to be silenced or marginalized, or to be defined as "deviant" simply because they differ in race, culture, gender, ability or sexual orientation from the so-called "normal" citizen. They demand a more inclusive conception of citizenship which recognizes (rather than stigmatizes) their identities, and which accommodates (rather than excludes) their differences. (Kymlicka 2002, 327)

Therefore, among the common claims that multiculturalists often voice, we can find the demand for special group rights, based on language and culture:

> The details of the argument vary, but each of us, in our own way, argues that there are compelling interests related to culture and identity which are fully consistent with liberal principles of freedom and equality, and which justify granting special rights to minorities. (ibid., 339)

With regard to politics, Anne Philips has put the central multiculturalist/feminist argument for group political representation nicely:

> Political equality is not guaranteed by the equal right to vote, nor gender neutrality by the abstractions of the liberal individual. Abstract individualism imposes a unitary conception of human needs and concerns, and this serves to marginalize those groups who may differ from the dominant norm. (Phillips 1995, 293)

Therefore something stronger than individual rights is needed, some 'more formal representation of group identities or group interests' is necessary 'in order to counteract the current balance of power' (ibid., 289). This is clearly a call for an institutionalised permanent representation of marginalised groups.

Group rights, understood as rights granted to groups as distinct entities and right bearers, stand in sharp contrast to the authoritative liberal view that the only subjects protected by civic rights can be individuals. Of course, the liberal legal theory knows exceptions to this concept that can be found in the laws on trade, corporations and civic associations. But these are not the same kind of group rights that the proponents of the politics of identity have advanced. The difference is, that according to the liberal understanding, there is and ought to be only one legal status for all citizens of a polity. The introduction of group rights based on language, religion, race or ethnicity on the other side would create different legal statutes, different classes of citizens with different and probably conflicting rights and duties. Naturally, liberal authors have opposed such thinking and policies. One of the most resolute critics of multiculturalism has been Brian Barry (2001). According to Barry, one of the many flaws of multiculturalism is the focus on identity and culture in defining disadvantaged social groups, while at the same time ignoring their social and economic status. While there are indeed marginalised groups in all western liberal societies, to him it does not make sense to define these groups in terms of culture or language. Rather, there often is a high coincidence of cultural *and* economic marginalisation, that calls for a policy of redistribution and a robust welfare state and not for a public flagging of social groups as discriminated and their endowment with special group rights.

The debate on the need for and the practical results of multiculturalist policies has been both extensively and fiercely fought. Several issues from this debate raise questions about the right representation of minorities. One particular concern is about the changes that multiculturalist policies can provoke inside social and cultural groups. It is about the danger of essentialising and freezing of cultures through public funding and special legislation leading to a loss in political accountability. The argument starts with one of the major multiculturalist claims – the demand for the introduction or extension of self-government of (national) minorities like Indian tribes and the restraint of the state to prevent 'violations of liberty and equality' by the minority leadership (ibid., 138). In other words, national minorities should enjoy self-government and the state should not interfere if they choose to violate the civic rights of their members. Will Kymlicka puts it this way:

> But if two national groups do not share basic principles, and cannot be persuaded to adopt the other's principles, they will have to rely on some other basis of accommodation, such as a modus vivendi. The resulting agreement may well involve exempting the national minority from federal bills of rights and judicial review.' And further: 'In cases where the national minority is illiberal, this means that the majority will be unable to prevent the violation of individual rights within the minority community. Liberals in the majority group have to learn to live with this, just as they must live with illiberal laws in other countries. (Kymlicka 1995, 168)

That is to say: Cultures have a right to be illiberal, and the best a liberal state can do is to try to persuade them to change, but without the use of force. It is easy to imagine that such a policy can seriously endanger the life and liberty of dissenting members of cultural groups and national minorities. But the argument does not stop here. Granting groups based on inscriptive characteristics exceptions from the general rules and the common civil rights system is not only opening the door to oppression and violence inside those groups but is also artificially cementing cultures, their elements and membership. Iris Marion Young, otherwise sympathetic to the general politics of difference has warned:

> The logic of identity expressed by separatist assertions and movements, finally, often tends to simplify and freeze the identity of its group in a way that fails to acknowledge the group differences within a social group. A strong nationalist separatist movement, for example, may reinforce or increase its domination of women or a religious minority, because it wrongly essentialises and homogenises the attributes of members of the group. (Young 1995, 165)

Cultures are fluent, they mix, they learn from each other. People are born into cultures but they leave them sometimes. People add values and customs to their culture. Cultures change and evolve. A multicultural polity that needs to publicly and legally define its groups in order to treat them 'equally' or 'according to their needs' will create artificial 'cultures' or will freeze rather superficial understandings of culture.

A telling example for the failings of a policy built around racial or ethnic categories is the current state of Bosnia and Herzegovina which is practically deadlocked between the conflicting political interests of the leaders of the three major ethnic groups. The source of this enduring political stalemate is the Dayton Agreement of 1995. Intended to end the war in Bosnia, the Dayton Accord organised the new federation in a complicated political and administrative structure consisting of several levels of legislative, executive and judicial institutions that was meant to guarantee each of the major population groups of Serbs, Croats and Bosniaks an equitable share in the political system of the new common state. But this explicit politicisation of ethnicity has made Bosnia and Herzegovina practically ungovernable:

> Bosnia and Herzegovina is today an ungovernable country where institutions are blocked, power is shared at the citizens' expenses, and democracy itself is in danger. [...] Bosnia and Herzegovina (BiH) at the moment is in a serious political crisis, to the point that it could be compared to a comatose state. (Almir Terzić quoted after Moratti 2012)

Not only has governing become almost impossible, the politicisation of ethnicity has also brought a massive de-politicisation and loss of political accountability:

> This systematic indoctrination conducted by ethnopolitics leads directly to a dangerous depoliticization of individual members of ethnic groups. They leave "political reasoning"

to their elected leaders, the watchdogs of their survival. [...] The Bosnian peoples and citizens have undergone political euthanasia. That is the final product of ethnopolitics. (Mujkic 2007, 125)

And lastly, the permanent institutionalisation of ethnic differences has created artificial barriers for the citizens of Bosnia and Herzegovina to identify the way they want:

Dayton adopted a closed definition of identity, whereby a citizen can only be Serbian, Croatian, Bosniak, or "other", the residual category that includes all minorities. If such a strict idea of identity is problematic in itself, it is even more so in Bosnia and Herzegovina, a country with a long tradition of intermarriage and, consequently, of multiple identities. In addition, many people in Bosnia reject any ethnic label and prefer to be considered simply as Bosnian citizens (civic option), without further specification. Paradoxically, even these Bosnians are today a minority and part of the group of "others." (Rossini 2012)

There is more in the debate on multiculturalism that is relevant in the evaluation of guaranteed minority representation in legislatures. Here it is enough to note that the granting of rights and privileges to groups defined by culture, ethnicity or race is at best ambivalent. While there might be a case for the introduction of cultural and political rights to such groups when these have been victims of longstanding discrimination, the instrument of group rights, especially if these are political rights, remains dangerous.

4. The pros and cons of descriptive representation

Descriptive representation is generally understood as the similarity in the social and ethnic or racial backgrounds of representatives and constituencies. The similarity is expected either in the visible characteristics of the representative and the constituency, or in the shared experiences or in both. The main argument for descriptive representation is that similarity in characteristics or experiences will promote the 'representative's accurate representation of and commitment to constituent interests' (Mansbridge 1999, 629). Therefore voices, asking for minority descriptive representation, expect that representatives who originate from a particular minority will better serve their constituency than representatives which are part of the majority population.

In a much cited article on gender parity, Anne Phillips has identified four groups of arguments for raising the proportion of women elected to parliaments. All four types can be applied equally well to minorities and disadvantaged groups:

There are those [arguments] that dwell on the role model successful women politicians offer; those that appeal to principles of justice between the sexes; those that identify

> particular interests of women that would be otherwise overlooked; and those that point towards a revitalized democracy that bridges the gap between representation and participation. (Phillips 1998, 228)

According to the first of those four groups of arguments, there is a distinct value of having role models in national politics for minorities and marginalised groups. Following this view, the voter can see that one of his own will be able to participate on equal terms with majority representatives in the national decision making and feel that he is represented by a co-ethnic. The role model of successful minority representatives could therefore inspire other members of the minority and help to further the minority's political participation.

The second group of arguments is about discrimination. For sure, the sole fact of political underrepresentation is not in itself a proof of existing structural injustice. But political underrepresentation can hint at discrimination in other spheres of public life, it can hint at structural discrimination. If a society is sufficiently just, insofar as every group and every citizen have equal chances of political participation, we could then expect a reasonable amount of ethnic or cultural or social diversity among the deputies in parliament. This does not mean that we should expect that all but the smallest social groups will be (somehow) represented. There is a multitude of reasons why parliamentarians form an ever changing elite that often does not mirror its constituency. But ideally, in a just and diverse society we could expect some mirroring of this diversity in parliament. If this is not the case and we find that a diverse society is represented by a homogeneous elite, we can then suspect that some groups are denied equal participation and they are therefore unjustly discriminated.

According to the third type of arguments, it is expected that descriptive representation will improve the *substantive* representation of minority interests. This belief rests on three assumptions: a) that a minority has a distinct interest, different from the majority; b) that this interest cannot be represented well by deputies from the majority; and c) that descriptive representation ensures the defence of this interest (ibid.). Each of these three assumptions can be challenged. For example, it is questionable whether minorities do indeed have an objective and identifiable *minority interest*. And if so, is this always different from the interest of the majority? Surely, this cannot be answered in either way in general. Minorities do have special and distinct interests in particular issues. In other issues their interest coincides with that of the majority. If a particular minority has a distinct interest in a particular case is to be judged in context. Looking at the second assumption: Are majority deputies unable to hold up this special interest? Clearly, there are cases where majority deputies have successfully defended the interest of disadvantaged minorities. But this does not dismiss the argument. Majority deputies can represent minority interests adequately, either by knowledge of these interests and the will to uphold them or by a coincidence of the preferences of the minority and majority. But descriptive representation is better than this with respect to another point. Anne Phillips gives the example of political issues that are new, not precisely delineated and quickly evolving (see Phillips 1998). In these cases, where it is not clear from the outset what the interest of the different social groups with reference to this new issue is, the representation by deputies mirroring their constituency is most important. Because they have the perspective of their constituency, they will be able to decide and act in accordance with the special preferences of the constituency.

Such an argumentation is part of the larger trend to interpret representation as a 'differentiated relationship among plural actors' and therefore as a part of a deliberative process of democratic decision making (Young 2000, 127). Jane Mansbridge discusses the two concepts of representation: the deliberative function

> aims at understanding which policies are good for the polity as a whole, which policies are good for a representative's constituents, and when the interests of various groups within the polity and constituency conflict. It also aims at transforming interests and creating commonality when that commonality can be genuinely good for all. (Mansbridge 1999, 634)

This deliberative function is complemented by the aggregative function of representative democracy that aims at producing legitimate decisions, especially in cases of conflicting interests. A focus on deliberation opens up a space for arguments in favour of descriptive representation, that are not possible with a narrow view on representation as a pure numerical aggregation and delegation of preferences.

Central to this are the notions of *social perspectives* and *uncrystallised interests*. The social perspective is a rather broad concept, but it can generally be understood as the personal experience, history and social knowledge that influence the interpretation of the meaning of actions, events, rules and structures (Young 2000, 136). Consequently, people in different social positions will understand the reality around them in a different way. The differences in social perspectives can be quite fundamental and can lead to a complete incompatibility of the interpretations of particular issues by different social groups. A specific social position does not necessarily determine a specific understanding of reality, but it does influence it. If this concept is accepted, it becomes clear, that a parliament composed solely of majority representatives will exclude the experiences and views of minority groups. The crucial point is that while majority deputies can be informed about specific demands of minority groups, they will at times not even *realise* that specific issues are of importance to or endanger the interest of minorities. Here special measures, that ensure descriptive representation, can improve the democratic process in providing that deputies who are *socially close* to their constituencies enter parliament and add to the perspectives represented in it. With respect to the deliberative function of representative democracy this is of critical importance. More points of view included in the deliberation make more dangers become apparent, and this leads to a better and more rational decision. This general argument for an inclusive deliberation combined with the idea of distinct perspectives of minority group members makes a strong argument for descriptive representation in the legislature (Williams 2000).

Additional weight to this argument is added in the case of uncrystallised interests. Although coined by Jane Mansbridge, this term follows the argumentation of Anne Phillips that new and quickly evolving political issues are those, where descriptive representation can make the biggest difference in deliberation. Mansbridge defines interests as uncrystallised, when they refer to issues that 'have not been on the political agenda long, candidates have not taken public positions on them, and political parties are not organized around them' (Mansbridge 1999, 643). When such issues have to be dealt with politically, the best predictor on the behaviour of the representative, and therefore of his defence of the interests of the constituency, is his social background. In a case like this, when the representative has not positioned himself on the topic in advance, and the political parties do not yet present unanimous standpoints on the issue, the voter can at most hope that the representative will decide as he would have done, on the basis of social similarity. And the crucial point in this is that issues of identity, discrimination and inclusion are in most cases relatively uncrystallised. Therefore the best voice in such a debate can be the voice of someone who has experience in these issues and understands their implications.

As there are several ways to defend the necessity for a social similarity of constituency and representatives, there are multiple ways and arguments to engage this statement. Critical but sympathetic views on descriptive representation see it as valuable, but only if linked to substantive representation. The argument goes that if members of parliament that represent minorities resemble their constituents but support majority policies without furthering the special interests of their voters, they will not be of much value to them. And depending on the electoral system minority deputies can be pressed to soften their policy agenda in order to gain enough majority support to win office, while at the same time betraying their minority constituents. Therefore a focus on composition of parliament can distract the analysis and debate from the real issue understood as the activities of the representatives (Pitkin 1967, 226). Perhaps the strongest argument against descriptive representation is a notion that is also employed against special group representation in general. Here, the argument goes that no deputy can be as diverse in his perspectives and preferences as his constituency and that therefore he will necessarily ignore or even suppress the interests of sub-groups. This is especially important in the case of deputies that do share social backgrounds and characteristics with their constituency and can therefore claim a higher legitimacy in representing it. And finally, the institutional promotion of descriptive representation through measures of reserved seats, racial redistricting, special constituencies and party list quotas can decrease the accountability of deputies in legislatures (Young 2000, 150). By seeing themselves as being represented by members of the same minority group, voters can be led to think that their substantive interests are being defended. And yet, this does not need to be so (Mansbridge 1999, 640). The research on ethnic representation in post-communist Eastern Europe also adds clues, that group representation and the politicisation of ethnicity can reduce the accountability of minority group representatives (Phillips 1995, Protsyk et al. 2008, Protsyk and Sachariew 2012). In emphasising the danger of losing any representation if they question their performance and divide the electorate, ethnic minority leaders can press their followers into unanimous support of their campaign.

5. Conclusion

This chapter offered a very brief review of the normative and empiric argumentation for and against group and descriptive representation. It has shown that there are a number of issues that speak in favour of both, and that there are not less weighty ones that can lead us to dismiss either concept.

The strongest argument in favour of all measures, that are intended to increase the political inclusion of disadvantaged groups, is an argument about justice. From a democratic point of view, political exclusion is unjust. This is easily accepted by most authors. But the question about the right instrument to end exclusion remains difficult. Regarding political group rights like guaranteed representation, there is a whole range of notions that advocates of political inclusion have compiled. Among them is the understanding that the lack of political group rights can be unjust, as it de facto favours the status quo of majority dominance and minority exclusion. Group rights are seen as a remedy for this. They are further believed to improve deliberation in the political process. Adversaries of group rights on the other side see the instalment of affirmative practices as morally arbitrary and politically dangerous. They claim that the granting of group rights to a particular group can discriminate other minorities, or the majority or sub-groups within the minority group. This can foster the divisions and create hostility inside a society, and ultimately lead to its disintegration.

The concept of descriptive representation faces similar justifications and critiques. Proponents of descriptive representation point out the importance of positive role models, the injustice of exclusion, the importance to incorporate the specific interests and perspectives of minorities in a deliberative process, and an expected revitalisation of democracy through the increase of chances for participation by disadvantaged groups. Critics of 'the policy of presence' see either no added value in the resemblance of deputies and constituencies, or point at the dangers of a weaker accountability of minority representatives.

As can be seen, most of the arguments refer either to perceptions of justice and injustice or to the value of minority representation for deliberation. The common conclusion in most of the literature on this topic is that every discussion of special rights and measures needs to focus on the context of particular societies. Even the advocates of group and descriptive representation admit that there is no standard answer on the justification and effectiveness of both in general and in particular.

Finally, coming back to the questions starting this review, we can find that minority representation is indeed valuable. Guaranteeing minority representation in legislatures, or even further guaranteeing *descriptive* representation through special measures, *can* be beneficial. But a social, cultural or ethnic mirroring of the constituency in parliament is not in itself valuable. It is the interests and perspectives of minorities that should be present in the legislative process in order to empower them and improve the democratic decision making. Put in other words, there are sound arguments in favour of a mirror representation for the sake of a better deliberation. But political theory does not give a standard answer, when and how special measures to improve minority representation are necessary or prudent. It simply cannot, as it is the history and complexity in the power relations in each individual society that may call for guaranteed representation of minorities or may warn against the instalment of special statuses.

References

Barry, Brian. 2001. *Culture and equality: an egalitarian critique of multiculturalism*. Cambridge (MA): Harvard University Press.

Bird, Karen, Saalfeld, Thomas, and Wüst, Andreas M. (eds.). 2011. *The Political Representation of Immigrants and Minorities*. New York: Routledge.

Dahl, Robert A. 1989. *Democracy and its critics*. New Haven: Yale University Press.

Dovi, Suzanne. 2002. Preferable descriptive representatives: Will just any woman, black, or Latino do? *American Political Science Review 96* (4): 729–743.

Htun, Mala. 2004. Is Gender like Ethnicity? The Political Representation of Identity Groups. *Perspectives on Politics 2* (03): 439–458.

Kymlicka, Will. 2002. *Contemporary Political Philosophy: An Introduction (2nd ed.)*. Oxford: Oxford University Press.
Kymlicka, Will. 1995. *Multicultural citizenship: a liberal theory of minority rights (Oxford political theory)*. Oxford et al.: Clarendon Press.
Manin, Bernard. 1997. *The principles of representative government*. Cambridge: Cambridge University Press.
Mansbridge, Jane. 1999. Should blacks represent blacks and women represent women? A contingent "yes." *Journal of Politics 61* (3): 628–657.
Moratti, Massimo. 2012. Bosnia and Herzegovina, a country in a coma. Osservatorio Balcani e Caucaso. [http://www.balcanicaucaso.org/eng/Regions-and-countries/Bosnia-and-Herzegovina/Bosnia-and-Herzegovina-a-country-in-a-coma-126111, accessed on 14.04.2013].
Mujkic, Asim. 2007. We, the Citizens of Ethnopolis. *Constellations 14* (1): 112–128.
Phillips, Anne. 1995. Democracy and Difference: Some Problems for Feminist Theory. In *The Rights of minority cultures*, edited by Will Kymlicka, 288–302. Oxford et al.: Oxford University Press.
Phillips, Anne. 1998. Democracy and Representation: Or, Why Should it Matter Who our Representatives Are? In *Feminism and politics*, edited by Anne Phillips, 224–240. Oxford: Oxford University Press.
Pitkin, Hanna F. 1967. *The concept of representation*. Berkeley: University of California Press.
Powley, Elizabeth (ed.). 2010. *Diversity in Parliament: Listening to the voices of minorities and indigenous peoples*. Geneva: Inter-Parliamentary Union.
Protsyk, Oleh, Sachariew, Konstantin. 2012. Recruitment and Representation of Ethnic Minorities under Proportional Representation: Evidence from Bulgaria. *East European Politics & Societies 26 (2)*: 313–339.
Protsyk, Oleh, Matichescu, Marius, Chatre, Baptiste. 2008. Representational Consequences of Special Mechanisms for Ethnic Minority Inclusion: Evidence from Romania. *ECMI Working Paper N. 41, September 2008*.
Rossini, Andrea. 2012. Bosnia: agony over Dayton. Osservatorio Balcani e Caucaso. [http://www.balcanicaucaso.org/eng/Regions-and-countries/Bosnia-and-Herzegovina/Bosnia-agony-over-Dayton-121036, accessed on 14.04.2014].
Urbinati, Nadia, Warren, Mark E. 2008. The concept of representation in contemporary democratic theory. *Annual Review of Political Science 11*: 387–412.
Urbinati, Nadia. 2006. *Representative democracy: principles and genealogy*. Chicago: University of Chicago Press.
Weymans, Wim. 2005. Freedom through Political Representation. *European Journal of Political Theory 4* (3): 263–282.
Williams, Melissa S. 2000. The Uneasy Alliance of Group Representation and Deliberative Democracy. In *Citizenship in Diverse Societies*, edited by Will Kymlicka and Wayne Norman, 124–152. New York: Oxford University Press.
Young, Iris. M. 1995. Together in Difference: Transforming the Logic in Group Political Conflict. In *The Rights of minority cultures*, edited by Will Kymlicka, 155–178. Oxford et al.: Oxford University Press.
Young, Iris. M. 2000. *Inclusion and democracy*. Oxford: Oxford University Press.

Contributors

Martin Belov chief assistant professor, Sofia University 'St. Kliment Ohridski', Bulgaria
André Brodocz professor, University of Erfurt, Germany
Wojciech Ciszewski PhD student, Jagiellonian University in Krakow, Poland
Stefan Ewert research associate, University of Greifswald, Germany
Balázs Fekete associate professor, Pázmány Péter Catholic University, and research fellow, Hungarian Academy of Sciences, both in Budapest, Hungary
Mariusz Jerzy Golecki associate professor, University of Łódź, Poland
Katalin Kelemen senior lecturer, Örebro University, Sweden
Rafał Mańko external fellow, University of Amsterdam, Netherlands
Marcin Pieniążek research associate, Andrzej Frycz Modrzewski Krakow University, Poland
Axelle Reiter lecturer, University of Verona (Vicenza), Italy
Karolina Ristova-Asterud docent, Ss. Cyril and Methodius University in Skopje, Macedonia
Konstantin Sachariew research assistant, University of Rostock, Germany
Szilárd Tattay assistant professor, Pázmány Péter Catholic University in Budapest, Hungary

Editors

Antonia Geisler coordinator, Graduate Academy, University of Greifswald, Germany
Michael Hein research associate, University of Greifswald, Germany
Siri Hummel scientific assistant, Alfried Krupp Wissenschaftskolleg Greifswald, Germany

Central and Eastern European Forum for Legal, Political, and Social Theory Yearbook

Edited by Jürgen Busch / Péter Cserne / Michael Hein /
Miklós Könczöl / Miodrag Jovanović / Marta Soniewicka

Vol. 1 Péter Cserne / Miklós Könczöl (eds.): Legal and Political Theory in the Post-National Age. Selected papers presented at the Second Central and Eastern European Forum for Legal, Political and Social Theorists (Budapest, 21–22 May 2010). 2011.

Vol. 2 Miodrag A. Jovanović / Bojan Spaić (eds.): Jurisprudence and Political Philosophy in the 21st Century. Reassessing Legacies. 2012.

Vol. 3 Péter Cserne / Miklós Könczöl / Marta Soniewicka (eds.): The Rule of Law and the Challenges to Jurisprudence. Selected papers presented at the Fourth Central and Eastern European Forum for Legal, Political and Social Theorists, Celje, 23–24 March 2012. 2014.

Vol. 4 Antonia Geisler / Michael Hein / Siri Hummel (eds.): Law, Politics, and the Constitution. New Perspectives from Legal and Political Theory. 2014.

www.peterlang.com

www.ingramcontent.com/pod-product-compliance
Ingram Content Group UK Ltd.
Pitfield, Milton Keynes, MK11 3LW, UK
UKHW021842100926
8556IPUK00019B/999

9 783631 654644